The Formation of the Italian Republic

Studies in Modern European History

Frank J. Coppa
General Editor

Vol. 5

PETER LANG
New York • San Francisco • Bern • Baltimore
Frankfurt am Main • Berlin • Wien • Paris

The Formation of the Italian Republic

Proceedings of the International Symposium on Postwar Italy

Edited by
Frank J. Coppa and
Margherita Repetto-Alaia

PETER LANG
New York • San Francisco • Bern • Baltimore
Frankfurt am Main • Berlin • Wien • Paris

Library of Congress Cataloging-in-Publication Data

International Symposium on postwar Italy (1989 : New York, N.Y.)
    The formation of the Italian Republic : proceedings of the
International symposium on postwar Italy / edited by Frank J.
Coppa and Margherita Repetto-Alaia.
        p. cm. — (Studies in modern European history ; vol. 5)
        1. Italy—History—1945- —Congresses. I. Coppa, Frank J.
II. Repetto-Alaia, Margherita.   III. Title.   IV. Series.
DG576.8.I57   1993   945.092—dc20   92-26677
ISBN 0-8204-1530-8   CIP
ISSN 0893-6897

Die Deutsche Bibliothek-CIP-Einheitsaufnahme

Coppa, Frank J.:
The formation of the Italian Republic : proceedings of the
International Symposium on Postwar Italy / Frank J. Coppa and
Margherita Repetto-Alaia.—New York; Bern; Berlin; Frankfurt/M.;
Paris; Wien: Lang, 1993
    (Studies in modern European history ; Vol. 5)
    ISBN 0-8204-1530-8
NE: Repetto-Alaia, Margherita: International Symposium on
Postwar Italy <1989, New York, NY>; GT

The paper in this book meets the guidelines for permanence and
durability of the Committee on Production Guidelines for
Book Longevity of the Council on Library Resources.

© Peter Lang Publishing, Inc., New York 1993

Printed in the United States of America.

Table of Contents

"*Il viandante ansioso di varcare il torrente getta pietre una sull'altra, nel profondo dell'acqua, poi posa sicuro il suo piede sulle ultime, che affiorano, perchè sa che quelle scomparse nel gorgo sosterranno il suo peso.*"

Nello Rosselli, *Carlo Pisacane nel Risorgimento italiano*, 1932

Publication of this Volume was made possible by a generous grant from the Banca Commerciale Italiana

PART ONE

THE INTRODUCTION AND OPENING OF THE INTERNATIONAL SYMPOSIUM ON POST WORLD WAR II ITALY

I

Introduction

Frank J. Coppa
Margherita Repetto-Alaia

The idea for the International Symposium on the Postwar Italian Republic held in New York City from October 19 to October 21, 1989 originated with Margherita Repetto-Alaia who was motivated both by her personal experience in Italy and the perspective born abroad. The prospect was presented to a small group of American scholars of modern Italy who shared her enthusiasm, examining both the academic parameters and the practical problems inherent in such a venture. Following a series of meetings a Program Committee was constituted which included James Beck, Director of the Casa Italiana and Center for Italian Studies at Columbia University; Jared Becker of Columbia University; Joel Blatt, of the University of Connecticut at Stamford; Frank J. Coppa, of St. John's University, New York; Ronald S. Cunsolo of Nassau Community College; Mary Gibson of John Jay College of Criminal Justice; Clara Lovett of George Mason University; Gianclaudio Macchiarella, Director of the Italian Cultural Institute in New York, and Richard Wolff of Kekst and Company. While the broad theme of the program was inspired by Professor Margherita Repetto-Alaia of Columbia University, it was clarified, amplified, and organized by the Program Committee coordinated by Professors Repetto and Coppa, who served respectively as chair and co-chair.

The work of the Program Committee was facilitated by an Honorary Committee and Sponsoring Committee, which offered both moral and material assistance. The Honorary Committee included Professor Jonathan R. Cole, Provost of Columbia University; Francesco Corrias, Consul General of Italy in New York; Professor Ainslie T. Embree, Acting Dean of the School of International and

Public Affairs, Columbia University; Ambassador Richard N. Gardner, Professor of Law and International Organization at Columbia University; H. E. Rinaldo Petrignani, Ambassador of Italy to the United States, and Professor Giovanni Sartori, Albert Schweitzer Professor of Humanities, Sociology Department at Columbia University.

Serving on the Sponsoring Committee, which provided both advice on the Program and suggestions regarding prospective participants, were John Cammett of John Jay College of the City University, Elisa Carrillo of Marymount College, New York; Alexander De Grand of North Carolina State University; Victoria De Grazia of Rutgers University; Charles Delzell of Vanderbilt University, Spencer Di Scala of the University of Massachusetts, Boston; Ira Glazier of the Balch Institute of Temple University; Raymond Grew of the University of Michigan; H. Stuart Hughes, Emeritus, University of California, San Diego; Norman Kogan, Emeritus, University of Connecticut, Storrs; Joseph La Palombara of Yale University; Emiliana P. Noether, Emerita, University of Connecticut, Storrs; Frank Rosengarten, Queens College of the City University of New York; Salvatore Saladino likewise of Queens College, and Roland Sarti of the University of Massachusetts at Amherst.

The Chairs of the sessions included Elisa Carrillo of Marymount College, New York; Norman Kogan, Emeritus, University of Connecticut at Storrs; John A. Thayer, University of Minnesota; Clara M. Lovett, George Mason University; and Giovanni Sartori, Columbia University.

Post World War II Italy has been of interest to scholars on this side of the Atlantic since the 1970's. These were difficult years for Italian democracy and for the Italian economy as well. Media coverage often came to alarming conclusions, depicting the country's political system on the verge of collapse under the pressure of terrorist plots, whose piecemeal disclosure often raised more questions than answers. Meanwhile economic commentators decried the spiralling inflation and the soaring deficit that threatened to undermine economic growth. The situation seemed to reach a climax with the kidnapping and assassination of Aldo Moro in 1978. It seemed to many, even those most friendly to Italy, as if the future of Italian democracy was compromised; some talked of its inner fragility now being exposed to all.

The existence of the crisis or even of a chain of crises, no one would deny. Equally undeniable the fact that for a large part of the decade of the 1980's, Italians continued to live under the shadow of that crisis. However as the decade came to a conclusion, it became possible to look back and see things in a different perspective, to assess the significance of the past decades and make projections for the future. In the eyes of many the postwar period had come to a close. The spectacular unraveling of events, first dismantling and then bringing to an end the postwar world, provided an international resonance to that perception.

As has been noted in the Western constellation of political systems, each is one of a kind. The Italian has been, and to a large extent remains, more unique than any other. Among other things one might mention the peculiarity of Italy's political parties, including the parties self and reciprocate legitimization as well as their historical identities, both in their hold on society and their interface between parties and society.

The Italian party system has been the object of some scholarly inquiry in the United States and the English speaking world. Though far from numerous, these earlier studies were often informative and perceptive. Within the last two decades this task has been assumed by political scientists rather than historians. Thus most studies of the Italian Communist Party produced in the United States are written from a political science perspective. There is far less scholarship on the major Italian Party, the Christian Democratic Party. In its case, as that of the Communists, the historical material available for such works remains scarce, with little primary material such as memoirs, speeches, and other writings available in English. A similar situation has confronted those wishing to reconstruct the role of the Socialist Party.

The situation has been compounded by the fact that the teaching and researching of contemporary Italian history in the United States remains limited. It has been suggested that this lack of academic appeal, which in turn stifles motivation, stems from an oversimplification of Italian political culture. Thus, for example, the equation that Catholicism equals conservatism has hindered the understanding of the complexities of the "Catholic world" and its many derivations, as well as the broad variety of strains of thought coalescing into the birth and development of the Christian Democratic Party. At the other end of the spectrum, much the same fate has befallen Italian Communism, branded simply as an appendix of Moscow. To be sure Italian Communism is better known than Italian Catholicism, nonetheless historical knowledge concerning the party's origins and peculiarities have never gone far beyond the few pioneering studies. A complete translation of Gramsci's work — essential for an understanding of the historical and cultural environment in which his thought developed — is only now scheduled to appear.

Our conclusion that the historical picture of the Italian parties of the postwar period is incomplete, led us to make them the focus of the Symposium. Around them were grouped a number of issues such as labor organizations and labor strategies; the gender impact on a society which finally experienced universal female as well as male suffrage; the judiciary and how it bridged the gap between the written law and the broader society, and the State's intervention in economic life. Issues such as labor and gender strategies, the interpretation and implementation of the law, and the restructuring of the economy are crucial in defining the democratic profile of a civil society. In a mature democracy one is likely to find that the dynamics in each of these areas, though by no means separate, have attained a high degree of autonomy from their political trappings. In the Italian Republic, which emerged from the Fascist experience, it was natural to seek to determine to what extent political institutions had chartered new spaces for that autonomy to expand.

The Symposium which sought these answers was structured in two parts with the first focusing on the political and intellectual forces in the formation of the Republic, and the second on institutional issues of the postwar society. Within the sessions of the former the perspective and contributions of the Christian Democrats and organized Catholics, the Socialists and Communists, as well as the parties and groups of liberal democratic orientation were considered. Within the sessions of the latter the role of organized labor, the evolution of the judiciary, and the impact of women on political and social developments were explored. While all the presentors were from Italy, the chairs and the commentators were drawn from this side of the Atlantic, rendering the dialogue truly international. The interaction was broadened by those in attendance, hailing mainly from the Eastern Seaboard of the United States, but venturing from further afield including Canada and Great Britain. Together with the participants, those in attendance worked to trace the historical reconstruction of Italy's republican institutions while examining the development of Italy's postwar democracy.

In session after session both presentors and commentators concurred that the major political parties, as they emerged from the formative period from 1943 to 1945, played a key role in rebuilding unionism in the postwar society and provided the groundwork for women's organized presence in the postwar world. As prime historical agents, they also exerted, as more than one of the essays in the present volume indicates, a prolonged tutorship, conditioning future union and women's political activities and policies in the subsequent years.

Regarding the judiciary in the immediate postwar years, its relationship with the various political forces appears to have been filtered through the state apparatus. In fact one might say that for a number of years (the essay in this volume sets 1948 to 1964 as the periodization), the judiciary in its higher ranks used the polarization in Italian politics to further its own self preservation and retain the continuity with the pre-1945 years. A pattern of substantial continuity also emerges in relation to the State's intervention in economic life. In the latter case it spelled out a potential continuation of a policy of modernization which had been infused into the industrial and financial structure since the mid 1930's. Considerable credit for this development must be accorded to Raffaele Mattioli, whose personality and policies are catalogued in one of the essays in the volume.

In our effort to examine another dimension of postwar society, we sought to shed some light on some of the individuals who left their mark on the course of events and the Reconstruction. In numerous cases the biographies of these men and women hold the answers to many of the questions concerning the Reconstruction which have yet to be deciphered by historical study. Many of the problems explored naturally extend back to the prewar period, including the state-society relationship, the cultural and ideological openness of society during the fascist years and the degree of "fascistization" of its cultural and intellectual enclaves. On some of these issues avenues of research have been opened both by Italian and American scholars, and we hope that these lines extend to bridge the hiatus between the prewar and postwar society.

For our Symposium, and this volume which flows from it, choices had to be made, marking broad paths of possible research. The decision to concentrate on intellectuals who were grouped about the journals of a liberal-democratic stamp found justification in the value — which is undeniable — of the cultural legacy they contained. Figures such as Adolfo Omodeo, Luigi Salvatorelli, Mario Paggi, Piero Calamandrei, Antonio Olivetti, to mention a few significant names, were links in the line of continuity with important areas of the prewar culture. In many cases their intellectual contribution was the result of many composite layers and had been filtered through conflicting personal experiences. Their political maturation antedated the rise of Fascism, resulting in diverse positions ranging from traditional liberalism to the critical revision of socialism.

"Croceanism" for some, the legacy of Piero Gobetti and Carlo Rosselli for others, provided intellectual and moral inspiration. The linkage to Rosselli was especially traceable in the cases of Calamandrei and Tarchiani. The analysis in the essay on the intellectuals of the "lay forces" focuses on the personality and contribution of Calamandrei. His influence in the reconstruction period, including the debate surrounding the drafting of the Constitution, is also traced in the essay on the judiciary. Tarchiani's contribution is assessed in the essay examining his role in establishing and developing diplomatic relations with the United States in the critical postwar period.

Regarding Mattioli, the Symposium called attention to the personality whose innovative financial and economic thought and policy between the mid 1930's well into the 1960's, played a key part in the economic reconstruction of Italy. Important in this assessment is Mattioli's role as an educator of several generations of economic thinkers and financial managers, many of whom were later found in diverse professional and cultural areas, but who shared a common current of intellectual and civil concerns. Within the volume a number of these are mentioned, including Saraceno and Vanoni to mention only two who belonged to this "think tank," which played an important part in the country's economic reconstruction.

The Symposium sought to uncover issues and meanings in the complex nature of Italian society as it emerged from the war. We intended to present a set of evaluations, many of which had already come together as a consequence of the increasingly multicultural scholarship, in this case prevailing Italian and American, but not all of which had experienced the crossfertilization.

Within this context the issue of political parties quickly exploded into the wider question of continuity versus change. This was critically posed at the close of the Symposium during the round table discussion, conceived and chaired by Professor Coppa, which provided an American coda to the Italian presentors. The participants of this final session were drawn mainly from the sponsoring committee offering additional suggestions, considerations, and insights on the previous proceedings. It also provided the opportunity for a truly spontaneous and unstructured exchange of ideas between the Italian and American scholars, while allowing the audience to pose questions and provide comments on the Symposium as a whole. During the course of this concluding, capstone session, continuities and discontinuities between the prefascist liberal regime and the republican state were also explored, providing an interesting long-range historical perspective to the post World War II age in Italy.

Long before it became an issue of historiographical debate, change versus continuity in the political parties was at the center of a heated political debate. Presently, thanks to new methodological approaches, we are witnessing a liberation of some analysis from the ideological baggage which long accompanied it. Furthermore scholars increasingly have examined the manifold aspects of postwar society, again downplaying the ideological confrontations. Social history and the support offered by sociological and anthropological research have contributed to diffuse the ideological issues. Increasingly researchers are aware that the picture presented varies with the indicators we chose, and that our understanding increases with additional perspectives and approaches. This multifaceted approach has been applied to a study of the Christian Democratic party. It examines layers of different generations of politically committed Catholics as well as the issues they pursued and actions assumed. Christian Democracy, a party of continuity, helped to shape the mass character of the postwar institutions as noted in Leopoldo Elia's essay on the Constitution. Another area where the question of continuity versus change is appropriate and intriguing is the essay on women and the gender question in postwar society. This focuses polemically, and perhaps rightfully so, on the historiographical "conspiracy of silence," which the author argues was instrumental in downplaying the role of "woman in the Republic." Looking at women from the perspective of this essay, the reader is led to conclude that what was novel was the trajectory of change. Furthermore, the mass character of the process represents another striking and essentially new quality of the postwar development.

Harper, in his essay, observes that there was no "zero hour" which served at the source of postwar Italian society, viewing Italian history as a pattern of "layers over layers, new grafted on old." The Constitution was indeed born of the effort to graft the new onto the old. In speaking of the Constitution, however, "old" rather than weight of tradition adverse to change meant the dignity of the diverse cultural heritages which the political forces in the Constituent Assembly each brought into play: the best, therefore, in the process of continuity. Really new were the lessons which were imposed by history. The catastrophe of war emphasized to many the value of restraint, of maintaining even in harsh confrontations, a clear divide between ideology and politics, setting common goals of humanity and decency, placing the preservation of the new political institutions above the single parties' interests. Postwar political forces therefore bore this sign of change. This is obvious in the various essays which trace the renovation of the postwar period.

We wish to point out another thought which guided the planners of the Symposium: our belief that passion, and personal involvement in the process can sometimes shed an additional dimension to the unfolding of historical events. We considered personal involvement an important feature in the assessment of the notion that an era — in this case postwar Italian society — had come to an end. Thus many of the participants who spoke at the Symposium did so with their memories as well as their mind. We consider this to be one of the interesting features of the endeavor.

Endeavors such as the International Symposium have a material as well as an intellectual cost, and the former were in part borne by the Center for Italian Studies of the Casa Italiana of Columbia University, the Italian Cultural Institute of New York, the Italian Ministry of Foreign Affairs, and the Banca Commerciale Italiana. The BCI also contributed to the event by offering a banquet for the participants and by funding the publication of the proceedings. We thank SVIMEZ for having made available for display works on the reconstruction and development of Southern Italy during the postwar period.

The International Symposium was above all a joint enterprise. Sponsored by the Center for Italian Studies of the Casa Italiana of Columbia University and the Italian Cultural Institute of New York, it was conducted under the auspices of the Italian Ministry of Foreign Affairs. Its work was facilitated by the Columbia University Seminar's office under Dean Aaron Warner, while ideas and inspiration were provided by a number of members of the interdisciplinary Columbia University Seminar on Studies on Modern Italy.

The opening of the Symposium, which set the stage for all that followed, was presided over by Professor James Beck and Professor Gianclaudio Macchiarella, respectively the directors of the Casa Italiana of Columbia University and the Italian Cultural Institute of New York. Following their remarks salutations were offered by Franco Riolo, Deputy General Manager of the Banca Commerciale Italiana, the Honorable Francesco Corrias, Consul General of Italy in New York, and Professor Jonathan R. Cole, the Provost of Columbia University. The latter introduced Senator Leopoldo Elia of the Italian Republic, Professor of Law and past President of the Italian Constitutional Court. In the opening address Senator Elia, who was then Chair of the Committee on Constitutional Affairs in the Italian Senate, examined the formation, implementation, and interpretation of the 1948 Constitution, stressing its unique character and impact. The Senator, like a good number of the other participants, had been personally involved in the issues which found expression in the Constituent Assembly and its aftermath. Their assessment and evaluation of the process is an important historical record, which we have gathered in the present volume.

In conclusion, the editors would like to mention that since this is a volume of presentations rather than one of commissioned essays, we have adopted a minimalist approach in our editorial responsibilities. A number of papers have been translated from Italian into English and in these cases we have sought to assure that the language reflects the original intent of the authors. Elsewhere, we have sought to adhere closely to the original text, restricting most of our revisions to usage.

II

Opening Address: The Republican Constitution and the Development of Democracy in Italy

Leopoldo Elia

In its afternoon session of December 22, 1947, the Constituent Assembly voted 453 out of 515 to ratify the text of the new Constitution. In the conclusion of his report, the President of the Commission that drafted the text declared: "There are defects, there are gaps, and perhaps redundancies as well, and there is uncertainty on some points; but word has reached me from prominent officials abroad that this Charter should be positively received, and that it is among the most noble Constitutions of the post-war period, if not indeed the noblest." The subsequent course taken by European Constitutionalism demonstrates just how well this description fits, especially the declaration that "no Constitutional charter contains as complete and as well-defined a system for safeguarding forms of freedom."

The Italian Constitution placed the declaration of basic principles in the body of the text, rather than isolating them in a preamble, as had been proposed and as the French had done the year before. It was a decision that was heatedly debated and gave way to later criticism on the programmatic nature of the Constitution. Pietro Calamandrei expressed the theory that "to compensate the forces of the left for a circumvented revolution, the forces of the right showed no opposition to a promised revolution in the constitution." In 1955, denouncing the failure to implement the constitution, the Florentine jurist and member of the Action Party (Partito d'Azione) revived earlier criticisms of a long and rigid Constitution that entrusted its "aspirations" to programmatic declarations of principles; these could be realized only with further precise legislation at a later time.

These aspects were also the focus of the first Anglo-Saxon criticism of post-war European Constitutions. The points made by John Clarke Adams were elaborated above all by Crisafulli. According to him, norms/principles (as for example the right to work sanctioned in Art. 4) are juridic norms of a relatively general nature that may also be somewhat overly de-ontological. At any rate, after the collapse of Fascism, a need was strongly felt to give direction to the democratic choices under consideration.

In this sense, the large vote passing the Constitution assumes a special meaning. The French Constitution, drafted in a comparable cultural and political climate, had also been recently ratified (1946), but only by a relatively slim majority. The decision to link traditional guarantees and programmatic principles becomes even more meaningful. The political forces were in agreement on how to safeguard the freedoms that had already been secured and to define the process that would lead to further reforms.

A careful examination of how these choices came about indicates that all the political forces that had fought against Fascism had reached a consensus revealing the strong influence exerted by democratic Catholic thought. Giuseppe Dossetti had opened the discussion by emphasizing that the basic rights of individuals and of social groups take precedence over any concession by the State. The instances of "Personalism" — one of the intellectual currents that had most rigorously analyzed the crisis of the state in the 1930's — came face to face with progressive liberal democratic thought and demands for renewal from Marxist inspired parties to design the outline of a "solidary legal state" ("stato sociale di diritto") (as defined in fundamental Articles 2 and 3). The recognition and guarantee of the inalienable rights of citizens as individuals or as part of social groups are closely related to the obligations of social solidarity and to the principle that public action must remove all obstacles — especially those of an economic or social nature which "limit the freedom and equality of citizens, and hinder the full development of the human person and the effective participation of all workers in the political, economic, and social organization of the country."

A convincing testimonial as to the breadth of consensus on Constitutional matters was provided by the Communist leader Palmiro Togliatti; he conceded to the Christian Democrat Dossetti that "today we have the opportunity to endorse the current struggle to install and strengthen democracy in our country. Even if we do not have a common ideological experience, we are starting out from a common political experience; this should allow us to come to an understanding." This understanding was to go even beyond solidarity among the parties which ended in May 1947, when the left was excluded from the government.

In fact, from the day of Liberation and throughout most of the deliberations of the Constituent Assembly, Italy was governed by coalitions hinged on the three major parties which together accounted for more than two-thirds of the vote: the Christian Democrat (DC), the Socialist Party (PSI), and the Communist Party (PCI). In the June 2, 1946 elections, the greatest strength was shown by the Christian Democrats with 35.2% of the vote, followed by the two parties of the left, the Socialists with 20.7% and the PCI with 18.9%.

These figures appear to express a contradiction: the DC and the two parties of the left were ideologically distant from one another, but all three had been legitimated by the liberation struggle. At the same time, all were united by the desire to build a new state, one that would not only break with the Fascist dictatorship, but also with the old Italy, the Italy of restricted suffrage that had capitulated to Mussolini as the "Savior of the Homeland." This newly formulated mandate explains the dynamics of the consensus of the parties on the "programmatic" points discussed earlier, and the "Constitutionality" of the parties sanctioned in Art. 49. The largest parties became the cornerstones of the new democratic republic. This also explains the impasses, the failure to express compliance, the delay in enacting not only the guidelines, but also in establishing the institutions envisaged by the constitutional text. It prompted the criticism of men like the great constitutionalist Mortati, a Christian Democrat, which came, however, long after the issues that Alcide de Gasperi, President of the Cabinet and leader of the reconstruction, brought up when he warned that the government must first strengthen and develop democratic institutions and defend basic rights when formulating administrative codes, before it sets about enforcing the policies. The party system was based on an intricate relationship that was cohesive and at the same time contradictory and polarized. This explains why more frequent disputes erupted during the draft of the second part of the constitution, and why the "governmental structures" of the Italian Republic, as well as the resulting compromises were somewhat weaker.

The Constitution itself and the labor of the Constituent Assembly had thus established the basic coordination necessary for defining the form of government of Republican Italy, but underneath it all there prevailed an attitude that can best be defined as dilatory. Once the fundamental choice for a parliamentary system based on parties with broad popular support had been approved, the Assembly did not proceed further. The proposed refinement of the parliamentary system through "rationalization" i.e. the establishment of limits, aimed to secure government stability avoiding the "parliamentarism" advocated by the Republican Perassi and supported by Mortati himself, was ignored by the leadership of the majority parties casting the vote.

The constitutional consensus, that characterized the birth of the Republic, thus implies another constitutional mandate to the parties for the building of the political system. One basic decision had already been taken in connection with the system for electing the Constituent Assembly and its internal regulations: the proportional representation, favorable to small parties, was substantially legitimated and no longer open to challenge. This was a reform which the PSI and the Catholic Popular party had succeeded in gaining in the first elections held on the basis of universal (male) suffrage in 1919, and to which they remained faithful after the Second World War as well.

Another distinguishing element is worthy of mention: the autonomy of the Constituent Assembly from the government headed by Alcide De Gasperi, and from the mounting international tension which led to the Cold War. The drafting of the Constitution thus connoted an optimist sense of promise, in contrast with the fierce ideological struggle then ravaging Europe.

The critical moment in restructuring the political system was the election of the first Republican Parliament on April 18, 1948. The Constitution had become effective on January 1 of that same year and the political forces had already been polarized into two opposing camps. The clash resolved itself in an unequivocal manner: the DC won 48.5% of the vote, and the Popular Front 31%. Compared to the election of 1946, the two parties of the left lost almost one third of the votes, and the Socialists suffered a clear loss resulting in an Italian peculiarity, a Communist Party much larger than the Socialist Party. The 1948 election was a turning point also because it showed how a "centripetal" structure of the party system can be the result of extreme polarization of the political forces.

De Gasperi won the election on the basis of the sound decision to defend and consolidate democracy during the very same months in which institutional governments in Prague and other Eastern European countries were toppled. The parties that substantially backed this decision (Republicans, Liberals, Social Democrats), supported De Gasperi's government for the full length of the legislature (1948-1953), while the two parties of the left, united in the Popular Front, and the small parties of the far right were opposed to it.

On April 18, 1948, the party system was thus structured on three elements, each different in size, each in a different position along the right-left axis, and each in a different stage of legitimization. If the right had been completely detached even from the constituent process, the left, despite its participation, by rejecting the concept of "western" style democracy raised a question of legitimization. Because of its position along the right-left ideological axis, and because of its stand on essential questions of legitimization, the Christian Democrats were the center party. Accordingly, and not only for its electoral strength, the DC was called to perform a vital role in all post-war governments. The overwhelming majority it carried in the 1948 elections (never to be marked in later poll returns), the result of an intense polarization that cut across the lines and voting power of the center parties, demonstrates the "isolation" of the DC — let us remember the title of De Gasperi's first biography, *De Gasperi: A Lonely Man* — but also its central character and its potential for uniting political forces.

Thus, Italian political life — as the April 18, 1948 results vividly demonstrate — exists in the antithetical positions of the PCI and the DC, a bipolarization strongly rooted in the social fabric, in ideology, and in politics. Yet, at the same time, it is based on a gradual consolidation of the center, on a "centripetal" dynamics within the political system, far from "bi-partisan" models, of which the pivot is the DC. The Christian Democratic party has been defined as the majority party, or as the national party, describing its centrality both in terms of legitimization, and in terms of right-left dynamics.

In the first twenty years of the Republic, this "centripetal" motion was characterized by three critical stages: the period of structural centrism, corresponding to the first legislative term; the period of unstructured centrism and the opening to the left (a conflict that lasted from the 1953 election to the end of the decade); and, lastly, the period of the center-left which characterized the sixties.

The juxtaposition of DC and PCI is at the root of the political system and deeply embedded in Italy's social and cultural heritage. The old division between Socialists and Catholics — which may be profitably remembered also in light of the substantial takeover by the PCI of the traditionally socialist electorate, such as the so-called red regions — carries all the further implications, linked in particular to international politics and social and economic dynamics. There remains, nonetheless, the idea of common popular roots, at the common origin of the two movements in their opposition to the old liberal state, of a common legitimization through the Resistance struggle and through constitutional work. Thus even in the fortieth year of the Republic, this juxtaposition has not stood in the way of mutual commitment or various, — even political — forms of collaboration.

The first Republican Parliament (ending in 1953) was guided by the steady hand of Alcide De Gasperi, in coalition governments where the DC was flanked by the Social Democrats, the Republican party, and the Liberal Party. Italy embarked on economic reconstruction, establishing the necessary infra-structures. It re-entered the international system, taking an active role in the process of European reconstruction. The first social measures were introduced in 1950 by the agricultural reform which set the foundation for the massive State intervention in the rural South. A long-term housing program had been initiated in 1949, and the reform of education in 1951.

Once the veil of ideological conflict between democracy and Communism was lifted, the period of the "centrist" coalition governments was re-evaluated by historiography, and credited with several fundamental achievements even at the institutional level. While it is true that only with the introduction of the law of referendum, at the beginning of the seventies, were the innovations provided for by the Constitution put into effect, the governments headed by De Gasperi were successful in a number of initiatives: 1950 saw the establishment of the Supreme Defense Council; in 1953 measures were approved for the establishment of the Constitutional Court, as well as for the first government decentralization in favor of Regions; 1952 saw the ratification of the law outlawing the Fascist Party, and the proposal to reorganize the presidency of the Cabinet. By becoming a member of the European Coal and Steel Community Italy took a step forward in implementing the provisions of Art. 10 of the Constitution as regards the possible abdication of sovereignty in favor of supranational organizations.

The centrist governments were thus faced with a complex situation: the need for loyalty to the Constitution in a climate marked by fierce ideological conflicts and urgent material needs. In order to illustrate the basic strategy of those years, we might invoke the famous "fourth party" (quarto partito) formula, i.e., the "party of the middle class." Several months after the dissolving of the tripartite coalition (May 1947), in the afternoon session of the Constituent Assembly on December 19, 1947, De Gasperi, in his response to Nenni, the leader of the Socialist party, declared: "We must do something to calm this "fourth party" which belongs to all social strata, but above all to the middle-class. Among the possible solutions, there was, then, a person who could have relieved the anxiety: it was the Hon. Einaudi. At that time, to speak of him was to speak of conservatism, of someone who would have put us under the yoke of the great plutocrats and industrialists. Today, I believe, nobody in Italy could honestly think something like this, when we see the collusion of interests on the part of great industrialists, and, unfortunately, also on the part of the workers who need to work in order to live. It is a collusion against Einaudi's politics, which is a deflationary one, and manifestly against speculative interests. The fourth party, Honorable Nenni, is not the party of the great plutocratic industrialists; it is the party of the middle-class who needed to be reassured beyond what the government formula might have succeeded in doing." These words, pronounced at the beginning of the centrist period, may serve also as a possible striking of balance, stressing the deep social grounding of the reconstructed Italian democracy.

The end of the first Republican parliament (1953) is a crucial mark of historical periodization. The equilibrium guaranteed by the alliance between the Christian Democrats and the "fourth party" was threatened by a strong electoral growth of the right. In the 1953 elections, the DC won only 40.1% and other center parties barely 10%, weakening the majority that had guaranteed and established government leadership in the previous legislative term. Although running on separate tickets, the Communists and the Socialists were still bound by the pact to present a united front, and collected 35.6% of the votes the former, and 12.7% the latter, confirming the trend towards a distribution of electoral consensus to the left that had begun in 1948.

The outcome of the 1953 elections presented an even graver problem in that it failed to enforce, as required by the new electoral law that had been passed, with much controversy, in 1952, the so-called majority reward. The law, defined by the left as a "swindle law," represented the attempt to lend institutional coherence to the structure of the political system, by further rewarding the coalition that won absolute majority with an extra number of parliamentary seats. This failure therefore confirmed that in the dynamics of the Italian system politics have the edge over institutional processes.

The second period in the history of the Republic, covering the entire duration of the second legislative term and part of the third, was thus characterized by the quest for new political balances that had not as yet been identified. It is a period that corresponds roughly to the seven year term of President Gronchi, elected on April 28, 1955, by a Socialist-backed majority that went against the plans of his own party, which had projected and counted on a centrists majority instead. The response to the "opening to the left" decisively orchestrated by the Christian Democrat leader Saragat after the 1953 election, was also contradictory: the centrist parties were left with only a limit space for maneuvering, due both to the presence of a very active MSI and monarchical right, and to the

Socialists' unwillingness to withdraw from the unity pact with the PCI. A disengagement would gradually take place in the two years following the vents of 1956, signalling the Communist Party's first serious setback in the history of the Republic.

During a series of weak administrations led by the Christian Democrats, two currents emerged in connection with the "opening to the left:" the strategy of Fanfani, Secretary of the DC from 1954 (the year of De Gasperi's death) to 1959; and the strategy of President Gronchi, both developed amid strong pressures from the right which at the end of the period drew closer to the government area. The former appeared to be focused on strengthening the DC's apparatus and platform, and on renewing its centrist position so as to launch a dialogue with the PSI according to the centripetal scheme; the second, instead, seemed more oriented towards identifying a number of potential shortcuts proposed by Gronchi himself (who was rather more of an interventionist than his predecessor Einaudi).

After the March 1958 election, when the Christian Democrats and the Socialists obtained 42.3% and 14.2% of the vote respectively (never to happen again in the following thirty years), Fanfani attempted to continue his strategy by moving from Secretary of the DC to President of the Cabinet. The tri-partite coalition (DC-PSDI-PRI), heavily leaning towards the left, was unable, however, to last beyond the second half of 1958 and Fanfani was forced to resign even his post of Party Secretary. Also Moro was called to take office in March of 1959.

The centrist crisis and the attempt to pursue the "opening to the left" ends with the cabinet headed by Tambroni, a DC prime minister only supported by the MSI. The entire period was contradictory and politically complex: though perhaps controversial, it was certainly not lacking in significant achievements. They were the years of the Vanoni plan, made public in 1955, which included economic and financial policies for Italian development through state-managed subsidy programs and the expansion of public enterprises. They were the years of Italian industrialization, which saw the transfer of 1.5 million laborers from the rural South to the industrial North. There was also progress at the institutional level: implementation of the constitutional provisions moved ahead with the creation of the Constitutional Court in 1956, the National

Economic and Labor Council in 1957, and the Superior Council of the Judiciary in 1958. The signing of the Treaty of Rome in 1957 set in motion the process of European integration. Notwithstanding the problems posed by government instability, these achievements follow a course of democratic development that in the early sixties received political sanction.

The start of the new phase, that of center-left, was delayed until the VIII Congress held by the DC in Naples in late January 1962. "The DC congress is of the opinion that at the current political juncture it is not possible for the DC and the PSI to form an effective alliance and join in a common policy, but it reaffirms its interest in a tenable and effective expansion of the democratic area which would lay the foundations for the political understanding necessary to make democracy in Italy stronger and more secure:" the text of the motion passed with a majority vote at the Congress expressed the dynamics of an agreement of the center-left, cautiously taking into consideration the views of the Catholic world and of the rather reluctant ecclesiastical hierarchy.

The policy of involving the PSI was started by the one-party Fanfani cabinet, which followed the collapse of Tambroni's Cabinet in 1960. It was called the "parallel convergence" government, because it was backed by the PSI and the PSDI, the right and left wings of the centrist coalition. Despite the growing intolerance of the Liberals, and while organic center-left alliances emerged in several important municipalities (the first was Milan), the one-party cabinet managed to remain in power until the DC congress. It was then replaced by a tri-partite DC-PSDI-PRI coalition, with the Socialists abstaining and the Liberals opposing it. This new government set its sight on ambitious goals, such as secondary-education reform, raising the minimum age for compulsory education, and the institution of regional governments. It was also successful in nationalizing the electrical power industry.

The Socialists did not enter the government until the next political election, when the DC suffered a 4% loss and the PSI a slightly lower, one, with corresponding gains of the right and the left, in favor of Liberals and Communists. The Liberals, in particular, won their highest numbers of votes ever (7%). But it was on December 4, 1963, when Moro formed a four-party coalition (DC-PSI-PSDI-

PRI) able to count on a large parliament majority, that the political balances and structures were formally modified.

It was this coalition that would lead the country in the years when Italy began to reap the fruits of the great economic and social transformations, of the "economic miracle," and when Italian society was embarking on a new road, a road that was finally leaving behind the problems of war and reconstruction. A new era thus began, with its bright lights and its shadows, a new phase in the development of Italian postwar democracy.

PART TWO

POLITICAL AND INTELLECTUAL
FORCES IN THE
FORMATION OF THE REPUBLIC

III

Political Catholicism, Catholic Organization, and Catholic Laity in the Reconstruction Years

Francesco Traniello

The last free elections to take place before the advent of Fascism were held on May 15, 1921. The electoral law provided for universal male suffrage and proportional representation. In 1921 58.4% of the electors went to the polls. The Partito Popolare Italiano (PPI) acquired 20.4% of the votes, of which more than half came from five regions, in Northern Italy: Piedmont, Liguria, Lombardy, Trentino and Veneto. Although the PPI did not consider itself a Catholic party, all of its leaders were Catholic and its Secretary, Don Sturzo, was a Catholic priest while its electoral base consisted almost entirely of Catholics. Vote-wise, it represented the third party after the liberal political groups and the Socialist party.

The first political elections after the Second World War were held on June 2, 1946. The new electoral law provided for both male and female universal suffrage and proportional representation. The electors voted for the Constituent Assembly and for the institutional referendum (monarch or republic) with 89.1% of the electors exercising their right to vote. The Christian Democrats (DC) earned 35.2% of the votes and topped the polls leaving the Socialist Party (20.7%) and the Communist Party (19.5%) well behind; the liberals earned 6.8% of the votes. The electoral stronghold of the DC, successor to the PPI, proved to be the Northern regions of Lombardy, Trentino, Veneto and Friuli. In 1946, however, it also did well in many Southern regions.[1]

Two years later, on April 18, 1948, in the first republican elections, the DC earned 48.5% of the votes in the elections for the

Chamber of Deputies acquiring an absolute majority of the seats. Between the two political elections, there had been an administrative election in November 1946 in many important Italian cities; the result had been disastrous for the DC which lost many votes, above all in the South and in Rome, to the right-wing "Uomo Qualunque" party.

The DC did not consider itself a Catholic party; but it was certainly "more Catholic" than the PPI, in the sense that the Catholic organizational structures of the Church and the ecclesiastical hierarchies offered it greater support than had been given its predecessor. Unlike the PPI, the DC could count on a real mobilization of Catholic forces. With the election of 1948, the DC became the fulcrum of the republican political system. This was paradoxical because in the institutional referendum in 1946 at least $^3/_4$ of the DC votes had come from electors who had opted for the monarchy rather than the republic.[2]

How was the DC, whose forerunner prior to Fascism could count on only $^1/_5$ of the electorate, able to become the leading party, supported all over the country, whose share of the votes had more than doubled? Furthermore, was the DC really a continuation of the PPI? These two questions encapsulate a whole series of important problems.

If we are to furnish an answer to these questions we must center our attention on the Catholic world in Italy. This expression, which might seem somewhat vague, refers to the organizations, the works and the activities which, from the 19th century on, acted as a bridge between the institutional and doctrinal structure of the Church and the social, cultural and political structure of the country. The laity constituted the principal force of this Catholic world, but it was bound to the ecclesiastical hierarchy by a relationship of obedience and cooperation at various levels and in different sectors of society. The Catholic world was populated by the most active, organized and militant part of Italian Catholicism.

The presence of a lay Catholic world, organized in institutions which differed from the traditional ecclesiastical ones, was not only an Italian phenomenon. Nevertheless the picture of the post-war Italian Catholic world exhibited certain special characteristics which were rooted in its history, and, above all, in the transformations it had experienced in the Fascist period.

During the Fascist regime both the sectors and means by which the Church exerted its influence over civil society, public bodies, and the collective *ethos* had increased. Whatever judgement we may make regarding the real relationship between the Church and the regime, it cannot be denied that the favorable conditions Fascism offered the Church enabled it to penetrate society, the state apparatus, and public opinion much more profoundly, compared to the liberal period. Although there were intermittent conflicts, something like an "exchange" of consent for concessions took place between the Fascist regime and the Church, both at the legal and institutional level, and at the administrative level. The special relationship between Church and regime was sealed by the Concordat of 1929, which was part of the Lateran Agreements requested by the Holy See in exchange for the definitive settlement of the Roman question. The Lateran Agreements had a very important symbolic value for the two contracting parties, but they could be interpreted and applied in different manners, like any other formal agreement. But it must be noted that, in one sense, the Concordat was only the tip of the iceberg: it gave legitimacy to the prerogatives claimed by the Church over certain delicate matters in civil life (marriage, education, associations) and consolidated the increasing influence of the Church both in public and Fascist institutions, as well as in the social and civil fabric. Therefore, for the Church, the Concordat represented a point of arrival, the end of a long conflict with the nation state, but also a point of departure. The Concordat could constitute the first stop along a much longer road which had as its objective that of "Catholicizing" the regime by utilizing a ruling class which was of Catholic faith, and above all, which was sensitive to the impulses which came from the Church to conquer strategic positions in the Fascist state. In this manner, the gulf which had opened in the previous century between the sphere of public institutions and the "Catholic nation" would finally be bridged.

The significance which was ascribed by the Church to the Fascist regime as a providential occasion was sanctioned by the restructuring of the Catholic world. Faced with the totalitarian demands of the regime over political control, the Church doggedly defended and managed to preserve control of some associations over which it had exclusive jurisdiction, while having to surrender others. The

most well-known case (though not the only one) was Azione Cattolica (Catholic Action) whose existence had been safeguarded,
but also delimited, by a special article in the Concordat. The
uneasy survival of this Catholic associative tissue in the body of a
state which defined itself totalitarian, had tangibly modified its
features, sometimes as a result of the direct intervention of the
Church. On the whole, the lay Catholic institutions expanded in
the Fascist era. The network of branches of Azione Cattolica
alone totalled about 5% of the entire population in 1939 with more
than 2,250,000 card-carrying members, of whom about a million
and a half were girls and women (that is, 7% of the total female
population).[3]

The evaluation of the qualitative transformations that occurred
in the Catholic world is more difficult to assess. In many respects,
it modernized its means of action and its organizational formulae.
Particular care was devoted to the mass-media (from the press to
the radio, to the cinema); a specialization in the forms of apostolate for social categories and professional sectors, which indicated a
renewed influence of the Church and of Catholicism among the
urban middle classes, which had previously been the social base of
the liberals' hegemony. The cultural background of the Catholic
world was also refurbished and updated, especially in the field of
economics, law and social sciences. The "social weeks" of the
Catholics, the activities of the Catholic University of Milan, the
cultural periodicals, the initiatives of the Catholic Institute for
Social Activities (ICAS), and the intellectual associations of
Catholic Action, such as the Federation of Catholic University
Students (FUCI) and the Catholic graduates, all provided their
own special contributions.

A totally different scenario emerges if we examine the cultural
policy of the Catholic world in this period. Apart from a few
exceptions, political subjects were avoided in favor of spiritual,
moral and philosophical themes,[4] or were substituted by simplified
and apocalyptical visions of the world or by simple references to
the social doctrine of the church. On the whole, the political
thought of the Catholic world was rather poor. This was a consequence of a negative conception the Church entertained of politics
as a confrontation between ideologies and forces which opposed
each other, and hence as a vehicle of secularization and conflict.

The crisis and the disintegration of the PPI had signified that the Catholic world had abandoned the possibility of the development of a pluralistic democracy.

In this general framework, a kind of division of labor began gradually to take shape in the Italian Catholic world. On the one hand, a fairly restricted *élite* was formed, which was ready to establish a bridgehead in the institutions of the regime, in order to transform it from the inside, without ignoring the industrial and public finance structures which Fascism had established in the 1930's in reaction to the great depression. On the other hand, a laborious and painstaking grass roots operation was carried out, summed up in the formula of the lay apostolate, which was directed at very wide social strata and which aimed at shaping the beliefs and behaviors, practices and convictions of the private and professional spheres.

Thus the spreading of a militant apostolate which was active on the religious and moral plane, with an almost obsessive attention to "decency" and to sexual behavior, combined with a total delegation of power to the upper echelons of the regime and/or the Church, in the political field. This was also a reflection of the changes made to the statutes which modified the organizational structures of Catholic associations, such as the changes made to the structure of Azione Cattolica first in 1923 and then in 1939-40, which rendered the lay movements even more subservient to the will of their ecclesiastic superiors in the organization and the function of the laity.[5] The net result of these changes was that the Catholic world became more markedly clerical.

Can one therefore conclude that Italy was more Catholic in the late 1930's than it had been in the early 1920's? From the Church's point of view, the answer is undoubtedly yes. Furthermore, there were numerous signs of a renewed consensus toward Catholicism, sometimes even as an alternative to the Fascist regime, to its control and indoctrination. Existing within the regime, but with its own distinct role and its right to proselytism, the Church and its lay labor force enjoyed a strong position. The regime itself began to become aware of the Catholic world as a potential competitor to be feared in the struggle for control over public institutions and as aspirants to the ruling class.

Neither the Catholic world nor the Church played a direct part in creating the political conditions which brought about the collapse of the Fascist regime, on July 25, 1943. However, as important forces capable of influencing public opinion and common sentiment, they played a part in the progressive and increasingly rapid loss of legitimacy suffered by the regime.

The theme of the so-called detachment of the Church from the regime is one of the most controversial in historiography. Here we cannot consider it analytically, if not to note that, in any case, the process was neither a linear nor a uniform one. We must therefore restrict our attention to identifying its different components and its various phrases. With regard to the Holy See, both the politico-military alliance of Italy with Nazi Germany and the enactment of the racial laws of 1938, which violated an article of the Concordat in the sphere of marriage, had been received with great concern. In the last years of Pius XI's pontificate, the problem of the totalitarian threat to the Church and to Christianity (a threat which came not only from Communism but also from Nazism) had become of central importance in the Pope's evaluations.[6] However, Mussolini earned a new line of credit from his role as mediator at an international level from the Munich Conference to the outbreak of the war. On the occasion of the latter event, Italy's proclamation of "non-belligerency" had been approved and strongly supported by the Church. But Italy's entry into the war crushed all illusions and convinced Pius XII, who had just been elected, to move the axis of the Vatican's political bearings towards the government in Washington, which was still neutral.[7]

The principle of impartiality among belligerent which Pius XII adopted as a norm could not be extended to the Italian Church and the Catholic world, because they were prey to the fate of a nation at war. Nevertheless, the messages which came from the Pope about the war in progress moved in an opposite direction to that of the Fascist propaganda, and traces of it were to be found in the relatively cautious and reserved attitude which was adopted by a large part of the Italian episcopacy,[8] especially that sector which was closer to the rural world. The differences as regards the support furnished the regime on the occasion of the war in Ethiopia and in Spain were conspicuous. The course of the war, which became increasingly less triumphant, did not create a widespread anti-Fascist consciousness in the Catholic world, at least at the beginning, apart from a few sectors which were already resolutely hostile to the regime. Yet it contributed to the crumbling of the quality of Catholic consensus, distinguishing between fidelity to the mother-country which was at war and the duty to serve one's country, and the Fascist system. In conclusion, even though there were many nuances along a continuum which went from exasperated nationalism to convinced pacifism[9], the Catholic world adopted the same attitude towards the regime as the one it would have adopted towards any established power, towards which Catholic morality imposed a duty of obedience, though not totally unconditional. On the other hand, the developments in the war, which already presaged an unfavorable result for the regime as early as 1942, stimulated a renewal of activity, even at a political level, on the part of the Catholic élites.

If the Fascist regime fell without immediate jolts, this was also due to the fact that the Catholic world had abandoned it in its soul. Moreover, the way in which the regime fell provided the Catholic world with an assurance, at least temporarily, of the legality and the institutional continuity of the state, which was guaranteed by the monarchy. This does not exclude the fact that a hard political game was begun which was also played within the Catholic world itself, the stakes of which were the future post-war settlement of the country.

The game which took place within the Catholic world was based on certain shared presuppositions. The first was the authority of Pius XII as the source of inspiration and orientation.[10] It developed, during the war, along a line which proceeded from the enunciation of the causes of the conflict, which were identified in the abandonment of the order of natural rights willed by God, to the enunciation of norms and principles which had to govern the construction of a new order regulating both the international community and the internal system of the single nations. In this regard, see the Christmas radio-messages of 1942 and 1944. Plus XII came to single out the democratic form of government as the system which best respected natural rights. The most problematic and debated points of the "political" teachings of Pius XII concerned the relationship between the order of natural rights and the role of the Church; and the tasks which Catholics would have had to fulfill in a democracy both as believers and as citizens of a nation.

A second unifying element of the Catholic world was its fundamental law-abiding, anti-revolutionary and markedly anti-communist attitude. The only exception was the young intellectual fringe of Communist Catholics, which was tolerated and even protected by the Church, for some time.[11] Catholic anti-Communist sentiment was destined to increase with the decline of the danger which was constituted by Nazism. The Church and the Catholic world became, to all intents and purposes, the principal guarantor, even at an international level, of a non-revolutionary transition from Fascism to post-Fascism. But the respect of legality and the aversion to Communism could have led to many other possible results.

The third factor of convergence was the common aspiration to build a "Christian order" on the ruins of Fascism, though utilizing many of the materials which had been prepared in Fascist times: an order, therefore, which had to grow from the roots which had previously penetrated society and public institutions. Nevertheless the outline of the new order and the means by which to realize it were the object of one of the most intense debates which have ever taken place in the Catholic world: many forces came into play including different theological, philosophical and spiritual currents of thought[12], difference approaches which had matured in the numerous intellectual circles such as that of the Catholic University of Milan, those of Catholic Action, the Florentine group that had gathered around Giorgio La Pira, and so on.

The solidarity and consistency of the reasons which united the Catholic world must not induce us into disregarding the great variety of plans which animated it. These must be considered in relation to the rapidly changing situations following the fall of Fascism, to the collapse of the political-territorial unity of the state, and to the beginning of the Resistance movement after September 8, 1943. It will therefore be necessary to distinguish between the different phases and protagonists.

Up until July 25, 1943 the political solution the Holy See would have preferred regarding Italy was the rapid conclusion of a separate peace, to be negotiated by a different government from Mussolini's. Was it the aim of this policy to safeguard the existence of the regime "without Mussolini," as has been argued elsewhere?

This interpretation cannot be substantiated. Certainly a transition phase was imagined, which was characterized by the restoration of the constitutional order and the prerogatives of the sovereign, and by the exercise of rigorous control over law and order, against the threats of "subversion." The idea of a Catholic leadership had not yet appeared on the horizon.[13]

The disastrous management of political and military affairs after July 25, and during the armistice phase played an important part in nullifying all hopes of a painless transition from Fascism to post-Fascism. The renewal of an intense political struggle conducted by the antifascist parties and the CLN (the Committee for National Liberation), together with the start of the Resistance movement which acted as a strong catalyst in stimulating a widespread increase in political consciousness, and though dominated by the left-wing movements, also found the support of many militant Catholics as well as a part of the clergy, radically modified future perspectives.

Thus, the policy of the Holy See was defined in more distinct terms and launched attacks on many fronts. Greater pressure was put on the government in Washington, in an anti-Communist stance, showing "the real situation of Italy" to be that of a nation which was deeply threatened by the risks of internal subversion and which was about to set up a system of multi-party democracy after a transition period. The personal fate of the king was divorced from that of the monarchy as a guarantee of institutional continuity and of national unity. The Holy See tried to temper the action of the armed resistance, as far as this was in its power, even by allowing the clergy to carry out their pastoral work among the partisan groups. A strong drive to mobilize the clergy and the Catholics in humanitarian works of solidarity, succour and assistance was undertaken. The activism of the ecclesiastical institutions of the Catholic laity was rallied, above all those of Catholic Action, and its decisive function as an agency of political education was stressed.

The practical results of this intensive mobilization however was rather indeterminate. Many policy documents which were elaborated by Catholic Action concentrated above all on preventing Catholics from becoming political militants in parties which were "contrary to the Christian faith and morality." Moreover, the Church and Catholic Action did not opt for a policy which was definite and binding, taking great care not to identify themselves in one party, to preserve a position which was *super partes*, to oppose the idea that one sole party "would seem to monopolize Catholicism."[14] This position also corresponded to the fragmentation of the experiences that the different Catholic groups which were spread over the country, were undergoing. This gave rise to tension between the central organisms of Catholic Action and the leaders of the Christian Democrat party (DC). The origins of the DC date back to the summer of 1942, and to the numerous meetings which took place between representatives of the old PPI and between these and the group of anti-Fascist Milanese "Guelphs," who both criticized the compromises the Italian Catholic world had made with the Fascist regime.

Only after July 25, 1943, when the DC had become part of the committee of the opposition groups and then of the CLN, and had come out into the open with its own programs (such as the *Milan Program* and the *DC's Ideas on reconstruction*), did the party show it was capable of acting as a real force of aggregation in the Catholic world, and attracting numerous men and groups of the new generation who had been trained in the Fascist epoch. The ensuing war of liberation further strengthened its cadres. Although the ties which bound the party members to the clergy, to the top ranks of the ecclesiastic hierarchy even (the well-known communion of opinion between Alcide De Gasperi and the substitute Secretary of State Giambattista Montini is a case in point), the party was not born of the initiative of the Church. It was born under the autonomous impulse of Catholic élites of various origins, whose central leadership was for the most part formed by long-standing PPI members. The choice of the DC as the party with which the Church established a privileged relationship was therefore the result of a process, not a foregone conclusion, nor a historical destiny. Such a choice could come about, as De Gasperi lucidly comprehended, on the basis of an "exchange" between the political unity of the Catholics in a democratic party, which was supported by the Church, and the guarantees that such a party could offer the Church in matters of politics, ideology and institutions.[15] It was however a conditional choice which was reversible and not even shared by all the top people of ecclesiastic hierarchy.[16]

At the end of the war many conditions existed in Italy which allowed the Church to accept the risks of a political democracy, including those of a religious nature. Religious practice seemed to be on the rise. The forecasts of those who had hoped the Church would find itself in troubled waters because of the compromises it had made with the Fascist regime proved to be wrong. When the state collapsed, the Church remained (thanks also to the abnegation of its clergy) the only efficient and substantially united institution. Its role as mediator had placed it above the parts, even in the civil war, whose effects were mitigated by its contribution; vice-versa, many believers had taken part in the civil war, thus legitimating their role as future members of the political class. Its international relationships had multiplied and become stronger, particularly those with the United States which had identified the Holy See as a prime interlocutor for the Italian theater. The disrepute into which the monarchical institutions of the Risorgimento had fallen opened up new spheres of influence to the Church. It was able to add to the successes obtained in Fascist times, the prestige and the consensus it gained in war time. Thanks to its wide networks and the solid texture of lay Catholic organizations, the Church could act as a force of social stabilization, a role which was facilitated by the spread of its interclass messages, of its invitations to social peace, of its appeals to social justice. Even without underestimating the reappearance of anticlerical forces and manifestations, especially among certain sectors of the intelligentsia and the working class as well as in some parties, very few of the new ruling élites seemed inclined to enter into direct conflict with the ecclesiastical institution taken as a whole; even less so the leaders of the Communist party. One of the principal components of the strategy the "new party" adopted by Togliatti was the special care with which it treated the Catholic world.

These basic elements could not but have a beneficial effect on the party around which the organized Catholic world gradually polarized. Many other factors also worked in its favor: the pressing appeal of the Church for political unity among Catholics: the gravitation of the new Catholic élites towards the party, and their relative homogeneity, at least with regard to certain general tendencies and aims; the widespread conviction that collective decisions of enormous importance even from the religious point of view would have been made in the new historical phase.

Even the opinion of those who hold that the expansion and rapid success of the DC is due exclusively to its direct and intimate ties to the Catholic world is open to criticism because the exact opposite might also be argued: that is, the capacity of the DC to mold the consensus of the Catholic world was also won in the field, in the heat of political battle, in its actions in local and national government. The relationship between the DC and its Catholic and ecclesiastical hinterland cannot be schematically summarized as a one-way relationship. It is precisely this two-way relationship that renders it an interesting object of historical inquiry.

The party which assumed the leadership of the government in December 1945 (the first De Gasperi cabinet) was extremely atypical. Although it already had a respectable number of card-carrying members, it had very little in common with mass parties exhibiting a rigid structure. Organization-wise, the party was weak. Almost all its adherents also participated in other organizations, which mediated, so to speak, their members' party political militancy. Most of these organizations were Catholic even when their name did not express the fact openly. Some of them had seen the light shortly before the end of the war. The central reference point continued to be Catholic Action with its four mass associations of men, women, young men (GIAC) and young women (GF), together with its specialized "movements": FUCI, graduates, primary school teachers. The ICAS (Catholic Institute for Social Activities) coordinated the various social associations: the Farmers' Federation, which was founded in 1944 and which had a strong following in the countryside, the Catholic Union of Entrepreneurs and Managers, the National Center for Artisans, the Confederation of Co-operatives, etc. The professional associations were linked to each other via the graduates' movement: Catholic doctors, chemists, secondary school teachers, etc. The ACLI (the Association of Catholic Workers), which was founded in the summer of 1944 in conjunction with Catholic participation in the unified trade union CGIL, and the boy scouts associations, reported to the President's Office of AC. The so-called "works," like the Sports' Center and the Tourist Center depended from the pertinent individual mass associations.

Another association which reported to the President's Office was the Entertainment Board which was organized into three Catholic bodies — one for the cinema, one for the theater and one for radio.[17]

This network, which, while not officially incorporated into the party existed side-by-side with it, furnished the supporting framework, much of its financial resources, and a large quota of its peripheral personnel. Furthermore, the party was organized around the different groups of which it was composed even at the level of its ruling class, most of whom had their own newspaper and afterwards acted as "currents" in attracting adherents. The weak organizational structure was in part compensated for by a constellation of notables, often at the center of a network of "political patronage," especially (but not only) in the Mezzogiorno.

On a mass level, a party of this nature operated as a basin in which were collected or deposited a mass of votes. Thus the real political physiognomy of the party was projected by its ruling group (which had been selected before the birth of the party or outside the party ranks) and by its manner of exercising the functions of local and national government.

One of the strong points of the Christian Democratic leaders who sympathized with De Gasperi was their full awareness of the structural limits of the DC. Ever since 1945 he had warned that the future of the country "will not be decided by our one million party members" (in truth there were far less). In fact, De Gasperi took it for granted that there was a certain lack of homogeneity between the cadres and party leaders, and the "so-called gray, lazy masses, the slow masses," whose action, in his opinion, it was the duty of the party to channel in the right direction. This emerged clearly on the occasion of the referendum on June 2, 1946, when, with the agreement of the upper echelons of the Vatican and AC, De Gasperi wanted the party (the vast majority of whose members were republicans) to leave the electors free to choose as they wished on the institutional question.[18]

De Gasperi's line sought to attract many of the voters who had a low level of political consciousness which Italy inherited from Fascism and the liberal era. They were composed prevalently, but not only, by the large constellation of the middle classes, both employees and self-employed, which in some estimates, accounted for

almost 50% of the Italian workers[19]. The data also indicate that in
1951, farmers — farm owners and tenant farmers — still outnum-
bered the entire industrial working class.[20] The objective of con-
structing the democratic system was thus to be achieved by sub-
tracting the largest part of the body politic from the influence of
the traditional right wing parties (the results obtained by the
"Uomo Qualunque" in the autumn '46 elections sounded the
alarm), or, at the very least, from electoral passivity: see the data
on the number of votes polled in the elections before Fascism.[21]
This project depended, of course, on the type of democracy that
the political class led by De Gasperi wished to create: a democracy
which would very quickly leave behind the "exceptional" phase of
the Resistance and the CLN, and find stability and mass legitima-
tion through universal suffrage with the popular parties playing the
role of guide.[22]

For a party such as the DC, this project could only be achieved
on certain conditions. In many cases, pragmatism had to be
favored over the integrity of the program. Care had to be taken to
avoid fractures in strategic lines of action: first and foremost with
regard to the Church, an indispensable ally especially when it came
to mobilizing a lazy, unstable and heterogeneous electorate. De
Gasperi's desire to re-establish normal relations for Italy with the
international community by accepting a peace treaty which many
considered unacceptable and punitive was also fruit of the same
logic.

Against the background, the line which prevailed among the
ruling class of the DC under De Gasperi's leadership achieved two
different objectives. On the one hand, a more moderate democratic political equilibrium was achieved. On the other hand, a
constitutional framework was defined which was open to the stimuli which came from the left-wing tendencies of the DC and from
the working class parties in the field of economic and social reform.
In order to enable the work of the Constituent Assembly to be
despatched, De Gasperi delayed breaking off the government
coalition with the Socialists and Communists until May 1947,
resisting the strong pressures to put an end to that coalition which
the Catholic world and the Church began to exert on him shortly
after the end of the war. The political and cultural ferments which
had animated the Catholic world, especially in the period between

1943 and 1945, now found their principal outlet in the design for the new constitution.

The formula which dominated the Catholic world after the fall of Fascism was the foundation of a new Christian order to be built on the ruins of the old one swept away by the war. This was the Papacy's fundamental message, one which millions of Catholics had internalized and made their own. The idea that the new order had first to be realized in a new constitutional order for the state enjoyed equal favor. Thus the phase of building the new constitution acquired religious value, creating religious expectations; it was not merely a political process.

The model of the liberal state, as a lay state in which religious institutions led a separate life from the institutions of the state, was alien to the view which was widely prevalent in the Catholic world. Indeed, the liberal state was now even blamed for the rise of totalitarian systems. With rare exceptions, the Catholic world was convinced that Catholicism had to be confirmed as the religion of the state.[23] Nevertheless, some of the various Catholic proposals could often be identified by their language alone. Some Catholics spoke of a Christian state pure and simple, by which they meant the direct application of the Catholic doctrine to the new constitution, especially as regarded the "rights" of the Church in the fields of morality, education, the family and social welfare.

Others preferred to use a more indirect expression: "a state inspired by Christian principles." This suggested a more complex relationship between Church and state, one which would be mediated by recognizing the primacy of the "rights" of the "person," which would therefore represent a middle way between ethical-religious principles and their embodiment in the constitution. The choice of "personalismo" as the axis of the new conception of the state was a reflection of the cultural changes which had come about in certain sectors of the Catholic intelligentsia under the influence of Jacques Maritain and, to a lesser extent, Emmanuel Mounier.[24] *"Personalismo"* claimed to have superseded the liberal and socialist theories in as much as it represented an 'integral humanism', without eliminating the possibility of debate.

Thus, in one sense, at the end of the war, the Catholic world was bent on going beyond the Concordat of 1929, which was however strenuously defended as the minimal condition which could ensure religious peace. But proceeding beyond the Concordat could mean quite different things. For some it meant using the Concordat as a springboard to place new spheres, both in public and in private life, and at the constitutional level, under the direct influence of the Church. For others, it represented an opportunity for Catholics to confirm their peace with the state so that they could devote themselves to drawing up a model of the constitution which would encompass those aspects of the doctrine of the state which one sector of Catholic culture had been developing[25]. These represented a new lattice of ideas on the themes of social welfare, local government, a plurality of legal codes, designed in opposition to totalitarian models, and which had many points in common with analogous developments in liberal-democratic and reformist-socialist thought.

Furthermore, it must be noted that at the end of the war, the Church and the Catholic world exerted exceedingly strong pressure for a new Christian order to be created without delay. This pressure assailed the DC and continually risked impairing its policy of alliance with other parties, even calling into question its status as a democratic party. De Gasperi was fully conscious of this risk. On the occasion of the XIX Catholic Social Week held in October 1945 and dedicated to the theme *The Constitution and the Constituent Assembly,* De Gasperi remarked that ideal perspectives could not always become reality "when the objective is to establish peaceful cohabitation in human society respecting the opinions of others and to find a formula which reconciles the principles one aspires to and the actions one can take."[26] It was a delicate manner for pointing out that the practice of democracy could not be divorced from the competition between different cultures and ideologies, and consisted in the laborious search after valid compromises.

During the war the conviction that the war itself marked the end of the old social order had already become widespread throughout the Catholic world. What was required was the drawing up of a blueprint of a new order founded on different principles and values.

For almost a century, the social sphere had been the primary field in which Catholic movements actively participated. Their declared aim was to recreate a Christian society. Their point of departure was their view that the Catholic doctrine alone contained in itself the principles and rules of a just social order. The teachings of the Popes, from Leo XIII to Pius XII, constituted the axis of the social doctrine of the church, and was taught in all the ecclesiastical schools and in all the educational centers for the laity. The characteristic of this doctrinal *corpus* was that it was prevalently "deontological," that is an indication of moral principles as applicable to the social order. Catholic social culture in its entirety had suffered the effects of this characteristic, exhibiting a certain degree of weakness in analyzing the structural mechanisms which regulated industrial societies. Nevertheless, some strides forward had been made to translate the general principles into more effective operational measures and guidelines.

Many of the documents written during the war took this stance. We may mention the "Code of Camaldoli" or "principles of social order", a document produced in 1943-1944 by a group of intellectuals linked to Catholic Action and published in April 1945; the programs of the DC; those of the other Catholic political groups, such as the movement of Communist Catholics (which later became the Party of the Christian Left, and which was dissolved at the end of 1945) or the movement of Social-Christians. Catholic magazines of all types, ecclesiastical documents, newspapers and educational pamphlets all trumpeted the social question.

The main thrust was in two directions: the abolition of the proletariat and the elimination of private monopolies, which were considered to be the product of a form of capitalism dominated solely by the law of profit. The most widely-accepted solutions envisaged the increase in the number of small and medium-sized farm owners (achieved by means of an agrarian reform, if necessary); the participation of the workers in the profits, the share capital and the management of firms; the defense of artisan modes of production.

The preference accorded to all forms of participation in property and management of the economy was rooted in an organic vision of the social structure which prevailed in Catholic culture and which separated it, with few exceptions, from antagonistic conceptions of social life. This led to placing great stress on the theme of solidarity between the various social groups, within a vaster framework of national solidarity. This was an ethical attitude which played an important part in the reconstruction phase.

The organic conception of social life was reflected in the attitude to trade unionism. The image of unionism which prevailed in the Catholic world was not that of an organization based on one class only, but of a collection of categories of workers (including the self-employed), which had to be granted public legal status. Opinion, however, diverged widely on the subject, especially with regard to the autonomy of the unions, the measures they could adopt, and the relationship to the Communist and Socialist trade unions. With the Pact of Rome in 1944, the leaders of the various tendencies in the union movement had stipulated a unitarian agreement: trade union unity, however, gave rise to varying evaluations. Some quarters, such as the Catholic leader Achille Grandi, who died in 1946, praised its value; others, especially those in ecclesiastical spheres, looked upon labor unity with diffidence, partly because the Christian component in the General Confederation of Workers (CGIL) represented a small minority.

But the most complex and politically important problem, the real cleavage which divided the Catholic world, was the question of the duties of the state in economic and social affairs. State intervention in defense of the weaker social strata, with functions of promoting social welfare and redistributing resources through the instrument of fiscal policy had, by now, been accepted, at least in principle. What gave rise to controversy was the subject of the real limits that were to be placed on state intervention.

The first point to be noted is that an extension of state powers went against the Catholic principle of the "subsidiary role" of the state: only in the case of real need could the state take the place of private initiative, of other bodies, or of the agreements between the parties. Nonetheless, the Catholic groups that belonged to or had arisen out of the intellectual movements, held that "society could not be defended without willing the state into existence." In this view, it was a contradiction to try to defeat the monopolies without having recourse to the functions of the state, which might even include resorting to the nationalization of certain economic sectors. According to Pasquale Saraceno, a brilliant young economist, the formation of monopolies could not have been opposed by the use of palliative, but only by the intervention of the state. For these men, the most effective weapon to achieve a socially just economy was the policy of economic planning. They had studied the experiments in economic policy in the 1930's, they were acquainted with and approved of the Beveridge plan, and they were soon to embrace Keynesian theories.[27]

Caution, however, was the catchword of the men who came from the Partito Popolare, as did De Gasperi himself: free trade ideas dominated their thought. This was due in part to their desire to dissociate themselves from Fascism, together with the conviction that economic freedom was an essential component of personal freedom. Even authorities in the ecclesiastical world, such as *La Civiltà Cattolica*, embraced free trade theories in opposition to socialism.[28] The industrial and financial sectors which belonged to the Confederation of Industry, chaired by Angelo Costa, a Catholic whose opinion carried great weight in certain ecclesiastical circles, were firm proponents of classic economic rules.

There are many reasons which account for the victory of a free trade economic policy in De Gasperi's fourth government in May 1947: political reasons, ideological reasons, and economic reasons. But what must be added is the fact that this type of economic policy was a powerful source of attraction in the Catholic world. The middle class, which provided the DC with its largest number of votes, was hostile to state intervention in the economy, and even to the "social" limits to property rights that the Catholic doctrine preached in theory. The strong interests of capital put pressure in the same direction.

It is not surprising therefore that the work of the Constituent Assembly on economic and social themes was extremely troubled despite the convergence of opinions which emerged on the theme of the "social state" among the adherents of the Christian Demo-crat Left-wing, led by Giuseppe Dossetti, and the class-based parties of the left. In any case the work of the Constituent Assembly did not weigh heavily on the present, that is on the economic policy which formed the cornerstone of the work of reconstruction. The republican constitution remained a future commitment on this topic.

Thus political and cultural cleavages had appeared in the Catholic world over the constitutional order and the tasks of the state in the economic and social spheres. A third cleavage which was no less important concerned the physiognomy and function of the Christian Democrat party.

In the elections held on June 2, 1946, the DC enjoyed the advantage of being selected by the Church and by the lay associations as the party of choice. Other political groups of Christian denomination, such as the Christian Left or the Social-Christians had disappeared from the scene or were on their way to extinction, partly because of the hostility the Church had manifested towards them. The call to Catholics to unite in one party was justified on religious grounds. The appeal to Catholic unity worked, but only to a certain extent. More than a few practicing Catholics had voted for other parties, both of the left and of the right. An analysis of the votes Catholics cast for other parties has never been attempted, and perhaps the task is an impossible one. Nevertheless, the Church continued to affirm that 99% of the Italian population was Catholic; this, it was claimed, was another reason why its institutions and the organizations connected to it could not identify themselves totally in one party. Furthermore, certain circles in the Vatican and some bishops were suspicious of a party which, in their opinion, exhibited excessive freedom in its movements. Its leader had defined it a party of the center which was moving towards the left; much of the clergy would have preferred it to move towards the right.[29] The experience of the Partito Popolare had taught the political élite which had militated in that party an important lesson: a shift in the political preferences of the Church could prove fatal to a party which had its roots in the Catholic world. The "ex-popular" élite therefore put great pressure on the top echelons of the Vatican, pointing out the risks the Church would have run on the subject of ecclesiastical politics if Catholics had divided up their votes among various parties. De Gasperi had already made this observation in a note he had written during the war[30]. Nevertheless they knew that a party which was reduced to acting as the bulwark of "religious interests" could not be a democratic party, because it would be directed from the outside. The defense of the Church and its rights was therefore a winning argument in favor of the political unity of Catholics; but it could not constitute the sole reason for the political existence of the party.

The leaders of the PPI who gathered round De Gasperi introduced other discriminating criteria which determined the physiognomy of the party. The first was antifascism: this excluded Catholic circles which were nostalgic for the old regime. The second was that of the democratic method: this elemented those who sympathized with the authoritarian regimes of the Iberian peninsula. In the end, the judgement on the party was left in the hands of the electorate, in free electoral competitions, that is, in the hands of the people, not of the Church. Naturally, this judgement was influenced by the numerous pressures exerted by the Church; but it was a much freer judgement than the one permitted in states with a one-party system. The third discriminating factor was that the party had to choose its allies with whom to form a government from among the anti-Fascist parties, which also helped (as we have already seen) to keep immoderate Catholic drives towards integralism in check. The fourth, and most important, discriminating factor was De Gasperi's design to expand the electoral base of the party beyond the confines of the organized Catholic world, to transform it into a "nation-wide party" which was capable of attracting the most disparate range of interests and social classes, thus occupying the "center" of Italian society as well as the center of the political spectrum.

A comparison with the Partito Popolare is instructive on this matter. Although the PPI had renounced employing the term "Christian", it had remained within the confines of the organized Catholic world. The DC under De Gasperi's leadership had set its sights much higher, pointing in all directions. The political situation and the onset of the great ideological divisions of the cold war gave it a helping hand.

Electoral consensus among divergent interests and opinion could be obtained provided certain conditions were respected: a) the party had to avoid following a rigid ideological line: the appeal to the Catholic social doctrine paid great dividends in realizing this condition; b) the party had to maintain a flexible structure; c) the party had to play a strong leading role in the government. This made of the DC a party which was much akin to the liberal model, with the fundamental difference that the core of its base was made up principally of organized groups.

The group which recognized Giuseppe Dossetti as its leader, and is therefore commonly referred to as the "Dossettiani", tried to furnish an alternative to this type of party[31]; it was composed of young people of the second generation, who had not militated in the PPI. They had received their cultural education either at the

Catholic University or in the intellectual movements of Catholic Action or in both. Their political initiation had taken place during the war and in the war of liberation. Dossetti had been able to observe the organization of the Communist Party in Emilia and the way it worked at close range. The Dossettiani were a far cry from the old world of liberalism. They concentrated their attention on the destiny of the proletariat, fearing that the DC would lose sight of it completely. They passed severe judgement on the level of the political culture of the Catholic world, on attitudes and culture of the clergy as well as on the structures which Catholic Action had created to organize the masses. These were the reasons they believed that one of the fundamental tasks of the party was to educate its adherents and direct their political action. They drew up a clear dividing line between Catholic Action which operated within the bounds of the religious function of the Church, and the party. Their design was based on the fundamental idea that the party could represent the opportunity and provide the means with which to bring about a cultural transformation of the Catholic world which would be in stark contrast to the clerical and bourgeois Catholic project. At the end of 1946, Dossetti published an article entitled "Beyond politics," in which he described a party which was capable of "engaging man in all his social relationships."

It is not surprising that dissent arose continually between Dossetti and De Gasperi, and the party leaders who supported him. Dossetti had already resigned as vice-chairman of the party in February 1946 because of his differences over the position De Gasperi had adopted in the institutional referendum. He would have preferred the DC to commit itself wholeheartedly to the republican cause. In September 1946, Dossetti also resigned from the party leadership, and as the party representative of the press office and for propaganda, criticizing the party's indifference to organizational problems. On the other hand, Dossetti's group devoted itself body and soul to the work of the Constituent Assembly, where it found more fertile ground for its ideas. Furthermore it began to act as a political and cultural educational group through the association "Civitas Humana." Planned in 1946, this association gathered together politicians, intellectuals, clergymen and trade unionists. More or less the same group later gave life to the review of political culture *Cronache Sociali* (*"Social Chronicles"*).

The first number was published on May 30th, 1947, the day before De Gasperi's fourth government was formed, the government which put an end to the coalition government with the Communists and the Socialists. Even Dossetti and his friends agreed that the split was by then inevitable; but they begged the DC to keep alive the political spirit which had characterized the collaboration between the three popular parties. This demand was unrealistic. While one member of Dossetti's group, Amintore Fanfani, entered the new cabinet, the situation became much more difficult for the others, given the climate of the approaching elections — those of April 1948.

In fact, the pressure exerted on the DC by the Church and the Catholic world had gradually increased, producing effects which were the opposite of those aspired to by Dossetti's group.

Men who were very close to the DC had reached the top ranks of Catholic Action in 1946. For example, Vittorino Veronese had become Central President and Monsignor Giovanni Urbani General Assistant.[32] But the result of the administrative elections in Autumn 1946 and the Sicilian elections held in April 1947, both of which were unfavorable to the DC, had made a great impression in the Catholic world. In January 1947, Luigi Gedda, president of Catholic Men (and ex-president of Catholic Youth) had argued that the cause of the Catholic failure to achieve political unity lay with the DC, and that a new organization which would bring together Catholics of all tendencies had to be created in order to combat *"pro aris et focis"*: the chief adversary was obviously Communism. In March, Gedda maintained that Catholic Action had to promote an electoral union; this harked back to the model of the Electoral Union of 1906. These proposals could have put the DC in serious trouble as a party, since they embodied the idea of a Catholic block which would be held together by its opposition to Communism. For the time being, Gedda's proposals were rejected, but Catholic Action committed itself to conditioning the political line of the DC in a more forceful and direct manner.

The breaking off of the coalition government with the Socialists and Communists was greeted with enormous satisfaction and regained for the DC the sympathy of many ecclesiastical circles and the Catholic world. But with the approach of the political elections, Gedda engaged battle again, this time having obtained the prior approval of Pius XII. His idea was to create a web of "civic committees", under the direction of a national committee with its own offices and agencies, which was distinct from Catholic Action but supported and sustained by the latter's structures.[33] They were to act as a vehicle of propaganda and electoral mobilization. The plan was linked to the models of mass organization that Gedda had successfully experimented with in Catholic Youth. Furthermore, the plan formed the part of the wave of mobilization and propaganda which stimulated the Catholic world into action at the end of 1947, and in which the Jesuit preacher Father Riccardo Lombardi was one of the main protagonists. Those leaders of Catholic Action who most feared the open use of the organization in a political commitment, obtained the assurance that the employment of the civic committees in the task of mobilizing the electorate would be limited to those elections. Although their activity on the occasion of the elections was massive and of great importance to the DC, the project for a Catholic bloc which would override the party did not result.

What conclusions can be drawn? The investment the Catholic world had made in the DC had undoubtedly increased between 1945 and 1948. That year also marked the end of the "constituent" phase of the physical reconstruction of the country. The Italian population was called upon to make decisions which would decide its future in a national and international situation which was tension-ridden; which system should they choose? This decision also involved the selection of the political entity they preferred.

The effect of all these factors was to make an irrepeatable number of tendencies, hopes, fears and interests converge on the DC. But the electoral success which placed it at the center of the political system was not simply the consequence of Catholic mobilization: the phenomenon was much more complex. It was also the realization of the project of transforming the "Christian party" into a truly "national party."

Notes

1 Electoral results referring to the PPI (Popular Party) in 1921 and to the CD (Christian Democracy) in 1946 and 1948 elections. Results are shown in percentages and subdivided by Regions.

	PPI 1921	DC 1946	DC 1948
Piemonte	22,1	35,2	47,9
Liguria	23,9	32,5	45,9
Lombardia	25,6	38,5	52,5
Veneto	35,9	49,1	60,5
Trentino	32,0	57,4	71,9
Vanezia G. (later Friuli e Venezia G.)	3,2	46,6	57,0
Emilia Romagna	19,3	23,3	33,0
Toscana	18,9	28,2	39,0
Marche	29,9	30,6	46,7
Umbria	16,2	25,7	36,5
Lazio	22,1	33,0	51,7
Abruzzi e Molise	7,2	42,4	54,3
Campania	13,8	34,0	50,1
Puglia	10,1	32,9	48,6
Basilicata	4,2	31,3	48,4
Calabria	18,8	34,3	48,8
Sicilia	13,2	33,6	47,9
Sardegna	11,4	41,2	51,2
(Italy as a whole)	(20,4)	(35,2)	(48,7)

2 A Spreafico, "La competizione elettorale e gli esiti del voto," in *La Nascita della Repubblica*, Atti del convegno di studi Storici, Roma 1987.

3 Catholic Action membership 1938-1941, subdivided by organizational branches and movements. (Source: M. Casella, *L'Azione Cattolica alla caduta del Fascismo*, Rome, Ed. Studium, 1984).

a) GIAC (Italian Youth of Catholic Action)
    GF (Young Women)
    UU (Men's Union)
    UD (Women's Union)
    Fanciulli (Boys)
    FUCI M. (Italian Federation of Catholic University Students-Men)

FUCI F. (Italian Federation of Catholic University Students-Women)
MAESTRI (Teachers)

	1938	1939	1940	1941
GIAC	385,256	387,843	382,060	395,562
GF	959,557	1,011,013	1,059,496	1,075,342
UU	193,843	196,870	195,664	190,303
UD	414,077	436,053	448,353	463,540
FANCIULLI	196,544	217,133	230,395	243,439
FUCI M.	2,158	1,715	1,811	2,111
FUCI F.	1,224	1,291	1,477	1,499
MAESTRI	3,347	3,417	3,268	2,923
	2,156,006	2,255,371	2,322,524	2,774,719

(As one can see, Catholic Action membership on the whole appears to grow over the years, slowly but steadily. Looking at the breakdown among the various branches, the growth appears to concern women's membership, while men's membership decreases at times, mostly on account of military draft.)

	1942	1943	1944	1945
GIAC	432,439	462,528	387,675	347,542
GF	1,164,388	1,150,842	737,636	851,384
UU	190,085	151,652	18,482	51,921
UD	486,211	483,633	335,560	273,292
FANCIULLI	270,201	281,923	172,469	135,620
FUCI M.	2,546	–	–	3,024
FUCI F.	2,099	2,000	–	3,325
MAESTRI	3,509	3,000	–	–
	2,551,478	2,535,578	1,651,822	1,666,108

4 R. Moro, *La formazione della classe dirigente cattolica (1929-1937)*, Bologna 1979.

5 L. Ferrari, *Una storia dell'Azione cattolica. Gli ordinamenti statutari da Pio XI a Pio XII*, Genova 1989.

6 G. Miccoli, "La Santa Sede nella II guerra mondiale: il problema dei "silenzi" di Pio XII," in *Fra mito della cristianità e secolarizzazione*, Casale M. 1985.

7 E. Di Nolfo, *Vaticano e Stati Uniti (1939-1952)*, Milano 1978.

8 F. Malgeri, *La chiesa italiana e la guerra (1940-1945)*, Roma 1980.

9 R. Moro, "I cattolici italiani di fronte alla guerra fascista," in *La cultura della pace dalla Resistenza al Patto Atlantico*, Bologna 1988.

10 A. Riccardi, "Governo e "profezia" nel pontificato di Pio XII," in A. Riccardi (ed.), *Pio XII*, Roma-Bari 1988.

11 C. Casula, *Cattolici-comunisti e sinistra cristiana (1938-1945)*, Bologna 1976.

12 A. Giovagnoli, *Le premesse della ricostruzione. Tradizione e modernità nella classe dirigente cattolica del dopoguerra*, Milano 1982.

13 F. Traniello, "Il mondo cattolico italiano nella seconda guerra mondiale," in *L'Italia nella seconda guerra mondiale e nella Resistenza*, Milano 1988.

14 M. Casella, *L'Azione Cattolica alla caduta del fascismo. Attività e progetti per il dopoguerra (1942-45)*, Roma 1984.

15 P. Scoppola, *La proposta politica di De Gasperi*, Bologna 1977.

16 A. Riccardi, *Il potere del papa da Pio XII a Paolo VI*, Roma-Bari 1988.

17 A. Parisella, "Mondo cattolico e Democrazia Cristiana," in F. Malgeri (ed.), *Storia del movimento cattolico in Italia*, vol. VI, Roma 1981.

18 F. Traniello, "La Chiesa e la Repubblica," in *La nascita della Repubblica*, Roma 1987.

19 P. Sylos Labini, *Saggio sulle classi sociali*, Roma-Bari 1975 (V. ed.).

20 Social stratification in Italy, 1936-1951. Percentages. (Source: P. Sylos Labini, *Saggio sulle classi sociali*, Bari, Laterza 1975, 5th ed.)

		1936	1951
1. Bourgeoisie		1,6	1,9
2. Middle Class		54,8	56,9
2.1	White Collar Employees	5,0	9,8
2.2	Small Entrepreneurs	47,1	44,4
2.2.1	Peasant Farmers	35,6	30,3
2.2.2	Merchants	5,4	6,7
2.2.3	Artisans and Other Trades	6,1	7,4
2.3	Other Middle Class Categories	2,7	2,7
3. Working Class		43,6	41,2
3.1	Agricultural Laborers	16,2	11,8
3.2	Industrial Workers	21,4	22,9
3.3	Other Activities	6,0	6,5

21 P. L. Ballini, *Le elezioni nella storia d'Italia dall' Unità al fascismo. Profilo storico-statistico*, Bologna 1988.

22 P. Scoppola, *Gli anni della Costituente fra politica e storia*, Bologna 1980.

23 M. Casella, *Cattolici e Costituente. Orientamenti e iniziative del cattolicesimo organizzato (1945-1947)*, Napoli 1987.

24 G. Campanini, *Cristianesimo e democrazia. Studi sul pensiero politico cattolico del '900*, Brescia 1980.

25 R. Moro, "I movimenti intellettuali cattolici," in Ruffilli (ed.), *Cultura politica e partiti nell'età della costituente*, vol. I, Bologna 1979; Pombeni, *Il gruppo dossettiano e la fondazione della democrazia italiana (1938-1948)*, Bologna 1979.

26 R. Ruffilli, "La formazione del progetto democratico cristiano nella società italiana dopo il fascismo," in G. Rossini (ed.), *Democrazia Cristiana e Costituente*, vol. I, Roma 1980.

27 P. Barucci, *Ricostruzione, pianificazione, Mezzogiorno. La politica economica in Italia dal 1943 al 1955*, Bologna 1978.

28 P. Roggi, "Il mondo cattolico e i 'grandi temi' della politica economica," in G. Mori (ed.), *La cultura economica nel periodo della ricostruzione*, Bologna 1980.

29 A. Riccardi, *Il "partito romano" nel secondo dopoguerra (1945-1954)*, Brescia 1983.

30 P. Scoppola, *La proposta politica di De Gasperi*, Bologna 1977.

31 P. Pombeni, *Il gruppo dossettiano e la fondazione della democrazia italiana (1938-1948)*, Bologna 1979.

G. Baget Bozzo, *Il partito cristiano al potere. La DC di De Gasperi e di Dossetti (1945-1954)*, Firenze 1974.

32 F. Fonzi, "*Mondo cattolico, Democrazia Cristiana e sindacato (1943-1955)*", in S. Zaninelli (ed.), *Il sindacato nuovo*, Milano 1981.

33 M. Casella, "La nascita dei Comitati civici", in *Rivista di storia della Chiesa in Italia*, XL, 1986, pp. 446-534.

IV

Catholics and the Establishment of the Italian Republic: A Commentary

Richard J. Wolff

Some years ago, Francesco Traniello began to encourage scholars of Italy to look at the experience of Catholicism and Fascism in an entirely new light. He and other historians, particularly Pietro Scoppola, Pier Giorgio Zunino, and Renato Moro, laid the groundwork for the general acceptance of the view that the Catholic experience in Italy was extremely complex.[1] Although they examined a variety of issues on the subject, they generally followed the same line of reasoning. They argued that to focus on the role of the Vatican and the hierarchy alone in discussing "Catholicism" represented a grave methodological error. In their work, they demonstrated that the exclusion of the grass root lay Catholic movements, labor unions, mutual benefit associations, Catholic Action branches, and the lower clergy inevitably results in a distorted and inaccurate interpretation of the relationship between Catholicism and Fascism.

This view of the Catholic experience or "Catholic world," as Professor Traniello terms it, both complemented and spurred the work of American scholars in this field. Richard Webster, for example, saw the merits to this approach early on, but did not fully articulate a methodology.[2] In the last decade, however, historians who are conscious of the complexity of Catholicism have contributed to the literature. More recently the wide appeal that this approach has gained can be gleaned from the volume *Catholics, the State, and the European Radical Right*, published in 1986, in which scholars examined the Catholic experience with the radical right in eight different European countries between the wars.[3]

Professor Traniello's present essay displays a clear understanding of the complexities and nuances of the Catholic world in Italy, both during the Fascist period and in the immediate postwar years. In January 1943 a gathering of Catholic leaders took place behind the Vatican walls. This meeting is of importance not only for its impact upon the course of events in Italy at the time, but also because it exemplified by its tone, content and participants the disparate and heterogeneous nature of Italian Catholicism. The 1943 annual meeting of the Movimento Laureati, the association of Catholic university graduates, assembled an impressive array of Catholic leaders to hear undisguised rumblings about the Fascist regime.   Intellectuals, ex-deputies and senators, journalists, prelates, and leaders of Catholic Action — all finally seemed united in their disenchantment with Mussolini. The mood of the conference was set at the outset, when one participant overheard another mention the name of the Duce. To clamorous applause and shouts of approval, he proclaimed: "Ormai, si deve dire: Mussolini, basta!"[4]

Even at this late date, the Fascist police had active informers and spies. They listened intently to the conference speakers. What they reported alarmed the Fascist authorities. The police report summed up the main points of the keynote speeches, delivered by Professor Fausto Montanari and Mons. Adriano Bernareggi. They had argued that:

> ... today's political theory has caused the war; that the regime has instigated war instead of peace and it is morally bankrupt; that the goals of the State are not the same as those of the individual and of universal society; that the Nazi theory of racism is a violence against God; that the Christian of today must build an apostolic conscience; and the Christian intellectual must combat every deviation from political, social and economic ideas that are not Christian; and that from the ruins of war, will come a new humanity.[5]

Obviously the *laureati*, the Catholic university graduates, were not the whole of the "Catholic world," as Professor Traniello defines it. In terms of numbers, they were not even a large part of the Catholic world, representing a fraction of a fraction. A small percentage of an élite, for Italy in 1939 graduated from its university faculties only about 2.5% of its university aged-population.

Why, then, mention an obscure meeting of a relatively obscure group in the context of remarks on Professor Traniello's conception of the Catholic world in the reconstruction years? Because this meeting in 1943 in some small way may be seen as the midpoint in the development of the "Catholic world's" role in the reconstruction of Italy. How, after two decades of Fascism, did Catholics arrive at the views expressed at the Congresso? How, in the ensuing years, did [or did not] those same views affect the Catholic world's attitudes toward reconstruction?

The 1943 meeting is, intellectually and methodologically, an arbitrary starting point. But these questions, after all, are those which Traniello has raised and attempted to answer. And perhaps we can focus on his answers, his interpretations a bit more clearly by first looking backward from 1943 and, then, looking forward from 1943 — with our midpoint the Congresso Nazionale of the Movimento Laureati. Of course, even if this arbitrary approach helps us focus on the questions with chronological clarity, one question must leap to the minds of many. Of what significance could so small a percentage of the population be in the large, diverse "Catholic world," no less in Italy's reconstruction?

To a certain extent, the Fascist views of the *laureati* shed a good deal of light upon that question. According to the fascists themselves, what did these Catholics want? They wanted a political, social and economic structure to reflect Christian principles. What role did they envision for Catholic intellectuals? To build this society and to combat, in an organized manner, any deviations from this Christian, this Catholic concept of society. To serve as a non-revolutionary force in the transition from Fascism to post-Fascism. Under what auspices did these Catholics operate? They were members of a branch — albeit somewhat independent — of Catholic Action. They spoke up those days in January 1943 against the regime behind the protective walls of the Vatican.

Traniello is correct when he argues that the Catholic world, in the closing months of the Fascist regime, shared certain basic assumptions. Those assumptions — dependence upon the authority of Pius XII, a non-revolutionary bent, and a common aspiration to build a Christian order on the ruins of Fascism — were alive, were spoken openly, and were duly noted by the worried Fascists at the 1943 annual meeting of the Movimento Laureati. But after 20 years of Fascism, how did Catholics arrive at this set of assumptions for their attitudes and actions? Traniello, along with Pietro Scoppola and Pier Giorgio Zunino, to name only a few, has pioneered the view that explanations of the relationship between the Church and the Fascist regime must go beyond the Vatican and the hierarchy.

It is true that the Church, from a variety of standpoints, was far better off under Mussolini than under the governments of the liberal period. The expansion during the Fascist years of work of Catholic Action alone would substantiate this interpretation, and the influence of the clergy and hierarchy on everyday Italian life in the 1930s only adds to this impression. But arguing that Italy was "more Catholic in 1939 than it was in the 1920's" — a statement with which I agree — is not the same as saying that Catholicism, because it may have benefitted from the political and social climate of the Fascist years, was subservient to the Regime. This is an important point that cannot be left unsaid when discussing the Church and Italian Fascism.

Furthermore, the issue of Catholic political thought during the 1920's and 1930's is worthy of some comment. Traniello claims that such thought was "poor," although this term is not defined. Does it mean that the Church appeared to lose faith in democracy in the 1930's? If it does, then there may be something to that argument. However, the loss of faith in a particular system is hardly an indication of "poor political thought." Nor can it be said that Catholics had not developed any serious socio-political viewpoint.

First of all, the Church articulated a political-social theory of sorts in Pius XI's encyclical *Quadragesimo Anno*, which was echoed in regimes such as in Austria, Ireland, and Portugal. Rather than ignoring political issues, many clerics, like the Jesuit Enrico Rossi, vociferously championed political systems and leaders like Salazar, Dollfuss, Schussnigg, and Franco. It is true, of course, that most of the members and lay leaders of Catholic Action did focus on non-political activities, but political-social issues were discussed by some groups throughout the 1920's and 1930's.

Secondly, if we see the Catholic world as essentially apolitical, measured by the activities of the majority of branches of Catholic Action, then how can we account for the fact that by 1943 — and perhaps even a few years before — a loose coalition of lay Catholics were beginning to articulate an alternative political and social system to Fascism? These Catholics, like Igino Righetti, Guido Gonella, Giovanni Battista Montini, Aldo Moro, and even Andreotti, were in the interwar years working out a Catholic social philosophy and outlook which also affected politics. They were, perhaps, not outspoken. They did not openly oppose the Regime. But in their writings and at their meetings they did ponder the tradition of the Partito Popolare and attempt to articulate a new Catholic social philosophy for Italy.

If the Catholic world as a whole suffered in the Fascist years from undeveloped, weak political thought, then where did the political thought of the post 1943 years which shaped Catholic attitudes toward reconstruction come from — if not from the minority of Catholic intellectuals melding with the still surviving tradition of the Popolari? Traniello notes the importance of this group, despite its size, when he points out the "division of labor" which arose in the Catholic world: an élite and a large grass roots organization. It was this élite, however, a not insignificant part of it formed during the Fascist years, which provided the leadership in the post-1943 period.

The themes sounded at the 1943 meeting of the Catholic graduates were carried forward in the ensuing years. Traniello points out the critical assumptions underlying the Catholic world at that time, unearthing the seeds of post-1943 Catholic thought by tilling the ground of the Fascist years. Relying upon Catholic Action, the DC party apparatus itself was weak, at the beginning almost non-existent. In fact, the issue of the élite versus the mass movements — which constantly surfaced in the 1930's as well — is again played out during these years. The gulf between the leadership — De Gasperi and his supporters — and the politically unsophisticated Catholic masses and their leaders was substantial. In certain respects, this gulf was reminiscent of that which existed between the Catholic intellectuals in the 1930's and the leaders of Catholic Action. In the post-1943 years the same differences existed. Those differences could be found in political consciousness, in matters of culture, in economic outlook, including the sickly obligations and role of the state, in tolerance for the necessary plurality of cultures and ideologies in a democracy.

There existed, however, one great, over-riding commonality within the Catholic world. It was held together by the assumptions, which Professor Traniello has rightly identified, and by the skill of De Gasperi who never lost sight of the organizational weakness and the disparate nature of his movement. That commonality was the belief that the new state must reflect Christian values, that the lay state — represented by Liberal Italy — which divorced religious institutions from the state was not acceptable. The problem as we have seen, was a common definition of the "Christian values" that would permeate the state.

It is precisely on this point that Professor Traniello's views are most convincing. By painting the complex picture of the various strains of Catholic thought competing with each other to influence the nature of the DC, the characteristics of society, and, ultimately, the constitution itself, he has displayed Catholicism in all its complexity. This, alone, is a major contribution. All too many misinterpretations of Catholicism have resulted from the failure of historians to recognize the disparate strains of Catholicism, focusing instead on the homogeneous symbols of the Vatican and hierarchy. Studies of Catholicism and Fascism throughout Europe, until the last decade were generally guilty of this error. Here as in his many prior works, Professor Traniello has aptly demonstrated the necessity of understanding the complexity of the Catholic world in historical inquiry.

On the whole, Traniello's interpretation of the role of Catholicism in post-war Italy presents a broad and comprehensive view of the Catholic world as it faced the tasks of reconstruction. At times, however, the manner in which research and viewpoints are presented has a significant bearing upon the effectiveness of the argument. One cannot, for example, give short shrift to the roots of the post-1943 Catholic world. These roots are critical to a full understanding of the events that came about after the fall of Mussolini. There is clearly a continuity in the Catholic World — pre-1943 and post-1943 — which is striking. It can be seen in the ebb and flow of particular strains of thought, represented by particular factions of Catholicism. By 1943, a certain element of the Catholic world, which had existed but been overwhelmed during the Fascist years, was fast gaining the upper hand. In the mass of interesting detail that Traniello's essay presents, this fact is somewhat obscured. Asserting this, however, does not negate the author's basic assumptions, interpretations or characterizations of the Catholic world.

Long after the reconstruction period, this continuity continued, in large measure, to exist. When in 1978 Aldo Moro was kidnapped, it was Giovanni Battista Montini who as Pope Paul, pleaded for his life from a balcony above St. Peter's square. And when the funerals of both Moro and Papa Montini were held that fateful year, it was Giulio Andreotti, as prime minister, who led the government in official mourning. These men had met, worked together, in the Catholic world of the 1930's, as members of the FUCI. This group of young Catholic students represented one, small but important, element of the Catholic world. In thought, in outlook, in personal relations, a continuity existed, from the Fascist years, to reconstruction, to, perhaps, the present day. It is this thread, however tenuous it appears at times, that is worth examining when discussing the Catholic world between the fall of Fascism and the birth of the new Italian Republic.

Notes

1 See Pietro Scoppola and Francesco Traniello, eds., *I cattolici tra fascismo e democrazia* (Bologna: Il Mulino, 1975); Pier Giorgio Zunino, *La questione cattolica nella sinistra italiana (1919-1939)* (Bologna: Il Mulino, 1975); Renato Moro, *La formazione della classe dirigente cattolica, 1929-1937* (Bologna, Il Mulino, 1979).

2 Richard Webster, *The Cross and the Fasces: Christian Democracy in Fascist Italy* (Stanford, CA.: Stanford University Press, 1960).

3 Richard J. Wolff and Jorg K. Hoensch, *Catholics, the State, and the European Radical Right, 1919-1945* (New York: Distributed by Columbia University Press, 1986).

4 *Archivio Centrale dello Stato, Ministry of the Interior, DGPS, AGR, cat.* G-1, *busta* 169; "Azione Cattolica," 22 January 1943.

5 Ibid.

V

The Italian Socialist Party:
Its Policies and Failure to Unite
With the Italian Communist Party

Giuseppe Tamburrano

When, on February 6th, 1957, the Socialist leader Pietro Nenni, his voice breaking with emotion, denounced the criminal invasion of Hungary by the Soviet Union, the "La Fenice" Theater of Venice seemed to collapse under the rumble of applause that exploded in the stalls among the delegates and in the gallery full of participants at the XXXIInd Congress of the Italian Socialist Party. It was a liberating gesture: thus the Socialist Party consecrated the break-ing of its more than twenty-year alliance with Communism.

The first pact to form a united front of the Socialists and the Communists was signed on August 17th, 1934, in France — on exile territory. It was Nenni who desired it more than anybody else. The Communists were hostile, as they considered the Socialists to be worse enemies than the Fascists. They were forced to come around when the tune changed in Moscow. Stalin — having lost all hope of promoting the revolution in Europe and having started seriously to fear the Nazi threat, set the way for a radical change of line, seeking alliances with democratic governments and parties, which culminated, with the VIIth Comintern Congress, in the politics of the Popular Fronts against Fascism and for democracy. The Italian pact followed by a few days the one signed by the French Socialist and Communist parties.

Pietro Nenni, whose cultural and political background placed him at some distance from the ideology and practices of the Third International, was, for political reasons, a determined advocate of the alliance with the Communists and the USSR. Convinced that reactionary politics was spreading all over Europe, "in Rome, Berlin, Budapest, Vienna, Warsaw, Madrid . . . ," he saw the alliance between the leftist parties and the support of the Soviet Union — natural enemy of the right — as the principal weapon in the fight against Fascism. The Italian and German experience showed, in his view, that when there was a division between Socialists and Communists, the politics of reaction triumphed: in Italy in 1922, in Germany in 1933. On the other hand, the successes of the Popular Front in the Spanish elections of February 16th, 1936, and in the French elections of May 3rd of the same year revealed that the right was defeated when the left was united, and that, within the unity, the Socialists prevailed over the Communists.

The united front between Socialists and Communists was upset by the trials that Stalin started in Moscow against internal antagonists, and it ended with the Soviet-German Pact of August 1939. Nenni, while strongly criticizing Stalin's politics, maintained the unity front met needs that had priority, and should be preserved. On account of his views, he remained isolated for some time, but subsequently he was proven right by the German invasion of the USSR and by the alliance between the Soviet Union and the Western powers.

In October 1941, at Toulouse, a third pact to form a united front was signed, in which also the liberal-democratic movement. "Justice and Liberty" joined in. The pact's main purpose was the fight against Fascism and the restoration of freedom in Italy. Socialists, Communists, and other democratic parties were united in their fight in the Resistance, and during the partisan war against the German occupation.

The climate fostered by the anti-Fascist struggle, by the alliance between the Soviet Union and the democratic West, by the heroic resistance of the Russian people and by the victory of the Red Army against the German troops gave birth to projects of putting an end to the 1921 schism and of unifying the two parties. On September 28th, 1943, a new document was signed, committing the Socialists and the Communists to pursuing the goal of forming a single party, and describing the Soviet Union as "the vanguard of the workers' movement and the people's most trusted ally in their struggle against imperialistic and reactionary forces."

After the fall of Fascism, governments of "national unity" were formed, articulating the cooperation between the Christian Democrats (DC), the Italian Communist Party (PCI), and the Socialists (PSI). But with the gradual deterioration of relations between the Soviet Union and the Western powers, it became increasingly difficult to preserve the government alliance between the centrist and leftist parties, and the differences among the factions of the Socialist Party on the issue of their relations with the Communists grew ever more acute. In the first political elections after the Second World War, on June 2nd, 1946, the Italians opted for the Republic by a slim majority, with the Christian Democrats getting 35.2% of the vote, the Socialist Party 20.7%, and the Communist Party 18.9%. Thus the vast majority of Italians rejected Communism, and more than half of the 40% of the electorate who voted for the left declared itself in favor of the Socialists.

It was a surprising result: everybody expected a Communist landslide. But while for Saragat this result indicated the way to the autonomy of the Socialists from the PCI, for Nenni, on the contrary, it acknowledged the role of the Socialists within the framework of working class unity.

Even though in October 1946 a new pact for united action was entered into over Saragat's signature, just a few months later, in January 1947, when the Christian Democratic leader De Gasperi was in Washington negotiating a loan in exchange for a reduction of the Communist ranks in the government, the Socialist Party split up and gave birth to Saragat's Social Democratic Party, the PSDI. In May of that year, De Gasperi ousted Nenni's Socialists and Togliatti's Communists from the government. In the opposition, meanwhile, the Socialists and Communists were closing ranks. In December, at Nenni's proposal, the Popular Front emerged with Socialists, Communists and "Independents," parts of other formations (e.g. the late Action Party). The Popular Front was intended to be an electoral ticket, but in fact it led to the Socialist Party's dependence on the Communists.

In the elections of April 18, 1948, the Socialists and Communists ran on one ticket as the Popular Front, but were defeated by the Christian Democrats, who won an absolute majority in the House of Deputies. This was a serious defeat for the Front, (31% of the vote, almost 9% less than two years earlier), while for the Socialists it was an utter disaster. Nevertheless, the PSI majority, headed by Nenni and Morandi, continued to uphold the policy of the united Front. In fact, it was Morandi who introduced a reform of the Socialist Party which rendered it more similar to the PCI, both as to its organizational structure, based on "centralism," and as to internal relations, which were regulated by rules preventing dissent and factions.

The policy of the PSI fell in line with that of the PCI and of the Soviet Union, and Nenni, who was the most outspoken opponent to the Atlantic Pact in Parliament, and Vice President of The Partisans of Peace, the international organization that supported Soviet strategy, won the Stalin Prize in 1951. Why did a Democrat and Republican, such as Nenni, side with Stalin's totalitarianism and agree to be Palmiro Togliatti's second in command?

The reasons were both political and ideological, and are closely interconnected. Nenni felt that the centrist governments dominated by the DC were focused largely on restoring capitalism, on repressing the workers who were demonstrating for jobs and decent wages, on making sure that all levels of power would remain in the hands of the Christian Democrats, that the schools would remain under the sway of the Church, and that Italy would subject itself to the United States. The PSI, a party of the working class, could not but oppose this policy. Furthermore, the Communists, who were much stronger than the PSI — controlling the trade unions and guiding the peasant organizations, with the support of the greater part of the working class and greatly influencing the intellectuals and the cultural institutions — were in the opposition as well. The merging of Socialists and Communists was an objective fact. But the Socialist Party could have established an uncompromising opposition without losing its identity to the Communists. This is where the second and characteristic element of Socialist strategy becomes apparent: the Party's acceptance and support of the Communist system.

Nenni's ideological choice was influenced by the memory of historical experience, which taught him that when the left is divided, the right wins. But this experience had little value in post-war Italy where the danger of authoritarian regimes, as the Fascist and the Nazi had been, did not exist, since the Demo-Christian governments, though moderate, were certainly not reactionary. On the other hand, a left controlled by the Communist Party was more than just "left": it was also an instrument of support of a great totalitarian power, whose armies were deployed in the heart of Europe. The PSI, and Nenni in particular, was convinced that the United States was using its atomic supremacy to threaten the Soviet Union (the roll-back doctrine of Dulles), or China (McArthur's theory of bombing the Chinese "sanctuary"), or at least to quell the struggle for national independence of the peoples of the Western colonies. The Soviet Union was instead seen to help those peoples in their struggle and, partly because of its atomic inferiority, interested in bringing peace to the world.

Moreover, the PSI did not clearly understand the reality of the Soviet world, to the extent that it approved the merger of the Socialist and Communist parties in Eastern Europe — which brought as a result the loss of autonomy for the Socialists in the so-called "Popular Democracies" — and approved the farcical trials by which the Stalinist Communists liquidated all forms of dissent among the leaders in those countries. Caught up in political logistics, for which there was some justification in terms of internal policy, the Socialists did not and, to a certain extent, would not see the reality of what was happening in the Soviet sphere. By 1956, after Kruschev's secret report, after the Polish repression and, above all, after the invasion of Hungary by the Soviets, it was no longer possible "not to see." At that point, the PSI was faced with the dilemma: whether, once and for all, to break away from or to join the Communist "camp." Nenni, who even as a militant was deeply affected by the tragedy of the Hungarian democrats and patriots, broke away. He rediscovered harmony with the principles of Socialism and greater freedom in pursuing the Party's policies, which had been so trammelled by the alliance with the PCI.

The breaking away from Communism produced not only a serious division within the Socialist Party, among the "autonomists" and the pro-Communist left, but also a great push towards a reunification between the PSI and the PSDI. Nenni and Saragat, the leaders of the two parties, met in August 1956 at Pralognan, a tourist resort in the Alps of the French Savoy, and decided to work resolutely for their return to their common "Socialist home". It was logical that the pro-Communists in the ranks of the PSI should go over to the PCI, and that the Socialists, no longer divided on the issue of the relationship to Communism, should come back under the same roof. But with a *coup de théâtre*, at the XXXIInd Congress which was mentioned earlier, the left, by manipulating delegates who, due to years of internal central rule, were completely unprepared to a confrontation between factions, insured for itself the majority of seats in the Central Committee. Such a development limited Nenni's political victory. He was elected Secretary and proceeded to work on autonomy lines, heedless of the criticisms brought against him by his internal adversaries. Saragat, however, used that *coup de théâtre* as pretext for refusing the unification, in which he no longer believed, while the left, counseled by Togliatti, the leader of the PCI, remained in the PSI in order to create difficulties to Nenni.

At the next congress, on 15th of January 1959 in Naples, they voted on separate motions, and the Autonomist faction won with a 58% of the votes. The majority of the PSI developed a two-fronted politics: on the one hand, denouncing the retrogressive tendencies, such as the pro-Soviet and Stalinist ones of the PCI leadership; on the other, denouncing the conservative immobilism of the DC and of the governments where it held the majority. Nenni attempted to use for the PSI the crisis unleashed at the grass-roots of the PCI and among Communist voters by the Soviet invasion of Hungary and by Togliatti's support to the Soviet move, and was also trying to gain the votes of the lower class population which had only voted for the DC because of their fear of Communism. The PSI was successful in certain significant aspects: important representatives of the Communist Party began to lean towards the Socialists; the left factions of the DC exercised strong pressure on the Party for a change of policy and an opening to the PSI; at the political elections of 1958, the Socialists gained 14.2% of the votes, compared to the 12.7% of 1953. Significant and encouraging successes as these were, they were limited: one must remember that the PCI, in spite of the grave repercussions of the dramatic events of 1956, lost in the 1958 elections only 0.1%: from the 22.7% of 1953 to 22.6%. Moreover, the DC, though pressed by a party no longer burdened by its identification with the Communists, instead of losing the vote of the popular masses in favor of the Socialist Party, saw its electorate grow from the 40% of 1953 to 42.2%.

The internal fight led against Nenni by the pro-Communist left of the PSI and the minor faction headed by Lelio Basso (who at the Congress of Naples had won over 40% of the vote), contributed to rendering more difficult a potentially wider and more rapid success of the Socialists. The projected Socialist alternative to the Christian Democracy was ambitious. It required one single party, organized and determined; a leading class well prepared for its task; modern ideas and presence at all levels of society. And it needed time. What was its objective? The PSI may well have taken away votes from the Communists and from the Christian Democrats, but in the end it had to take into account the PCI — when creating an alternative to the DC — or the DC for the center-left alternative. The possible options were therefore limited even if the negotiating power resulting from a wider electoral consensus was important for the Socialists.

In the meantime, the general political situation was increasingly deteriorating. The Christian Democratic Party was not capable of producing stable governments: there was not an ample and clear centrist majority. The Center-right option was difficult because it must include conservative forces tied to the old Fascist regime. The opening towards the PSI was opposed by the Vatican, by the United States, by the corporate world and met with the strong resistance of the Party's majority, especially among the Socialist representatives in Parliament.

The governments which followed each other were weak and short lived, often the result of majorities collected at random. At the beginning of 1959, a great crisis traumatized the DC: the powerful Secretary and Prime Minister, Amintore Fanfani, in the course of a few days, lost both posts. Among the reasons that motivated the greater part of Fanfani's followers in the party, composing the faction of "Democratic Initiative", to abandon him and to bring into existence a new current — the "Dorotei" — was their hostility to Fanfani's favorable disposition to an opening towards the PSI. In March 1959, Aldo Moro was elected Secretary of the DC. He was nominated to that office apparently for his indecision and his political weakness. It was a kind of *ad interim* solution, waiting for the approaching Party Congress that could make clear the internal power relations among the various groups. The

Congress of October 23, 1959 confirmed Moro as Secretary and resulted in a majority hostile to the opening towards the PSI.

Between 1956 and 1960, the situation in Parliament and government became increasingly precarious. The DC's traditional allies were in diametrically opposed positions. Malagodi's Liberals were totally against any overture towards the PSI, La Malfa's Republicans (joined later by Saragat's Social Democrats) were in favor of the center-left. Any opening towards the PSI was also fiercely opposed by the U.S. Embassy and the Department of State, by the Confederation of Industrial Employers, by most of the press, and above all by the Catholic hierarchy which, through its publications and by way of direct pressures, threatened to encourage the emergence of a second Catholic Party. On May 18, 1960, the newsorgan of the Holy See, *L'Osservatore Romano*, in an editorial entitled *"Punti fermi,"* condemned all forms of collaboration with Marxist Socialism, and exhorted the Catholics to obey the Church's political guidelines.

The only majorities numerically feasible were either with the PSI or with the MSI (the Italian Social Movement, i.e., the Neo-Fascist Party). Although it seemed morally and politically impossible for a democratic and anti-Fascist party like the DC to be dependent on Neo-Fascist votes, eventually it was precisely those votes that tipped the scales in favor of an all-Christian Democratic government, headed by a man from the Christian Democratic left, Fernando Tambroni, who up to that point had been known to be a supporter of the alliance with the PSI.

That government generated widespread resistance among anti-Fascist groups and even among Catholic ranks, and survived just a few months. It left a long trail of blood in the streets of Italy. That was the summer of 1960.

This political crisis occurred while Italian society was enjoying an economic development hailed as the "Italian miracle." In the very year when the DC aligned itself with the flotsam of the Fascist regime, statistics on the national income over the ten-year period showed an average increase of 6% per annum. In ten years the income, in constant lire, had almost doubled. Per capita income had almost doubled. Imports had more than tripled and exports had exceeded even that level. The lira won the Financial Times "Oscar" for its stability. Consumption increased spectacularly.

Between 1953 and 1962, meat consumption tripled, expenditure in household durable consumer goods tripled, and expenditure for the purchase of private vehicles doubled. Nonetheless, Italy was still behind the other industrial nations in terms of over-all consumption and standard-of-living indicators.

Trends in the Italian political situation were caused by a combination of various factors. Internationally, the opening towards the Socialists reflected President Kennedy's New Frontier policy. In fact, the new Administration rejected the concerns expressed by former Ambassador to Rome Clare Boothe Luce, and cautiously favored political change. The Kennedy Administration's approval of the turn towards the center-left became fully evident during the U.S. President's trip to Italy. During a reception in the gardens of the Quirinale Palace (the Italian President's official residence), Kennedy had a long, friendly and affable conversation with Pietro Nenni, whom he showered with compliments and congratulations. (Spencer M. Di Scala recounts in abundant detail the story of the relations between the "Neo-Socialists and the New Frontiersmen" in his *Renewing Italian Socialism.*) The turn to the center-left was in keeping with the objectives of the New Frontier and with the new climate of detente between the USA and the USSR. It was also favored by the process of decolonization, the birth of new players on the international scene which constitute the so-called "Third World," and which remained on equidistant positions between the great powers.

Developments in the Church also proved helpful. Cardinal Roncalli, who became Pope John XXIII in October 1958, had a very different view of the Church's mission compared to that of his predecessor. Pius XII, worried about the advance of atheistic Communism, thought he could stem it through excommunications and support to all the forces and governments fighting Communism. The Church ended up by closing in on itself, ignoring and confusing with "Communism" the struggles and aspirations for justice and freedom (particularly in colonial countries), and compromising itself with reactionary governments and movements.

The new Pope wanted to restore to the Church its evangelical and pastoral mission and, instead of fighting waywardness, to dialogue with the wayward. John XXIII liked to say that it did not matter where the wayfarer came from, but where he was going, so that the road may be travelled together. Thus, as he wrote in his encyclical *Pacem in terris*: " . . . it is quite possible that a basic approach or meeting, which yesterday would not have been considered appropriate or fruitful, would today be considered so, and could become so tomorrow." And perhaps it should also be remembered that when in 1957 he was Patriarch of Venice, he published his welcoming address to the PSI Congress which was held in the city on the lagoons.

The runaway and disorderly economic growth had raised new problems. Industries were operating at peak capacity and new small businesses — many of them improvised — were sprouting like mushrooms. Unemployment was down and in several areas there was a shortage of skilled labor. Consequently, wages were climbing, and the principal factor that had made Italian industry competitive, namely the low cost of labor, was disappearing. Economic development, concentrated in the industrial regions in the North, had attracted enormous numbers of poor peasants from the South. This heavy migration widened the breach between North and South in absolute and relative terms, as the migrants flocked to the cities and land costs soared, generating real estate speculation and saddling the local governments with enormous budget expenditures as they struggled to provide the services necessary for the chaotically expanding cities.

The economic "miracle" was the result of a long term policy that had freed trade and led to Italy's entry into the Common Market. This policy had kept wages down due to severe unemployment and the consequent erosion of the power of the unions (as well as a repressive and discriminatory domestic policy directed at the Socialists and the Communists), it had invested heavily in public capital spending, particularly in construction and in the South (as through the Cassa per il Mezzogiorno), and benefited from a number of other contributing economic factors, principally the strong demand following the end of the Korean War. The boom could continue if a new policy was instituted to bring development under control, eliminate the imbalances, equip the country with the necessary services and infrastructure and stimulate modernization of industrial technology.

Wages were a decisive factor both in keeping production costs competitive with those of other countries, in particular the European Common Market, and in assuring a high level of reinvested profits, as well as in avoiding severe inflationary pressures. This policy required the approval of the unions, and an opening towards a leftist party might have facilitated it. After the crusade of the 50s, social issues required room for dialogue. It was no accident that the president of Fiat, Vittorio Valletta, was one of the few voices in favor of the center-left, amidst the chorus of "no's" coming from the Confederation of Industrialists.

As for the political situation, under Tambroni the DC government had shifted to the far right. It was an experience they could not afford to repeat. But if this direction was set, a majority government would automatically require an opening towards the PSI. The new DC Secretary, Aldo Moro, was convinced of this, but he also knew how much resistance he would have to overcome within his own Party. Navigating cautiously, he led the united DC to the meeting that could no longer be put off. Moro was successful, Nenni was not, for on the way to that meeting he lost a large contingent of the PSI – the left, which split off from the Party and created the PSIUP when the PSI joined the government.

Almost two and a half years passed between the fall of the Tambroni government and the Socialists' entry into the government. Initially, it was a government of "decantation" and "transition," with a politically flexible structure that would avoid immediately and exclusively committing the DC to the PSI. It was described in terms of the politically untranslatable expression "of parallel convergence," a formula which implies a trend towards a meeting point ("convergence"), while keeping one's distance ("parallel"). It was presided over by Fanfani, advocate of the center-left.

Finally, at the Christian Democratic Congress in Naples (January 1962), the DC made up its mind. It took Aldo Moro seven hours to read his 100-page report and to convince his opponents within the Party that the DC had no other option. But government with the Socialists was not yet a *fait accompli*. There was still another stage, although a more demanding one. The Socialists negotiated the Fanfani government's program, they considered it acceptable, but did not vote on it. They abstained. Moro and Nenni had decided, in order to overcome gradually the internal opposition of the two parties, to try out their new relationship. And yet, according to some, such as Riccardo Lombardi, leader of the new left of the PSI (as soon as one vanished, another one sprung up!), those few months, less than a year, of the Fanfani government constituted the true, brief but intense experience of the center-left.

Here we must carefully explain what the center-left meant for the two protagonists, beyond the economic and social issues connected to the end of one phase of development, that is to say, to the transformation of Italy from a prevailingly agricultural economy to a prevailingly industrial one, inserted in the vast European Market and in competition with more modern production systems.

The DC and Moro viewed the purpose of the center-left as that of undermining the Italian Communist Party, by depriving it of its Socialist ally and fighting it with a social policy that would isolate it in its "demagogic protest." It was the "democratic challenge" theorized by Moro. The PSI was also aiming to compete with the PCI by focusing on a policy of reform which, by resolving the real problems of the workers and the country, would convince the voters and the militants of that party that the right policy was the Socialist one. While the DC could not agree to any radical or anticapitalist reforms, the PSI needed these reforms to compete effectively with the PCI.

Actually, the PCI was in serious trouble even in the early days of this change of course. The center-left included in its platform issues for which the Communists had been fighting for years. What could they do? By voting for those reforms, the PCI would have been supporting a coalition from which it was excluded and which was actually planning "to challenge it." But could the PCI afford to vote against reforms that were of increasing urgency, simply because the majority would be carrying them out without and against the Communist Party?

The Fanfani government undertook major reforms that would have an impact on powerful economic and financial interests, such as urban reform, nationalization of the electric power monopolies and economic planning. Some of these reforms were carried out, such as the nationalization of the electric industry, and the law on stock dividends that introduced the principle of registered securities. All hell broke loose! The Confederation of Industrialists screamed that the DC wanted to collectivize the economy, the stock market plummeted and capital fled. The Christian Democrats lost more than 4% points at the 1963 elections, almost all of it captured by the Liberal Party that had run a fierce campaign against the Fanfani government as defenders of industrial interests. Pressured by the capitalistic and financial world which had supported it throughout those years, the DC worried about losing large blocs of votes to the Liberal right, applied the brakes, opposed the "structural" reforms advocated by the PSI, and actually raised the ante for the Socialists by demanding a more decisive and uncompromising anti-Communism. The PCI, confronted with the "moderate involution" of the center-left, regained its inner peace and party unity by way of the strongest possible opposition. Meanwhile internal differences were becoming sharper in the PSI between the faction of Lombardi, who was insisting on the "structural reforms" and that of Nenni, who was defending the politics of the center-left, which he regarded as the PSI's historical opportunity of becoming a "government party."

After the 1963 elections, the question arose of how the center-left would enter the second phase once the Socialists joined the government. After long and exhausting negotiations in the Roman sultry weather the Moro-Nenni government seemed settled, but a change of heart at the last moment — caused perhaps by differences between Lombardi and Nenni — made Lombardi's faction dissociate itself from the agreement stipulated by Nenni. The Moro government died before it was born. It took months of discussions and clarifications within the Autonomist faction in order to arrive at a common understanding, that took the form of an economic platform that proposed all the "structural reforms" dear to Lombardi, which the majority in the DC rejected. At this point it took all of Moro's ability to avoid having the reforms become so many unexploded bombs. He chose the "drowning" strategy, placing Lombardi's and many other reforms in his own program, and including the policy requested by the Bank of Italy to cope with the economic crisis. Such an over-extended program was deemed impracticable. The Parliament and its well-known sluggishness would take care of the rest. Content with the Lombardi platform, the PSI joined the Moro government, Nenni became Deputy Prime Minister, while the left wing split off from the Party.

But the irreconcilable differences between the vision of the Christian Democrat majority and that of the PSI were quickly becoming insurmountable. The economic situation was rapidly deteriorating. Demand exceeded supply, inflation was heating up, the trade deficit was soaring and investments were flagging. The DC majority, headed by the Treasury Minister Emilio Colombo and with the support of the President of the Republic Antonio Segni (leader of the "Dorotei faction", elected to the highest office in May 1962 to balance to the right the opening towards the Socialists), was aiming for a policy that would bring down inflation, as insistently demanded the president of the Bank of Italy, Guido Carli, and the European Common Market. The Socialists, particularly the minority headed by Lombardi which was represented in the Cabinet by the Minister of Budget and Planning, Antonio Giolitti, were resistant to that policy which meant unemployment, wages containment and reduction of consumer demand on the part of the working classes, implying that the "special" reforms — such as the urban reform, the Factory Workers Act and economic planning — be abandoned. But the Socialists were unable to devise any alternative economic policy that would be as specific and effective as the deflationary policy. Moro was stalling for time, waiting for Giolitti to bring in the trade unions' commitment to autonomously moderate the requests for wage increases. The trade unions, however, controlled by the Communist Party, made promises but did not deliver and all the while, the DC was applying pressure.

A chance vote in the Chamber of Deputies on a marginal issue — but which ran into another thorn in the relations between the DC and the PSI, namely the relations between State and private schools — enabled Moro to declare a crisis in his government and to bring the situation back to square one. It was a long and difficult government crisis, the most serious of all (and the overall count today would come close to 50). The Socialists insisted on the "structural" reforms, they rejected an unpopular economic policy. The Christian Democrats wanted an economic policy that would combat inflation and the deficit of the balance of trade, and rejected the "reforms" that would aggravate the deficit, discourage capital and frustrate the deflationary economic policies.

The crisis dragged on. The President of the Republic Antonio Segni urged not only a rapid end to the crisis, but, behind the scenes, was pushing for a program that would exclude the reforms demanded by the PSI, particularly the Land Act, which he felt would cause the Christian Democrats to lose several million votes.

The Communist Party and the union it controlled, the C.G.I.L., played a very important role in the crisis. The crux of the matter was labor costs. The wages were still far from approaching the European average, and from this point of view, the workers were not wrong in asking for substantial increases. But the productivity of the Italian industrial system was itself far from the European average, and a big increase of labor cost would, under those conditions, negatively influence both investments and the stability of the lira. It would have been necessary to allow for gradual increases while at the same time introducing significant across the board technological innovations in a productive system which until then had been competitive above all on the basis of the low labor cost. The situation called for a planned economic effort, in which the unions would responsibly do their share.

The Budget Minister, the Socialist Giolitti, told the Socialist-Communist union that they could have the reforms if they would contain their wage demands within *real* limits, consistent with an inflation-free growth of the economy. But the Communist majority of the C.G.I.L. rejected the proposed so-called "income policy" on two counts. First, the automatic growth, according to pre-determined parameters — such as the average increase of the national income — would replace negotiations between employers and labor, thus depriving the unions of their main function as negotiating and conflict regulating agents of the wage system. Second, it was not possible to trust the sincerity and the credibility of the commitment to reforms of the center-left coalition, which excluded the strongest party of the working classes, the PCI, and which was dominated by moderate and conservative elements. The Communist union leader Lama summarized the position of the C.G.I.L. when he affirmed that wage was an "independent variable" of the system. Subsequently, he himself defined his theory as "silly".

The economic situation was growing worse and there seemed no way out of the political crisis, which was at a standstill during the interminable negotiations between the Socialists and Christian Democrats. President Segni, suffering from blood circulation problems that were giving him anxiety attacks, sent out worrisome public messages and received General De Lorenzo, Chief of the Carabinieri and former Chief of Intelligence, and the Joint Chiefs of Staff. Moro revealed to Nenni and Saragat that Segni would never sign a law providing for the general expropriation of building land (and Saragat rebelled). General De Lorenzo was very active and met Moro and other DC leaders in secret, in a private house. Nenni was informed by someone at the Quirinale Palace — he has never disclosed who — that a plan of actions by authorities had been set up to back conservative solutions to the crisis. So Nenni threw in the towel, realizing that if it came to armed conflict, neither the Socialists nor any of the leftists would have the slightest hope of prevailing. The Socialists renounced the "special reforms" at the cost of a new internal crisis that shifted the Lombardi faction into the opposition, and joined the government again — the second Moro government. They gave in to a threat, but they saved democracy. Later on, judicial and journalistic inquiries revealed that the dangers that Nenni had feared were real.

The economic situation showed some recovery, the government situation stabilized in its entrenched position. Conditions were ripe for the resumption of a process that had emerged almost ten years before, that is to say unification between Nenni's Socialists and Saragat's Social Democrats: in the PSI there were no more pro-Communists, the maximalist Lombardi and his faction being in the internal opposition. Thus the PSI was "normalized" even if, on the subject of relations with the Communists and on the Socialist unification itself, the new Secretary De Martino's positions did not coincide with Nenni's.

Another circumstance favored the unification: Saragat was elected to the presidency of the republic. Nenni thus remained the only leader of the new Party. The unification was carried out, but a climate of distrust and suspicions between the top levels and the apparatuses of the two Parties remained. And yet, both the Communist Party and the Christian Democrats were very concerned about this resumption and afraid that it might lead to the formation of a third force that could, as Nenni commented in a felicitous slogan, "challenge the DC's hegemony over the State and the PCI's hegemony over the workers." Indeed, a leftist democratic party was seen as a potential alternative to the DC, which had long been in power. It could attract Communist votes that had been frozen in sterile opposition.

Due to the way in which the new Party was born — devoid of ideas and divided by internal strife between groups that waxed and waned — it was unable to meet the dual challenge. The unification was celebrated at the Sports Palace on a splendid October day of 1966, amidst the enthusiasm of the militants and many red flags. It faced the test two years later, at the election of May 20, 1968, and lost. In the previous election, the two separate Parties had won 18.6% of the votes; on May 20, they won a total of 14.5%. Logically speaking, from these votes one should subtract the 4.5% won by the new Party born of the split from the PSI four years earlier, the PSIUP, which was participating for the first time in the election. Common sense indicated that one should correct past mistakes while going ahead. Instead, the new Party underwent a crisis at birth, and it broke apart a few months later, in July 1969.

In the summer of 1968, great events shook Europe. The youth protests unraveled in Italy too; the crisis of Soviet Communism sent armored tanks in to squash the flowers of the Spring of Prague. But Italian Socialism, which had an historical right to interpret the youth protest against injustice and false idols, and to offer a democratic alternative to Communism, was not aware of what was happening, concentrating as it was upon internal divisions, under the pressures of personalities and power interests.

An analysis of the PSI's first experience at government shows two contradictory phenomena: the results during those years were generally positive, but instead of emphasizing their decisive contribution to this success, the Socialists were harsh critics of that experience.

Italy experienced great economic and social development during that period, as well as considerable civil growth. As it entered the 1970's, Italy was a very different country compared to what it was at the end of the 1950's, not only in terms of per capita income, but also because of its evolving values and patterns.

It was a country that was growing increasingly European, both in its consumer preferences and demands, and in its mentality. Illiteracy was being stamped out, backwardness and taboos of rural society were disappearing, relations between the sexes evolved, women joined the work force and demanded equal rights with men, and the power of authority was waning, both the spiritual authority of the clergy and the bureaucratic authority of the uniform. Politics were less defined by ideologies, discrimination against Socialists and Communists was out, the dialogue advocated by Pope John was taking root, class differences were attenuating, privileges bestowed through breeding and status were no longer tolerated, the outcry against corruption and abuse of power was widespread and no longer the exclusive expression of intellectual elites. In short, the mores and values of a mass industrial society were taking hold.

I do not mean to imply that Italy was becoming another Scandinavian country. On the contrary, civil development was unequal like economic development, and generated new problems which were to explode in the 1970's. The ruling class did not know how to, or could not, resolve the widening gap between the North and South, how to provide the nation with modern social and civil services, and how to plan urban and territorial development. In short, there were assets and liabilities on the balance sheet in those early years when the Socialists first participated in the government. But the voices coming from the Socialist Party were almost always negative. Even Nenni, who was more balanced in his judgement, said: "The bottom line of the achievements is considerable . . . (but) what we have been able to accomplish with the DC remains entirely inadequate compared to what needed and still needs to be done."

The Socialists expected much more from their collaboration with the DC than what that Party's moderate nature and the tugging forces between "progressives" and "conservatives" in the coalition could give. They expected some help from the Communists and particularly from the C.G.I.L., and met only with hard-nosed opposition. They expected understanding from public opinion and a growth in the electorate that could rebalance the forces of the left, but the gap between the PSI and the PCI actually grew wider during those years (in the 1958 election, on the eve of the center-left, the PSI stood at 14.2%, the PCI at 22.7%; in the 1976 elections, the year in which the center-left coalition yielded to a majority with the PCI's participation, the PSI had dropped to 9.6% and the PCI had risen to 34.4%.)

During the ensuing years, De Martino's PSI would increasingly lose faith in its function and resign itself to a minor role compared to that of the PCI of Euro-Communism, and an auxiliary role in the understanding reached between Christian Democrats and Communists — until Craxi, in 1976, started the long climb back up to make the PSI a major player in the political life of Italy and Europe.

Bibliographical References

1 AA.VV., *La politica estera della Repubblica italiana*, 3 vols., Ediz. di Comunità, Milano, 1967.

2 M. Bonanno, in *La politica estera della Repubblica italiana*, Ediz. di Comunità, Milano, 1967.

3 G. Candeloro, *Storia dell'Italia moderna*, Vol. X, Feltrinelli Editore, Milano 1966.

4 V. Castronovo, *Storia d'Italia*, Vol. IV, Part 1, Einaudi, Torino 1976.

5 E. Di Nolfo, *Le paure e le speranze degli italiani*, Mondadori, Milano.

6 A. Gambino, *Storia del dopoguerra*, Laterza, Bari 1975.

7 P. Ginsborg, *Storia d'Italia dal dopoguerra a oggi*, 2 vols., Einaudi, Torino, 1989.

8 A. Graziani, *L'economia italiana 1945-1970*, Il Mulino, Bologna.

9 G. H. Hildebrand, *Growth and Structure in the Economy of Modern Italy*, Harvard University Press, Cambridge 1965.

10 N. Kogan, *A Political History of Italy: the Postwar Years*, Praeger, New York 1983.

11 N. Kogan, *The Politics of Italian Foreign Policy*, Praeger, New York 1963.

12 D. Mack Smith, *Italy: A Modern History*, University of Michigan Press, Ann Arbor, 1969.

13 G. Mammarella, *L'Italia dopo il fascismo: 1943-1973*, Il Mulino, Bologna 1974.

14 P. Nenni, *Diari*, 3 vols., SugarCo, Milano 1981.

15 E. Ragionieri, *Storia d'Italia*, Vol. IV, Part 3, Einaudi, Torino 1976.

16 M. Salvati, *Economia e politica in Italia dal dopoguerra a oggi*, Il Mulino, Bologna.

17 S. DiScala, *Renewing Italian Socialism*, Oxford University Press, New York 1988.

18 F. Spotts, T. Wieser, *Italy*, Cambridge University Press, 1986.

19 H. Stuart Hughes, *The United States and Italy*, Harvard University Press, Cambridge, 1979.

20 G. Tamburrano, *Storia e cronaca del centro-sinistra*, Feltrinelli, Milano 1971.

21 S. Turone, *Storia del sindacato in Italia dal 1943 a oggi*, Laterza, Bari 1976.

22 E. Wiskemann, *Italy since 1945*, Macmillan, London; New York, St. Martin Press, 1971.

VI

The Lives of Pietro Nenni:
A Commentary

Spencer Di Scala

As time goes on, historians will have an increasingly difficult time judging Pietro Nenni. Unlike his great rival Giuseppe Saragat, who committed political suicide for consistency's sake — and turned out to be right — or Rodolfo Morandi the rigorous thinker whose ideas dominated the Socialist party (PSI) during the immediate second postwar period — and who turned out to be wrong — Nenni will never be cited as a model of consistency. Indeed, at different times, Nenni adopted the policies of both these leaders.

Professor Tamburrano and I have had a friendly discussion about this issue before. He believes that my analysis of Nenni (*Renewing Italian Socialism*, New York, Oxford University Press, 1988), seems discontinuous. I replied that, in the end, Nenni redeemed himself, unlike most politicians. In these comments, I have no intention of being mean like the city of Rome, which has bestowed Nenni's name on a miserable little iron bridge over the Tiber, instead of honoring him with a major thoroughfare.

In his paper, Tamburrano reviews for us the early unity pacts between Socialists and Communists, correctly and succinctly stating Nenni's motivations for the alliance. Given his experiences in Italy during the rise of Fascism and in 1930's France, Nenni concluded that wherever the left split, the right won. In addition, with the victory of Communism in Russia, a united left would have the support of a great power. Since the price of achieving that aid was the subordination of Socialists to Communists (PCI), as Tamburrano correctly emphasizes, Nenni should have exercised greater care to avoid PCI "imperialism" towards the PSI.

There are extenuating circumstances behind Nenni's reasoning and actions. First, he appeared to be fascinated with Rodolfo Morandi, who theorized an imminent third world war between the United States and the Soviet Union in which the US would lead the forces of capitalism and the USSR those of socialism. Second, the considerations and actions of the US during the period could indeed have appeared aggressive to impartial observers, as Professor Tamburrano points out. However, the constant, one-sided condemnation of US foreign policy coupled with the constant, one-sided absolution of the USSR characterized Italian leftist interpretation of world affairs until fairly recently.

Given the imminent state of war, Morandi concluded, the USSR's Italian agents should captain the nation's proletarian forces, and, as all good soldiers in just wars, the Socialists should follow orders, not question them.[1] Clearly the Nenni-Morandi cabal's cloudy judgement caused a serious misreading of the world situation and produced the subordination of the Socialists to the Communists in all fields.

It is true but hardly a defense that the Christian Democrats (DC) had a similar messianic view of the world and acted in the same manner by subordinating themselves to the United States. Catholics, however, have a longer tradition and greater experience in the struggle between good and evil and seem to do better at it then their supposedly modern-minded leftist counterparts.

In addition, more mundane considerations indicated that Nenni had chosen the wrong path in allying with the Communists so tightly. As Tamburrano recalls for us, the Socialists emerged as the largest party on the left in the first national free elections in post-war Italy (1946). In light of the greater Communist grassroots organization and Russian support, this result surprised everyone. Given Socialist material inferiority, a reasonable interpretation of these results pointed to a decisive rejection of Communism by leftist voters, who clearly selected Socialism and its democratic tradition over a Communism whose methods smelled of the regime from which they had recently been liberated.

Rather than Nenni, Saragat's vision has been historically validated, even if Nenni's superior political acumen defeated it within the Socialist party and forced Saragat out of the organization. As Tamburrano states, the Piedmontese statesman seized upon the election results to bolster his idea of converting Italian Socialism into a great, autonomous, and European force independent of both Communists and Christian Democrats. Misled by his vision of the world, Nenni instead interpreted the results as a victory for the Socialists within the context of popular unity, i.e., a PCI alliance.[2]

Even conceding Nenni's fear of a split left producing a Fascist resurgence, his policies remain difficult to justify. Brushing aside the Socialist electorate's emphasis on the democratic traditions of Italian socialism and blinded by a simplistic historical analysis, Nenni and Morandi demanded an intimate alliance with the PCI, even at the cost of Socialist subservience.

Instead, it was possible to meet whatever threat of a new Fascism which might have existed with a loose PCI coalition, an agreement committing the parties to cooperate case by case when they judged it necessary to do so against resurgent authoritarianism. By acting in a staunchly independent manner, by criticizing DC *and* PCI where warranted, while striving for an understanding on how the left would react in case of a Fascist recrudescence, and by defending its democratic tradition instead of allowing Communist denigration of it to go unchallenged, the PSI would have justified the faith that many voters on the left still retained in it.

This contention does not necessarily mean that the PSI should have moved to the right, a conclusion which is based upon the mistaken assumption that the PCI was a revolutionary party. In fact, the PSI of this period, when it acted independently, pursued leftist policies while the PCI backed conservative ones supported by the DC out of an excessive fear of wounding public opinion. Nenni, unlike Togliatti, opposed backing the authoritarian Badoglio, believed a real purge of Fascist elements from Italian society possible, did not suggest De Gasperi as Prime Minister, and did not vote to include the 1929 Concordat in the Italian Constitution. Within the PSI, then, the idea of a revolution emerging from World War II died hard.

Togliatti claimed that his Socialist comrades lacked "realism," which is still the Communist position when interpreting the immediate postwar era. Communist writers, however, view Italian history as a series of "failed revolutions," for example, uncompromisingly criticizing Risorgimento liberals or the Socialists after World

War I for failing to "make" revolution in what they label revolutionary situations. Yet, in neither of those cases did the protagonists act as cynically as did the PCI in what was arguably a more revolutionary situation, i.e., consciously abandoning all pretence at revolution and throwing their lot in with the Christian Democrats in the hope of being accepted by the Italian establishment. In fact, by abandoning as well the hope of significant reform and helping perpetuate some of the major deficiencies of Italian society without a real attempt to correct them, the PCI helped shove under the rug important issues which reappeared later. What a strange way for a revolutionary party to behave!

At least Nenni and Morandi tried to bring these problems to a head — and were defeated by superior Communist force. Thus, Nenni should have understood early-on that the PCI played above all its own game guided by Realpolitik, not by Socialist ideals, but, with Morandi, imposed alien Communist methods on the Socialist party. Certainly, had the PSI followed Saragat instead of Nenni and become a party on the European Social Democratic model in the 1940's rather than in the 1970's this fact might have profoundly altered the course of the Italian republic. Had the Socialists acted decisively, I believe that they could have created an alternative force to the Christian Democrats; had that happened, scholars would not be lamenting about over forty years of DC domination of the political system and the deleterious effects of that stranglehold.

Instead, Nenni conceived of a Communist alliance so strict that he once refused to join the government if the Communists were excluded, although, the Communists were not so understanding where he was concerned.[3] The result of Nenni's close cooperation with the PCI was Socialist exclusion from the Italian government in May 1947, along with the Communists. In fact, this whole affair should be reevaluated. The left held the event up as an example of DC unfairness only after the electoral loss of 1948; at the time Nenni believed that the exclusion would help the left during those crucial elections.

Nenni's policy of strict Communist collaboration made his ostracism likely. After all, his policy, and Morandi's, drove Saragat and the reformists out of the party, "bolshevized" the organization, lost the labor movement, transformed Nenni into the point-man of the left's opposition to NATO and all aspects of American foreign policy — good as well as bad — and made the PSI into the PCI's John the Baptist. In short, as Tamburrano points out, Nenni aligned himself completely and unquestioningly to Communist and Soviet strategy.

Professor Tamburrano quite properly poses the correct question: why? Part of the answer is the chafing of leftists at the subservient position in which Italy found itself with regard to the United States. Tamburrano provides an excellent account of this situation, so I will not repeat it here. The rebellion of workers and intellectuals against American high-handedness was reasonable and justified, although their slavish acceptance of the Soviet system and the naïvete with which they would have substituted a different and worse kind of subservience arouses substantially less sympathy.

In this respect, I find it hard to accept the statement that the PSI "did not clearly understand the reality of the Soviet world." After all, the Italians had been among the first to have tasted totalitarian methods, even if they lacked Soviet subtlety. Moreover, Nenni and Morandi had fought those methods, one in exile and the other underground in Italy, and were familiar with them. Saragat understood the totalitarian values of the Soviet Union very well, and I do not believe that Nenni was any less intelligent or worse informed. Nenni could have requested information from the international Socialist organizations to which the PSI belonged, especially during the proceedings which led to the PSI's expulsion for parroting the Soviet line.[4]

Quite clearly, for his own political and ideological reasons, Nenni did not wish to acknowledge Soviet reality. Next came the Popular Front defeat in 1948, which produced a sobering effect on Nenni. First, he did not expect it. Second, the defeat transformed the PSI into a second-class party, dropping its electoral percentage, as nearly as could be calculated, to 10 percent. Third, within the Front, the PCI took advantage of the disorientation and organizational weakness of its Socialist comrades to assign a lower number of seats to the PSI. Finally, given international conditions, it now seemed unlikely that the left either in Italy or France had a realistic chance for power.

In a particularly vivid interview, President Sandro Pertini described for me Nenni's immediate reaction to the 1948 defeat.

Undoubtedly, by then Nenni understood the seriousness of the Socialist situation.[5] I believe that even at this early date he already harbored the idea of loosening Socialist ties with the Communists, but several factors made this course particularly difficult. By now, the PSI was completely embroiled with the PCI, organizationally and emotionally. Italian police reports reveal Socialist financial dependency on the PCI, threats to cut off support if the party adopted an independent course, packing of Socialist Congresses with Communist sympathizers, and Socialist leaders holding secret dual membership in the PCI — the *doppia tessera*.[6] PCI members dominated common Socialist-Communist committees set up by the Popular Front. Moreover, battered by the 1948 electoral defeat, the loss of labor movement influence, the downgrading of their historical tradition, and the acknowledgement by their own leaders that their party had only an auxiliary role to play, PSI members suffered an inferiority complex not completely obliterated until the 1980's.

In addition, Nenni's foreign policy role had alienated the American Embassy, which, nursed by Christian Democratic and Liberal party politicians, simple-mindedly repeated the Socialist equals Communist equation — even after that formula had ceased to be operative.[7] In short, like Jacob Marley in Dickens's Christmas tale, Nenni had forged this heavy heritage link by link; unlike Marley, he would not carry the chain forever, although, politically, it seemed that way and it certainly produced more ghosts. One other factor contributed to the difficulty of reversing Socialist policy: Nenni himself. The Socialist leader incorrectly computed the practical difficulties of backing away from the Communist embrace, clinging to his idea of the necessity of unity of action while underestimating how tenaciously the Christian Democrats would keep turning a deaf ear to the Socialist overture.

The 1953 elections eroded the basis of the centrist coalition which had ruled Italy since 1948. At the same time, the rise of a social-minded Christian Democratic Left created the premise for a center-left with the DC by bringing close to power an interlocutor with whom the Socialists could begin a dialogue.

As the ever-observant Italian police noted, Nenni's attempt at a gradual retreat from the Communist entanglement began in 1950 at the administrative level. In that year, the Romagnol leader fought with Lelio Basso over the substitution of the Bologna Province PSI secretary. The Bologna Prefect wrote in one of his reports that Nenni "apparently intends to adopt a PSI policy tending . . . toward a certain autonomy from the PCI."[8] Several hostile encounters of this kind with party bureaucrats followed in the next couple of years, and in 1952 Nenni advocated an independent Socialist slate allied but not subordinated to the Communists in the Rome city elections. He viewed this policy as the practical start of Socialist disengagement from the Communists and as an opportunity for the voters to judge the PSI's new course and provide feedback.[9]

Both Togliatti and the procommunist Socialist left wing objected to these initiatives. Most importantly, Morandi still controlled the party apparatus. Nenni understood after the 1953 party congress (Milan) that he must go slow if he wished to effect a radical change of policy with his party intact because the Communists wielded an emotional, ideological, and financial ascendancy over the Socialist party and actively interfered in its internal affairs.

For the Communists, loss of their Socialist allies spelled isolation, while the DC right wing had the Americans and the Vatican in tow (or was it vice versa?). Thus, these groups powerfully resisted Nenni's plans. Indeed, Nenni initially underestimated the opposing *de facto* coalition's power and seriously miscalculated the resistance he faced. Still overly influenced by a popular front mentality and expecting applause from the DC because the PSI would bring the state the support of an important segment of the working class, Nenni offered to loosen his Communist ties, but he did not drop the PCI decisively enough. At the same time, he continued his sorties against NATO and endorsed some radical reforms. Ironically enough, Nenni anticipated the proposals of other European Social Democrats, but given the Italian context and his reputation as a Communist "stooge," his unwillingness to break cleanly from the PCI allowed his opponents to cast doubt upon his sincerity and to exploit the idea that he was a "Trojan Horse" for Communism. Incredibly, this tactic worked into the 1960's.[10]

Only the Hungarian Revolution afforded Nenni the emotional and political opportunity to break ideologically with the PCI.[11] But ideological changes take years to filter down to the rank and file; furthermore, PCI sympathizers controlled the PSI apparatus, making the situation much worse. Tamburrano's account of the Venice Congress is only one illustration of a problem never fully resolved.

Lack of control over the apparatus, furthermore, was only one of Nenni's worries. Despite the troubled parliamentary, political, and economic situation of the late 1950's, the credentials which Nenni had established by then, and the see-saw rise of the DC left to quasi-power, Italian ruling groups preferred to govern with the Neo-Fascists rather than with the Socialists.[12] The Tambroni affair, which produced civil agitation throughout the country, illustrates the non-existence of an alternate ruling coalition to the center-left. This coalition, however, did not actually gel until it received overt support from President John F. Kennedy's New Frontiersmen, skillfully led by Presidential Advisor Arthur M. Schlesinger, Jr. The capacity of the center-left to divide opinion can also be traced in the fight it ignited within the *American* bureaucracy.[13]

On the other hand, Nenni received valuable support from important industrial, commercial, and financial sectors anxious to strengthen ties with the Communist world; these supporters included ENI's Enrico Mattei, FIAT's Vittorio Valletta, publisher Angelo Rizzoli, and the Banca Commerciale's Raffaele Mattioli.[14] The exasperating and drawn-out struggle for the center-left testifies to the immobility of the Italian political and social situation in the 1950's. If it is true that Nenni helped create many of the most serious problems he himself faced during this period, observers cannot but admire his tenacity in reversing a disastrous course during this period — a change which, despite its initial disappointments, salvaged the Italian Socialist Party's future.

Professor Tamburrano gives a good summary of the events which produced the first "organic" center-left cabinet in December 1963 and of the conservative attempts to sabotage that government, especially by utilizing financial power. I would like, however, to expand on two points mentioned by him.

The first is the pernicious role which the Communist party played throughout the center-left period. In criticizing the PSI for "selling out," for being "reformists," etc. — the kind of technique American talk show hosts would envy — the Communists bolstered their immediate political fortunes but helped sabotage the kind of reforms they themselves had advocated and which would have spared their country untold grief. During the financial crisis following installation of the Aldo Moro government, the Communists did not help; throughout the center-left period, CGIL labor leaders refused to meet with Budget Minister Pieraccini to discuss structural reforms, the destructiveness of which Pieraccini himself emphasized to me.[15] In short, instead of encouraging the Socialists — even by constructive opposition — the largest party on the left helped derail the reform effort, and then criticized the supposed failure for partisan reasons. Instead of statesmanship, the PCI selected petty politics. Ironically, as the PCI became more mature, responsible, and independent, it discovered that it could do no better than follow in Socialist footsteps.

Second, the military threat to the center-left posed by the SIFAR affair, and the implications of the response to it, deserves greater attention and analysis than it has hitherto received. Professor Tamburrano states that Nenni's fear of a coup had substance. In order to head off the *putsch* and salvage Italian democracy, the Socialists dropped some of their more significant reform demands. As a result, the center-left did not produce the electoral advantages it should have because narrow leftist interpretations of the legislative "balance sheet" made the experiment seem a failure, even though it was not. Leftist competition enters into the equation here as well; Italian leftists have always been quick to denounce the supposed Italian penchant for authoritarian governments, but at the time one threatened, they ridiculed Nenni's fear of a coup, and they still fail to give the Socialist leader and the center-left credit for saving the Italian democratic system.[16]

More important, however, is this point: once such tactics "worked," opponents of Italy's "leftward" drift invoked them again. In short, SIFAR was the first "deviation" of the Italian secret services, a model which eventually culminated in the "strategy of tension" of the 1970's. At the same time, leftists reacting to such tactics initiated terrorism on the left.[17]

Ironically, many of these problems stemmed from a mistaken interpretation of the center-left, which did produce important results even more remarkable considering the difficult political context in which it operated. Despite tremendous obstacles, the center-left managed to help Italy adapt to the modern world, even if that transition is less than perfect. The interpretation of the center-left as a "failure" is as unjustified as it is partisan. Observers as diverse as Giovanni Pieraccini, Mauro Ferri, and Antonio Giolitti consider the center-left a success because it fostered a new and modern mentality and spirit in Italy, even if impartial observers could have hoped for a stronger legislative "balance sheet" and "bottom line."[18] Accountants, however, are hardly the best judges of historical development, be they of the right or the left.

Here we may quote Nenni, who responded to a question from Professor Tamburrano by stating: "It is said about rightist political systems and authoritarian regimes that everything functions and nothing lives. Of the political system which has taken its name and dates from the center-left, we may say the opposite, i.e., that nothing functions and everything lives. . . . [19]

Eventually, even the PCI grudgingly recognized the significance of the center-left, late, as usual, and after having skillfully helped sabotage and exploit to the hilt this valiant attempt to launch the Italian left on the path to positive political action. In 1976, Enrico Berlinguer acknowledged that the center-left had marked a new beginning in Italian politics.[20] Despite the PCI's skill in making immediate political hay from the center-left, the Communist failure to act positively during the experiment can be considered a milestone on the road to the PCI's ultimate bankruptcy.

Notes

1 Aldo Agosti, *Rodolfo Morandi. Il pensiero e l'azione politica*. (Bari: Laterza, 1972). pp. 423-24.

2 Pietro Nenni, *Tempo di guerra fredda. Diari 1943-1956*. (Milan: SugarCo, 1981), p. 299.

3 Ibid., pp. 100-07.

4 Suspicious of Italian Socialist double-dealing with regard to the Communists, European Socialists demanded a PSI commitment to democratic socialism and, when it was not forthcoming, expelled the PSI from COMISCO. See U.S. Department of State, *Foreign Relations of the United States. 1948*. Volume 3: Western Europe (Washington, D.C.: Government Printing Office, 1974), p. 856.

5 Spencer M. Di Scala, *Renewing Italian Socialism. Nenni to Craxi*. (New York: Oxford University Press, 1988), p. 75.

6 See, for example, Paolo Emiliani, *Dieci anni perduti: Cronache del Partito Socialista Italiano*. (Pisa: Nistri-Lischi, 1953), p. 29; and Giogio Galli, *Storia del socialismo italiano*. (Bari: Laterza, 1983), p. 83.

7 Di Scala, *Renewing Italian Socialism*, pp. 122-23.

8 See *Archivio Centrale dello Stato, Ministero degli Interni, Direzione di Pubblica Sicurezza*, PSI, *Categoria K*, Pacco 57/1, documents dated June 13, and 18, 1950; December 14, 1950; and *Pacco* 93, documents dated November 24, 1952 and December 20, 1952.

9 See Nenni, *Tempo di guerra fredda*, pp. 522-24.

10 Di Scala, *Renewing Italian Socialism*, p. 97.

11 Nenni's articles on this subject are collected in his *Le prospettive del socialismo dopo la destalinizzazione*, 2nd Ed. (Turin: Einaudi, 1962).

12 Giorgio Galli, *Storia della Democrazia Cristiana* (Bari: Laterza, 1978), pp. 200-01.

13 Di Scala, *Renewing Italian Socialism*, pp. 123-32.

14 *Archivio Centrale dello State, Ministero Interni, Direzione Pubblica Sicurezza,* PSI, *Affari Generali, Fascicolo* 175/P193, *busta* 49, document dated 27 March 1957 and marked "Visto dal Ministro."

15 Author's conversation with Giovanni Pieraccini, 14 November 1984.

16 Di Scala, *Renewing Italian Socialism,* pp. 152-58.

17 Author's conversation with Giuseppe Tamburrano, 18 December 1984 and Giuseppe Tamburrano's, typescript of an untitled article on the twentieth anniversary of the SIFAR affair.

18 Di Scala, *Renewing Italian Socialism,* pp. 158-60.

19 Pietro Nenni, *Intervista sul socialismo italiano.* (Bari: Laterza, 1977), pp. 106-07.

20 Editorial, *Rinascita,* July 23, 1976.

VII

Italy During the Reconstruction: The Communist Party Policy of National Unity, 1945-1949

Giuseppe Vacca

It is an accepted fact that, when war broke out, the PCI, the Italian Communist Party was a political formation comprising a few thousand persecuted militants, scattered over the country with very little communication among members. What enabled this party to become a decisive force in Italian postwar politics was without doubt the role it played in the resistance movement and the war of liberation. Equally important was the *plan* the PCI proposed for both the country's political and economic reorganization and the guidelines for its subsequent development. This is the main focus of my essay.

What is striking about Palmiro Togliatti's report to the PCI's Fifth Congress (Rome, 29 December 1945), the document which more than any other established the fundamental principles on which the plan was based, are the wide-ranging references made to the history of Italy. These references represented the analytical basis of the program and were based on the thinking of the "gruppo ordinovista" (which ruled the party after 1926) concerning the crisis of the Liberal state and the "great war" and the analysis of Fascism as a European phenomenon made by Togliatti himself with increasing determination between 1928 and 1936 and on Gramsci's thinking on *characteristics* (the "long duration") of the history of Italy, published in *Quaderni del carcere*, which Togliatti had been able to study as early as 1945. I begin my essay with this reference in order to stress a fundamental aspect of the PCI's political makeup, which has affected all its developments over the forty years of Togliatti's leadership. I shall attempt to sum it up as follows: parties put down roots and become a permanent part of a country's political life to the extent to which they prove to be a "necessary" factor for its historical development. One prerequisite of their political effectiveness is their *cultural independence*. Throughout the period marked, in Europe, by the (comparative) independence of "national development", the parties established themselves and grew by developing their own ideas concerning the relations between the domestic factors and the international factors of historical development, i.e. they made their own personal "combination" of the national and international ingredients of development (Gramsci). Whether or not they were aware of the theoretical basis behind this, their *political autonomy* was based on their capacity to develop *their own ideas* about their country's historical development.

These brief theoretical considerations are, I think, necessary to at least outline an approach which can do full justice to the formula of the "policy of national unity" in which Togliatti encapsulated the program developed for the "reconstruction" of Italy.

Togliatti summed up the strategic content in the concept of "progressive democracy." There is an acknowledged affinity between this strategy and the experimentation of "new paths," of "the advance to socialism in democracy" tried out by the communist parties of many European countries, both in the East and the West, between 1945 and 1947, involving their participation in coalition governments. However, in the case of the PCI, partly because it operated in the American "sphere of influence," there is no doubt in my mind that it was a genuine "national path," that is, "different" not only from the Soviet experience but also from the experiments in progress in other European countries at the time.[1] The essential difference lay in the relationship set up between *democracy and socialism*. It was not so much a question of attaining socialism (in the sense of a *model* of society basically defined in advance by the Soviet experience and of which only variants determined by different historical conditions were allowed) by peaceful, gradual, democratic means, but rather of setting off a *process* of interrelated political and economic transformations leading to a "new idea of socialism" (Togliatti was to use this expression later). However, I shall not pursue this idea further here.[2] What I shall examine, instead, is what plan for democratic order and economic development was pursued by the PCI in Italy after the fall of Fascism.

Together with the Christian Democrat and Socialist parties, the Communist party made a decisive contribution to the drafting of the Constitution. As the parties were gearing up for the election of the Constituent Assembly, Togliatti laid down the guidelines to be followed by the Party in the Assembly. "To those who ask us which republic we want," he declared, "we answer without hesitation that we want a democratic workers' republic, we want a republic organized on the basis of a representative parliamentary system, that is, a republic which remains within the confines of democracy and in which all the reforms of a social nature can be achieved while respecting the democratic method."[3]

"Democratic workers' republic" was the formula supported by the Communists at the Constituent Assembly. As the result of a compromise with the Christian Democrat representatives, this was subsequently changed to that of "democratic republic based on work" which is still contained in article one of the Italian Constitution. But what must be stressed here is the equation set up by Togliatti between political democracy and "representative parliamentary system." This point sets the PCI apart from the rest of the communist movement and has been the cause of most of its conflicts with the latter, from the Cominform incident to the 1957 Moscow conference and the 1981 "laceration."[4] It would be interesting to reconstruct the influences and paths followed and thus trace back the origins of *an independent, non-Stalinist, Communist tradition*, which has characterized the history of the PCI, at least starting from Togliatti's conclusions concerning the Spanish republic of 1936, and has its broadest and most solid theoretical basis in the *Quaderni del carcere*.[5] However, this too lies beyond our present scope and I shall therefore simply stress the difference which exists between "progressive democracy" and the other "transition" experiments carried out in those years in Europe which are commonly referred to as "popular democracy."[6]

Togliatti stated in his report to the Naples Communist organization leaders on April 11, 1944 that "should a national constituent assembly be convened tomorrow, we should urge the people to turn Italy into a democratic republic, with a Constitution to guarantee the freedom of all Italians; freedom of thought and speech; freedom of the press, to associate and to meet; freedom of religion and worship; freedom of small and medium size property owners to develop without being crushed by the greedy and selfish groups of plutocrats, that is, by the large monopolistic capitalist groups. This means that we shall in no way recommend a form of government based on the existence or the dominion of a single party. In a democratic and progressive Italy there will be different parties corresponding to the different ideas and interests of the Italian people; however, we will recommend that these parties, or at least those among them which have a popular basis and a democratic and national platform, should remain united in order to combat any attempt by Fascism to rise again. We do not want to ban democracy or democrats, nor liberals, only Fascists."[7] He went on to emphasize in his report to the Fifth Congress: "We have yet to achieve any great social conquests that can be ratified in a constitutional document of the State;" and therefore "We need a constitution, the originality of which, in a certain sense, lies in the fact that it represents a program for the future"[8]. The economic content of this program can be summed up in the formation of a mixed economy in which the constitutional recognition of "forms of ownership of the means of production different from the private, namely ownership by cooperatives and the State", of the legitimacy of economic planning instruments and institutes of "control over production by all categories of workers in the interest of society as a whole"[9] will lead to the promotion of "reforms of the country's social structures"[10] such as will "destroy reaction and fascism at their roots"[11]. "How much of all this", Togliatti asked, "must we write into the Constitution?" And he answered: "Just so much as is necessary to point the way to be followed by the legislative assemblies in their work of materially organizing economic and social life."[12]

A *programmatic* and *anti-fascist* constitution therefore signifies a fundamental law of the state which makes provision for and safeguards also "the advent of a new, democratic, innovative, progressive ruling class". However, Togliatti stresses that "we are not demanding a Socialist Constitution". The substance of economic and social change are to be achieved by political and government action. The constitutional charter can make provision for it and guarantee *that it is possible,* "but the only real, serious, guarantee that this will be done is for new forces, which are by their very nature democratic and innovative, to arise and lead the State." "These forces," he concludes, "are those of the workers."[13]

The political system to be traced out by the Constitution must therefore be democratic and *pluralistic* in the classic sense. In its political and governmental action the PCI has striven to achieve permanent collaboration between the mass parties in the belief that these are the sole conditions under which "reforms of the social structure" and the advent of new ruling classes could be promoted in postwar Italy. Of course, the constitutional charter cannot contain *prescriptions* to this effect. It must merely not exclude them and indeed also make provision for this possibility. In its fundamental aspects, therefore (a State based on legality, representativeness, majority principle), "progressive democracy" is in essence a form of parliamentary democracy; in this it differs from the contemporary experiences of "popular democracy."

The economic aspects of the reconstruction were defined after the liberation of Italy, as soon as the attention of the anti-Fascist coalition government could be brought to bear specifically on this objective.

In his address delivered to the economic congress of the PCI held in August 1945 (aptly entitled *Ricostruire*), Togliatti made a number of points which should be noted. In the first place, he called for a *market economy,* to be regulated through action taken by the State, the trade unions and the CLN (National Liberation Committees), aimed at increasing the country's overall *productivity.* The relationship between plan and market was clearly stated in terms of an "open economy." Togliatti thought that "at the present time, it is utopian to call for a national economic plan, particularly one imposed as a condition for a large-scale development of the country's reconstructive activity." By demanding such a plan, he continued "we would be asking for something that we ourselves are incapable of achieving." Therefore, he concluded "even if all the power was in our hands alone we should appeal to private enterprise for the reconstruction."[14]

The economic measures to be taken thus involved the stability of the lira (anti-inflation campaign and exchange rates),[15] elimination of the "ordinary deficit" by means of fiscal reform, special employment measures (including a reduction of working hours and a generalized unemployment benefit). With regard to economic control measures, Togliatti had no hesitation in declaring that "we must call for forms of action, supervision and restriction of the absolute speculative right of the private entrepreneur whenever necessary for the purpose of imposing what we term a line of national solidarity. We (therefore) call for *control over production and trade of the same kind as that which still exists in England and the United States*"[16] (italics mine).

When speaking of the "aid" (provided by the US through the *lendlease* program) and more generally of "foreign relations," he declared that "one of our fundamental directives in this field will be to demand that what is done be made public so that the people will know how economic relations are built up between our country and other nations. . . . In particular, the public must be informed about loans made both to private groups and to the State, and the collateral provided by the latter." He concluded that "if this is not done, we shall fail to establish a truly democratic form of government in Italy."[17]

The policy followed by the PCI thus formed part of the "politics of productivity."[18] The strategy adopted embodied specific aspects related to peculiarities of the Italian development model. These peculiarities emerged in particular from the analysis made of Fascism. Ever since 1922 the party leaders had endeavored to grasp the endogenous reasons for which, in Italy, the "recasting of bourgeois Europe"[19] (or, if one prefers, Tayloristic modernization) had taken the form of Fascism (a "mass reactionary regime," according to Togliatti's classic definition of 1935).[20] The depression afflicting the domestic market had been identified as the factor leading up to the formation of the system of dominant alliances ("national" nature of the "North-South question"), the political choice of the dominant block aimed at guaranteeing its reproduction, a permanent feature of the capitalistic management of the country's development and the main obstacle in the way of its democratic modernization. This explained the political, economic and social aspects of the "anti-Fascist revolution," the link between development and need to overthrow the dominant classes, in other words, the national specification of a program of modernization led by the working class[21] and the peculiar interrelationship between economic reforms and political transformation (democracy and social-ism).

The "reconstruction" program thus can be intended as a bridge between a "policy of productivity" and the "progressive democracy" plan. In his report to the Fifth Congress, Togliatti traced out the links between these complex interrelationships in terms that are worth citing. "Today work is less productive here than in other countries and this is due not only to autarkic policy, which was entirely based on the principle of producing at higher costs everything that was produced elsewhere more cheaply, but also to all the action previously taken by the groups heading the Italian industrial and agrarian classes. The economic policies of these groups was aimed mainly at consolidating their own privileges and at increasing their profits at all costs, to the detriment of the producing and consuming majority. They achieved this by implementing a customs policy and a wages and social policy which gradually restricted the domestic market and created a situation in which labor productivity and living standards were lower than in the other countries, while production costs were higher. Italian economic policy had thus to be reversed. It was necessary to attempt to gradually reorganize the entire national production on the basis of low production costs, high labor productivity and high wages. I agree that a formula of this kind does not yet contain a concrete program. However, it does provide a general guideline which can be gradually applied over a period of years." "In conclusion, what kind of reforms are we proposing? Do they have a class nature?" Togliatti concluded: "They certainly have, in the sense that they tend to increase the prosperity and standard of living of the working classes." "But," he added, "they are *national* insofar as, both by increasing the wealth of the working masses and by eradicating Fascism completely, they allow a start to be made on the economic rehabilitation of the country".[22]

It is no coincidence that with this stance Togliatti was concerned with explaining the difference between the program of the "new Party" and the action of the old Italian socialist "reformism." The limits of the latter were evident in its incapacity to link together reform objectives that were partially valid ("class" objectives, but in an "economic-corporative" sense) into an overall plan for the country's economic and political modernization. In this way, "on the one hand this split the unity of the working classes and their action, which was deprived of the necessary national significance; on the other, socialism itself was infiltrated by hostile influences."[23] At the same time, however, Togliatti praised the whole of Italian socialism,[24] identifying the "new party" as the heir to its better traditions.[25]

Shortly before this, in a lecture given at the Scuola Normale Superiore of Pisa, he had made a special effort to explain how, at the theoretical level, the distinctions which existed inside the European workers' movement could no longer be applied to the old alternative between reform and revolution but referred rather to the different ways of conceiving a national plan of economic, political and social reform.[26]

The left-wing parties made a disappointing showing in the elections of June 2, 1946. Communists and Socialists together accounted for little more than 40% of the Constituent Assembly and played no decisive part in the formation of the government coalitions. Doubts and hostility over the "national unity policy" obviously arose in the PCI. Unfortunately, no minutes are available for the meeting of the party executive in which the election results were discussed and the critical positions probably emerged quite clearly. However, from Togliatti's speech at the Party's Organization Conference, held in Florence in January 1947, there seem to be no doubts that the Conference itself had been called because of the need to reaffirm party strategy.

Attention must be drawn to the way Togliatti countered the criticism. In the teeth of rising anti-communism, encouraged both by developments in the international situation[27] and by the inequality of forces revealed by the elections, he attempted to build up broader alliances around a program of open "national reformism." "The anti-democratic and anti-communist tendencies which are emerging more and more clearly on the Italian political scene," he said, "can be the cause of misunderstanding and doubts also among us, they can contribute to the adoption of falsely extremist positions and can cause certain groups of comrades to lose sight of our objectives and of the path to be followed to attain them. If it is true, as indeed it is, that the reactionary and conservative groups are carrying out a systematic action and converging from a number of directions to reduce the scope of the democratic form of government and place all kinds of obstacles in the way of the development of democracy, the action we take must be diametrically opposed to this. Our policy must not be a narrow policy of class, but wide-ranging and democratic and national in scope. This is why, when we were attempting a general formulation of our economic policy we spoke of an 'economic new deal.'[28] This term is intended to convey to all concerned that we realize that in order to renew the Italian economy it is necessary for contacts and alliances to be formed between the working class and the other classes of workers involved in the modernization, and that these alliances can and must reach as far as certain groups of the hard-working and property-owning classes of industry and commerce."[29]

Perhaps the "moderation" with which the PCI responded to De Gasperi's move to oust it from the government in the first six months of 1947 was also the result of a misplaced evaluation concerning the possibility of persisting in anti-fascist collaboration even at a time when the "cold war" was now gaining the upper hand and it was clear that the European capitalist countries were becoming part of the international reorganization of the North American "economic-world."[30] Of course, the decisions of the PCI were above all a response due to its independent conception of the problems involved in the renewal of Italian politics and economy. It is therefore not surprising to see how the Communists reacted to their ousting from government in June 1947 and the setback suffered on April 18, the following year. Indeed, it is in the firmness of the PCI strategy that we must seek the reasons for which, precisely as a result of these processes, it became the main left-wing political force in Italy and established firm roots in the country.

In establishing the policy to be implemented in order to oppose the move to oust the Communists and Socialists from the government, Togliatti did not fail to point out the link between that decision and US foreign policy. Nevertheless, he placed the emphasis on the initiative taken by the Italian economic and political forces which had sought out these links and used them for domestic purposes.[31] And when, after the elections of April 18, 1948, in which the DC won an absolute majority, anti-Communism tended to lead the centrist governments to take on the appearance of a "regime," the PCI chose to shift the main thrust of the mass movements and its policy of alliances formed around the objective of the *defense and the implementation of the Constitution*.[32]

The examination of the "national unity policy" must be completed by an analysis of the PCI's decisions concerning foreign policy and Italy's international status. The basis for this point is again Togliatti's report to the Fifth Congress which lays down the general guidelines of an approach to international relations that the PCI has never ceased to follow:

> We believe that Italy is above all in need of peace. We do not believe in Utopia. We know that to eliminate all causes of war completely it is necessary to change the economic structure of society. However, we also know that today peace can be maintained by means of a given policy, which tends towards maintaining the unity of the great democratic nations, those which defeated Fascism by means of their unity and which, through their unity, must reconstruct a peaceful Europe and a peaceful world.

> I do not think it is in the interest of our country to belong to, or to promote even to a limited extent, a bloc of powers of any kind whatsoever, whether Mediterranean or Western, whatever it may be called. I think that a country which has reached our level of economic destruction and disintegration cannot have a bloc policy because whatever bloc it belonged to, it would be the slave of someone in that bloc. The material actions of our foreign policy must tend towards the reestablishment of friendly relations with all peoples, in the first place with those to whom a debt of gratitude for the contribution they have made to the liberation of a part of our territory. Our foreign policy is therefore one of peace and collaboration with all democratic countries, of reestablishment of normal political and business relations with the three great powers to which it befalls to reconstruct a Europe and a peaceful world as leaders of the great organization of the United Nations.[33]

These principles were used by the PCI as a basis for the positions taken on the occasion of the most important foreign policy decisions made by the Italian government during those years: the ratification of the peace treaty, the ERP aid agreement, and membership in NATO. Whatever the limits inherent in a strategy based on the concept of "national independence" in a world that was becoming increasingly interdependent, albeit permanently organized into two opposing blocs, this was undeniably the guiding principle on which the positions of the PCI concerning Italian foreign policy were based. Despite the advent of the "cold war," this principle was consistently applied.

The debates on the Marshall Plan and NATO membership are those which most accurately reflect the position of the PCI. Furthermore, 1949 has been chosen as the final date of the "reconstruction - PCI" issue because Italy's membership of NATO was the final act in the advance of the "cold war" and made the irreversibility of its effects on the everyday life of the country fully visible. As far as the "national unity policy" was concerned, the year 1949 can, to some extent, be taken as the end of the "reconstruction" period.

The parliamentary debate on the formation of the fourth De Gasperi Cabinet provided the PCI with its first, exacting contact with the Marshall Plan. The link between the intention to utilize American "aid" to further bloc strategy, and the ousting of the left wing from the Italian government, was quite obvious. However, in his speech to the House, Togliatti not only concentrated what he termed the "fire of his criticism" on the initiative and behavior of the national forces, but actually adopted a balanced stance on the topic of "foreign loans," making a distinction between acceptance of the loan and his unwillingness to accept this as an occasion for locking Italy into the "western bloc." His arguments are worth considering.

Togliatti agreed that Italy should offer her creditors (the US government) guarantees which were not only economic in nature ("that is, guarantees as to how the capital would be used" for the purpose of "developing our economy,") but also political ("I consider the requirement of a certain political stability to be legitimate" and "that our country should not be engaged in a foreign policy hostile to the country helping us.") On the other hand, he rejected "the opinion that a specific government, indeed, a government with a specific political color and a specific structure should be placed at the head of the country so that it can be entitled to receive the aid that it needs." "This," he said, "represents direct intervention in the domestic political life of our country, and any intervention in the domestic political life of our country, means that lend-lease is no longer a policy to help reconstruction but a power policy aimed at gaining certain positions."

This position was the exact opposite of the one that only the right wing defended openly.[34] It was based on the general guidelines for international policy laid down in the Report to the Fifth Party Congress. These were now being appealed to and emphasized with reference to a vital turning point in the country's political life:

> No one will object to these guarantees because, I repeat, the thinking shared by all good democrats is that the new Italian democracy must adopt a foreign policy which does not involve membership in either power bloc, insofar as such blocs exist, which may be questioned. Let us keep out of such competition. We have enough to do to reconstruct our homeland, to treat and heal our wounds.[35]

It could be argued that this position was now anachronistic as far as the possibility of influencing the policy of the country's government was concerned. However, it is undeniably consistent with the overall policy of "national reformism" pursued by the PCI. Indeed, at this point, it is worth stressing the similarities between this approach and the "new deal" type outlook characterizing the postwar international collaboration between the great powers aimed at the establishment of a world order of prosperity and peace. Until the creation of the Cominform, this was in no way in contrast with the tenets of Soviet foreign policy. However, this does not diminish the value of all this. The belated idea that despite the "Truman doctrine" and the announcement of the Marshall Plan the game was not over was held not only by the PCI but was still current also in certain sectors of the *liberal* wing of the new deal bloc.[36]

When the Sixth Congress of the PCI met (January 1948) the "Cold War" had now become the dominant feature of international and Italian politics. The creation of the Cominform marked a change in the fundamental analytical paradigm of the Communist movement: no longer "anti-Fascist unity" but the counter-position of socialism and capitalism at the world level. The PCI had subscribed (at least partially) to the Cominform and had accepted its criticism and new tendencies.[37] Only in 1974 was there an open criticism of those decisions.[38] In his Report to the Sixth Congress, Togliatti followed the general lines of the Cominform's analysis of the international situation. However, he persisted in the opinion that "the blame for the new forms of foreign intervention in our affairs lies with the present leaders of the Italian state, with the parties heading the government."[39] With regard to the Marshall Plan he was thus able to reaffirm that he acknowledged "the utility of, and even the need for, American aid," provided that it was possible "to discuss the conditions of the aid itself and to reject those conditions which jeopardize our economic and political future."[40]

During the House debate in July 1948 prior to the approval of the ERP-linked economic agreement with the USA, the contrary vote of the PCI was thus justified not only in view of its opposition to the Marshall Plan as a "Cold War" instrument, but also because, in accordance with the "Truman Doctrine" and "in contrast with our constitutional legality," the agreement was aimed at "restoring" the old model of Italian development.[41]

The most noteworthy point made by Togliatti in his speech against the approval of the NATO is the appeal to the centrist block for the majority and the opposition to steer a common course on the most important foreign policy issues.[42] This was much more than an ultimate attempt to save at least the principles of "national unity policy." In his speech on the Marshall Plan the year before Togliatti had made cautious mention of the change in the nature of war due to the atomic situation and the implications this had on political action and on political ideas themselves:

> Any intent of world dominion must necessarily lead to a new world war, at the end of which who knows what would be left of our civilization, both European and American. The truth is that we have reached such a point in the development of the balance of forces between peoples and the awareness of the masses that, if we wish to maintain a future of civilized life for the masses of men and women of this and future generations, we must strive and fight in order that the 20th century may be the century, not of the impossible dominion of a single people, but of international collaboration between the peoples of the entire world.[43]

In the first debate on NATO (December 2, 1948) he stated a general thesis concerning the *evitability of war*, which was clearly implicit in these analyses:

> We believe, in the first place, that it is no longer true that war is inevitable. Historically, we know how wars start in our era; we know that they are the result of the leaps and bounds by which the capitalistic and imperialistic countries develop, and which lead their ruling classes to affirm their power over all the others, to want to conquer the whole world and to reduce the other peoples to slavery. Although this is true, as it is true that the laws of development of capitalism are far from having changed, it is however equally true that we have reached a point in world history in which the opinions and will of peoples carry increasing weight and are increasingly asserted. An

awareness of political problems, or even just an interest in political problems, is extending ever more widely and involves larger and larger masses of people. Workers take an interest in problems of international politics, take sides for or against given solutions, actively defend their own interests or their very existence, first and foremost, that fundamental interest which consists of maintaining peace, on which their lives depend. Furthermore, the working masses are now organized, into professional organizations, into great political parties and, in most parts of the world, are at the helm of the State. In such a situation, can war be avoided? our answer is: Yes, it can.[44]

It is interesting to note not only the profound difference on this fundamental issue between Togliatti's position and the ideas current in the Cominform. Subjected to even further specification and development these opinions gradually gave rise, for instance in *Intervista a 'Nuovi argomenti'* and in the *Promemoria di Yalta*, to cite but the best known documents, to a line which prepared the way for the "new way of thinking" and the present Soviet "new deal."[45] In the light of these analyses and thinking, the unremitting defense in the postwar period by the PCI of national autonomy as the mainstay of Italian foreign policy has no narrow-minded nationalistic aspects. Nor can it be considered as a mere appendix to Soviet foreign policy. On the contrary, it outlines the only system of international relations in which the "national reformism" of the PCI could be seen to be founded. It contained a combination of internationalism and national outlook, rendered unfeasible by the reorganization of the world into spheres of influence and opposing blocs. However, to some extent it still satisfied the profound need for the country's political and economic renewal. Communist-socialist unity was maintained on this basis until 1956 (and, in many respects, until the center-left, as far as international politics is concerned) and the PCI succeeded in emerging as a decisive force in Italian politics.

What remains to be explored, though not in this paper, are the details of the main instruments of political action developed by Togliatti after the fall of Fascism: the trade union[46] and the "new party."[47] Nonetheless, I should like to propose a few final considerations.

In a scathing article on the work of Alcide De Gasperi, written barely one year after the latter's death and still strongly marked by the "Cold War" atmosphere, Togliatti took stock of the "reconstruction" years, which had just ended, in what was intended as a historical judgement. I should like to draw attention to two points: the evaluation of the foundations of De Gasperi's political inspiration and that of the results of the "reconstruction." According to Togliatti "In continental Europe, De Gasperi was one of the main inventors, if not the main inventor, (of the) Cold War. The difficulty lies in successfully measuring exactly what, in such an attitude, was part of an autonomous view of Italian political and social relations and what instead was imposed by international constraints. Perhaps on occasions some perturbing and deforming influence did come from abroad;" "but," he concluded, "we repeat that it is a difficult task to separate this element from the rest of the man's personality and behavior, and give it its correct weight. This is all the more true in that international relations developed at the same pace as internal relations."[48]

"From 1947 on," Togliatti continued, "after the expulsion from the government of Communists and Socialists, 'economic reconstruction' took on its clear, final, appearance of restoration, with the exclusion of all dreams of change. Those really responsible for this were the Americans on the one hand, and the leaders of the old dominant groups, on the other. The former acted saying openly that their economic aid, to Italy as to other European countries, was intended to allow their way of life to triumph, that is, old traditional capitalism. Not only did the old dominant groups regain control over the national economy but they reinstated the same habits they had got into under Fascism, demanding that the government take measures and action to place both the wealth of the country and the State budget at their disposal. The budget was not brought under control; in fact, prices rose; the funds from America were used haphazardly and without any control, mainly to the benefit of private enterprise; after industrial property had been revalued by the State, profits and capital began their flight abroad; tax evasion reached a peak and the country emerged with a devastated budget, and millions unemployed." What prevailed, in other words, was "an economic polity which proved incapable of detaching itself, in order to attempt to improve working conditions, from narrow-minded monetary and financial orthodoxy, but on the other hand capable of extravagance if this was imposed by a group of powerful speculators or demanded by the organizers of the international cold war." "What emerges from the entire research, in other words, is the figure of De Gasperi who is not a 'reconstructer,' much less a modernizer of our country's economy, but merely a restorer of the traditional economic structure."[49]

Togliatti did not perceive the new and dynamic factors inherent in American capitalism and in the reorganization of European capitalism under its leadership. Furthermore, he failed to see that, during the years of centrism, the foundations had been laid for a reorganization of Italian capitalism, which was partly different from the traditional variety.[50] Lastly, his essay is one-sided concerning numerous aspects of De Gasperi's work.[51] It is also inspired by a political aim of setting his own work off against that of De Gasperi's, in order to bring out the former's farsightedness and its "national" value. However, there is no denying the accuracy of the remarks concerning De Gasperi's overall role and the fundamental features of "reconstruction," which have been confirmed by the increasing and ever-widening consensus of later historians.[52]

Emphasizing the difficulties encountered in providing an unbiased judgment of Alcide De Gasperi's work, Togliatti himself observed that "we in no way consider it necessary to revise the fundamental positions of principle and policy which, from 1946 on and even earlier, we proposed to counter those of De Gasperi, as did the Socialists and a good number of Italian democrats."[53] After the defeat of centrism and at the first signs of an emerging policy of "coexistence," he again began to cobble together the elements of the "Italian road."

In several parts of the essay which appear to refer to the difference between his figure and that of De Gasperi, Togliatti reproaches the latter for being a second-rate "practical politician" (that is, incapable of dominating events, and indeed being dominated by them). On the other hand, he stressed that "even the practical politician furthest removed from theoretical discoveries and constructions is always tied to certain positions of principle, which he invokes to justify his work, and which represent, or at least should represent, the starting point and guideline of his action. Facing these positions of principle are the real relations, both objective and subjective, that present a vast range of different problems that have developed with time and await solution. This is the acid test for the politician, that is, "to grasp the course of events, to work out, in the midst of the confusion of the individual events, what is essential and above all what is new and which therefore contains the germ of the future." In other words, the test of the "practical politician" is his capacity "to draw from his principles a line of behavior which allows him to dominate the events, in such a way that they receive and retain the mark he wished to leave on them."[54]

At the end of the cycle of the "cold war" and of the "capitalistic restoration," Togliatti therefore proposed a "return to basic principles." It was on the strength of these principles that he evidently considered the behavior of the PCI during the "reconstruction" should be evaluated.

It is true that the "Italian road" had a theoretical basis which was intended to fix the general characteristics of the era introduced by World War II and its consequences. A necessary premise at the international level was the collaboration between the great anti-Fascist powers. The working classes had set themselves "tasks of a constructive nature which they (had not) set themselves in the past and that they alone (were) capable of performing." It became "historically inevitable that this progressive action (should take place) inside the individual national States."[55] Against this background the "Italian road" and the contemporary experiences of 1945-1947 were viewed as examples of the possibility that a new and more advanced form of socialism (compared with the Soviet experience) could be constructed. In this connection, there seems to be no doubt about the assertions Togliatti made before the Organization Conference of January 1947, in which he proposed a generalization of these experiences:

> The action of the working class has today reached a point in which, in order to develop further, new paths must be found, which have not been followed in the past. To trace these paths, work out ways and means of developing them, is the task that the leaders of a marxist workers party must prove capable of performing today. Past approaches and formulae cannot be repeated: ways must be found of creating something new, by means of political and organizational action suited to the national and international conditions in which the fight for democracy and socialism is carried out the world over. International experience itself already tells us something very important, something that perhaps even those of our companions who have studied most have not yet thought about. International experience tells us that, in order to achieve socialism, that is to develop democracy to its extreme limit, which is represented precisely by socialism, in the present conditions of the class struggle the world over, the working class and the advanced working

masses may find paths which are different, for example, from those followed
by the working class and the workers of the Soviet Union.[56]

In this perspective, how do we evaluate "the fundamental positions of principle and policy" which had guided the action of the
PCI during the years of the "reconstruction"? Although historically valid, the "Cold War" had rendered them politically anachronistic. In a world split into two opposing blocs the "Italian way"
(and any other "national way" in Europe) was deprived of all practical feasibility. Objectively, to persist in this direction, above and
beyond the declarations made, involved a "choice of side" which
doomed the PCI to the opposition for one whole historical cycle.
National autonomy, which was to provide the backdrop for its
political plan, had been overtaken by events. The link between
"national reformism" and internationalism proposed by the PCI
had been drained of all credible and actual content as soon as
internationalism coincided in practice with the foreign policy interests of one of the two "super-powers." The PCI, just like the
European social democracies in another sense, was thus deprived
of any basis of autonomy in order to propose its own combination
of national and international elements for the development of their
respective countries.

It cannot be denied that the contradiction was quite obvious. In
the main debates on foreign policy during those years (Marshall
Plan and NATO), while acting as spokesman for the PCI, Togliatti
recommended a position of autonomy for Italy in its international
relations, but at the same time spoke as a member of a supranational political movement whose guide and pivot was one of the
two "poles" of world politics — the USSR. In vain the PCI
claimed that this was not contradictory, but merely an inevitable
link between the national element and the international one in the
advance towards socialism, a movement that was supranational by
definition and the establishment of which was the main item placed
on the agenda of the political struggle by the ripeness of the times
and the actual historical moment. In fact, this link amounted to a
coincidence between the prospects of socialism and those of Soviet
international policy.

Togliatti himself was forced to admit this many years later: the
choice of bipolarism also by the USSR, whether free or con-

strained, frustrated all the innovations of the "new ways" tried out by European communists immediately after World War II. Furthermore, Togliatti did not fail to point out that the consequent imposition of the Soviet model on the countries of central and eastern Europe was Stalin's greatest error and a major tragedy for the destiny of world socialism.[57]

Although Togliatti and the PCI were aware of this, they rightly or wrongly decided to "put up with the contradiction" rather than resolve it in the only way possible in those years (although, to tell the truth, not recommended for and perhaps inapplicable to Italy) — to change sides.

Notes

1 P. Togliatti, "La nostra lotta per la democrazia e per il socialismo," in *Critica marxista*, luglio-ottobre 1964, pp. 191-192.

2 See A. Guerra, *Gli anni del Cominform*, (Milan, Mazzotta, 1977,) Chap. IV; for a more general discussion of the "Italian way," see G. Vacca, *Saggio su Togliatti e la tradizione comunista*, (Bari; De Donato, 1975).

3 P. Togliatti, "Rinnovare l'Italia," now in *Da Gramsci a Berlinguer*, edited by S. Bertolissi and L. Sestan, (Venice: Edizioni del Calendario, 1985), p. 106.

4 A. Guerra, Chap. IV; G. Vacca, *Saggio su Togliatti*, cit., idem. *Gorbaciov e la sinistra europea*, (Rome: Editori Riuniti, 1989), Chaps. V and VI.

5 G. Vacca, *Gorbaciov e la sinistra europea*, Chap. III.

6 A. Guerra, pp. 36-37 provides a concise review of the differences between eastern European countries on this point. The closest to those of Togliatti are the formulations by Gomulka, who proposed the term "popular democracy" to describe the Polish experience.

7 P. Togliatti, "La politica di unità nazionale dei comunisti," in *Da Gramsci a Berlinguer*, pp. 36-37.

8 Ibid., p. 16.

9 P. Togliatti, "Per una costituzione democratica e progressiva," in *Critica marxista*, pp. 220-221. This is actually the speech of March 11, 1947 delivered to the Constituent Assembly on the planned Constitution. In it Togliatti repeated the six points referring to the country's economic organization proposed by the PCI to the first sub-committee.

10 P. Togliatti, "La nostra lotta per la democrazia e per il socialismo," p. 171. The concept of "social structure" is a reference to the inseparable link between the economic system and the political system. It indicates a conception of the relationship between structure and superstructure which is typical of the Italian communist tradition. The latter dates back to Gramsci and was first systematically used in the *Tesi di Lione*. This is worth noting as this was much criticized in the PCI during the 1950's and 1960's by the "orthodox" communists who preferred the term "reforms *within* the structure." Although apparently academic, the difference profoundly affected the choice of party objectives, priorities and tactics.

11 P. Togliatti, "Rinnovare l'Italia," p. 107.

12 P. Togliatti, *Per una costituzione democratica e progressiva,"* p. 221.

13 Ibid., p. 204.

14 P. Togliatti, *Intervento al convegno economico del PCI*, in Id., *Opere scelte* edited by G. Santomassimo, (Rome: Editori; Riuniti, 1974), pp. 380-81 and 383.

15 Through Mauro Scoccimarro, Finance Minister, the PCI had prepared a draft bill governing currency exchange which the right wing succeeded in sabotaging, mainly through the action of its most capable representative in the anti-Fascist coalition governments, Epicarmo Corbino.

16 P. Togliatti, *Intervento*. He followed with great interest the action of the British Labor cabinet. (Ibid., p. 382).

17 Ibid., p. 387.

18 I do not think I am forcing this concept here. As is known, it was proposed by C. S. Maier in a well known essay *"The Politics of Productivity: Foundation of American International Economic Policy after World War II"* in *International Organization*, XXXI, 4). Maier used the concept — for instance, in the essay "The two Postwar Eras and the Conditions for Stability in 20th Century Europe," *American Historical Review*, 1981, n. 2 — to provide a useful conceptual framework for a differential analysis of the processes of economic and political integration in the West after World War II.

19 According to the title of the acclaimed work by C. S. Maier, of which the Italian election was published by De Donato in 1979.

20 Noteworthy are *Le Tesi di Lione* and then Togliatti's writings in *Opere*, edited by E. Ragionieri and Spriano-Andreucci, (Rome: Editori Riuniti, vols. II, III and IV, 1972, 1973, 1979). A. Tasca, *Nascita e avvento del fascismo*, (Bari-Roma: Laterza, 1965, first edition appeared in 1938); P. Grifone, *Il capitale finanziario in Italia*: (Torino: Einaudi, 1945).

21 This expression was proposed by Paggi to refer to the strategy developed by the PCUS during the NEP. Cf. L. Paggi, *Le strategie del potere in Gramsci*, (Rome: Editori Riuniti, 1983).

22 P. Togliatti, "Rinnovare l'Italia," pp. 109-110 and 111.

23 P. Togliatti, "Ceto medio e Emilia rossa," Lecture delivered at Reggia Emilia on 24 September 1946, now in *Opere scelte*, p. 471.

24 The essential reference is to "Po Valley reformism" as opposed to "Milanese reformism." Ibid., pp. 470-71.

25 Ibid., p. 471.

26 The text of the lecture has been published partially, in *Rinascita*, 25 April 1967.

27 For an overview of the origins and development of the Cold War and its impact on Europe and Italy, see: E. Collotti, *"Collocazione internazionale dell'Italia dall'armistizio alle premesse dell'alleanza atlantica,"* in *L'Italia dalla liberazione alla Repubblica* (several authors), Milan: Feltrinelli, 1977; R. Quartararo, *Dai documenti inediti del Policy Planning Staff: Gli USA e l'Europa (1947-1949)*; P. P. D'Attorre; "Il Piano Marshall. Politica, economia, relazioni internazionali nella ricostruzione italiana," in *Passato e Presente*, 1985 n. 7; R. Quartararo, *Italia e Stati Uniti. Gli anni difficili (1945-1952)*, Naples: ESI, 1986, E. Aga Rossi, ed., *Il Piano Marshall e l'Europa*, Istituto della Enciclopedia italiana, 1983; Idem., *Gli Stati Uniti e le origini della guerra fredda*, Bologna: Il Mulino, 1984; J. L. Harper, *L'America e la ricostruzione dell'Italia. 1945-1948*, Bologna: Il Mulino, 1987.

28 In abstract and in the article by P. Togliatti, "Nuovo Corso," in *Rinascita*, September 9, 1946.

29 P. Togliatti, "La nostra lotta per la democrazia e per il socialismo," pp. 175-178.

30 S. Galante, *La fine di un compromesso storico, PCI e DC nella crisi del 1947*, Milan: Angeli, 1980.

31 P. Togliatti, "Rapporto e conclusioni al VI Congresso del Partito comunista italiano," in P. Togliatti, *Opere*, ed. by L. Gruppi, vol. V, (Rome, Editori Riuniti, 1984), p. 370.

32 P. Togliatti, "Sul V governo De Gasperi" in Togliatti, *Discorsi parlamentari*, Rome: Chamber of Deputies, 1984), pp. 297-323.

33 P. Togliatti, "Rinnovare l'Italia," pp. 98-99.

34 A typical representative is Epicarmo Corbino who, at the Liberal party Congress held in May 1946, declared; "Is it conceivable that we can ask the United States for aid when we intend to implement an economy and a policy which are diametrically opposed to those of America? We have the right to impose upon ourselves any economic and political system that we wish, but we must accept that the United States has the right to give a hand and send their aid to those countries which set themselves up according to their lights." Reported by Harper, p. 120.

35 P. Togliatti, "La rottura dell'unità democratica," in *Opere scelte*, pp. 514-515.

36 J. L. Harper, passim; F. Romero, *Gli Stati Uniti e il sindacalismo europeo - 1944-1951*, Rome: Edizioni Lavoro, 1989, especially Chap. I; P. P. D'Attorre, "Il piano Marshall . . . "

37 A. Guerra, Chaps. six, seven and nine.

38 E. Berlinguer, *La questione comunista*, ed. by A. Tatò, Rome: Editori Riuniti, 1975, pp. 823 ff.

39 P. Togliatti, "Rapporto e conclusioni al VI Congresso," p. 370.

40 Ibid., p. 370.

41 In the cited speech against the Marshall Plan, Togliatti rejected above all the idea of "restoring" the free-trade model in the countries benefiting from "aid." "This is one of the famous principles on which American economic life is based and which Mr. Truman was referring to when he spoke of defending "free enterprise" by all possible means. But, gentlemen, have we not instead approved a republican Constitution containing a clause stating the need for the Italian people to curtail this principle of free enterprise, explicit articles stating the need to limit monopolistic capitalism by means of structural reforms in agriculture and industry?" (p. 481).

42 "Sulla adesione al Patto Atlantico," in Togliatti, *Discorsi parlamentari*, pp. 423-24. At the session of December 2, 1948, speaking against Italy's membership in military alliances or blocs (a motion by the Partito d'Azione that Italy should participate in the projected European Union was also under discussion), Togliatti had summed up the PCI foreign policy guidelines as follows: "Foreign policy, and more exactly, national foreign policy, begins exactly where those who disagree over belonging to different systems of ideas, feel the need, in the supreme interest of the nation, to work out a common policy which both arrive at in different ways, from different starting points." (Ibid., p. 370).

43 P. Togliatti, *Opere*, p. 476.

44 Togliatti, *Discorsi parlamentari*, pp. 374-375.

45 G. Vacca, *Gorbaciov e la sinistra europea*, Chap. IV.

46 The influence of the PCI's strategy on the reconstruction of the unified trade union at the fall of Fascism is documented in the classified reports by Giuseppe Di Vittorio to the party secretariat concerning developments in the negotiations with the socialists and Christian Democrats. The latter were subsequently to lead to the "Rome pact." For these reports, see M. Pistillo, *Giuseppe Di Vittorio - 1924-1944*, Rome: Editori Riuniti, 1973, pp. 217-259.

47 The main features of the originality of the "new party" are summed up in two well-known editorials by Togliatti published in *Rinascita*, "Classe operaia e partecipazione al governo," n. 1, June 1, 1944, and "Partito nuovo", October-November 1944.

48 P. Togliatti, "Per un giudizio equanime sull'opera di Alcide De Gasperi," in P. Togliatti, *Momenti della storia d'Italia*, ed. by E. Ragionieri, Rome: Editori Riuniti, 1963, pp. 190-191.

49 Ibid., pp. 201-203.

50 M. Salvati, *Stato e industria della ricostruzione. Alle origini del potere democristiano (1944-1949)*, Milan: Feltrinelli, 1982.

51 P. Scoppola, *La proposta politica di De Gasperi*, Bologna: II Mulino, 1977.

52 As well as the cited works of J. L. Harper and M. Salvati, and the article by P. P. D'Attorre (with extensive references); see also J. S. Woolf (ed.), *Italia 1943-1950. La ricostruzione*, Bari, Laterza, 1973.

53 P. Togliatti, *Momenti della storia d'Italia*, p. 190.

54 Ibid., pp. 225-226.

55 P. Togliatti, "Partito nuovo", *Rinascita*, Oct.-Nov. 1944.

56 P. Togliatti, "La nostra lotta per la democrazia e per il socialismo", p. 191.

57 P. Togliatti, "Viaggio in Yugoslavia," in *Rinascita*, 1964, no. 21. Togliatti wrote: "Much has been said concerning the origins and circumstances of the 1948 split, but I do not consider that everything has already been clarified completely (. . .). No study of how unity and discipline could and were to be guaranteed after the Communist International had been dissolved, and in the face of a situation and tasks which differed radically from the past and from country to country, has ever been carried out (. . .). However, the worst thing was that the 1948-49 controversies (linked, of course, also to other causes) brought the ideological and political growth of our movement to a standstill in many, in too many, countries (. . .). According to Togliatti, "the profound reasons for the split [between the USSR and Yugoslavia] are to be sought in the way the existing situation and future prospects of the popular democracies set up after the war were viewed vis-a-vis the internal developments taking place in each country and the international situation. It is significant that an interesting study had already been undertaken and developed concerning the political, economic and social novelties which represented the main features of these regimes. The whole matter was cut short and everything reduced to the reductive scholastic formula that popular democracy was "synonymous with" the dictatorship of the proletariat which had been implemented in the Soviet Union. This practically reduced to a question of mere terminology the greatest historical issue that our times had placed before the workers movement, namely the search for new ways of progressing towards socialism, of new forms of progressive democratic power and, by the same token, of new ways of organizing a socialist economy, as suggested and imposed by new objective and subjective conditions."

VIII

Commentary on Giuseppe Vacca's "The Communist Party Policy of National Unity, 1945-1949"

Charles S. Maier

Professor Vacca has written a provocative and stimulating, indeed remarkable, account of the premises of Italian Communist party policies in the reconstruction period. His presentation of PCI policy, and especially of the leading ideas of Palmiro Togliatti, is filled with intriguing suggestions: the comparison with the New Deal, and the insistence on Togliatti's belief that the unity of the anti-Fascist coalition must be preserved as the postulate of Communist policy, are among two of the most important suggestions. I must acknowledge at the outset that I cannot criticize the paper from the textual viewpoint. I accept Professor Vacca's proven expertise on Togliatti, and will not challenge his reading of texts. Nor can I offer counter-texts: I will accept those chosen by the speaker as typical of Togliatti's ideas. What I want to do is consider further some of the implications of Togliatti's position as interpreted by Professor Vacca.

In a sense the key to the paper comes where Professor Vacca suggests that Togliatti's reflections of 1948 look forward to the current Soviet "New Deal." Presumably Professor Vacca's recent work on Gorbachev amplifies this concept. Nonetheless, I am not sure that "New Deal" best describes the current Soviet turn, for the American New Deal was a policy that sought to take the United States from its dominant laissez-faire traditions and introduce larger measures of state intervention, whereas the Soviet initiative is precisely the reverse! Nonetheless, it is clear that Professor Vacca wishes to suggest a "mixed economy," and in that spirit I can understand the terminology, although he might wish to make clearer what he intends by it.

Togliatti, in short, emerges as a prophet of *glasnost* avant la lettre. This is, to be sure, a very appealing image of Togliatti, who appears as the advocate of a policy of broad social and economic reconstruction that tends toward social democracy. The formulation is reminiscent of the celebrated remark by the United States' wartime Communist leader, Earl Browder that "Communism is as American as apple pie." Of course, that was the period of the Popular Front; and as Professor Vacca points out, the Togliatti strategy was a product of the Resistance coalition. Indeed he might have looked even further back at the period of the Spanish Civil War, for as Franco Sbarberi suggests, "L'ipotesi della 'democrazia progressiva' perseguita da Togliatti nel secondo dopoguerra costituisce infatti una variante soltanto *normale* della 'democrazia di tipo nuovo' progettata per la Spagna."[1] Perhaps to update Browder's famous metaphor, we could say (in the spirit of this paper) that Togliatti was as Italian/American as pizza pie.

Nonetheless, as the author rightly emphasizes, the premise of a reformist policy — one that both emphasized Italian national independence and support of the Soviet Union — was continued cooperation among the wartime allies. Of course, this ended during 1947-48. As Professor Vacca rightly stresses — I certainly agree with this reading of events — the PCI hoped to minimize the consequences of the division and of their exclusion from the government. They probably hoped to come back into the government and were even willing to accept the Marshall Plan. As late as the moment when NATO was being organized, Togliatti allegedly advocated a new plea for centrist collaboration. Professor Vacca cites at length Togliatti's eloquent plea against the notion of inevitable war.

But we must ask some hard questions about the premises of both international and domestic options. Was Togliatti's policy more than a last-ditch effort to prevent Italian adhesion in NATO? After all, the anti-war rhetoric marked many other Communist statements, especially in France ("Les communistes pour la paix"). And after the Czech coup in February 1948, was it not apparent that a really independent course vis-a-vis the Marshall Plan was hardly acceptable to the Soviet Union? Surely Prague must have taught the limits of a policy that refused to accept the encroaching division of the world. Certainly Professor Vacca recognizes the limits of Togliatti's policies, when he terms the principles "politically anachronistic." The question that he leaves open is whether, and when, Togliatti himself understood the anachronism.

Consider next the alternatives for internal development as Togliatti envisaged them. The party leader's program — Professor Vacca usefully argues — was to overturn the economic premises of the dominant bloc — that is, the alliance of capitalist and landowners who sought to perpetuate high tariffs and inexpensive labor costs. Instead, Togliatti apparently sought a regime of high investment, productivity growth and a corresponding rise of wages: a competitive "American-model" economy that would decisively depart from the conservative political economy Fascism had allegedly sought to entrench.

But was Togliatti's analysis sufficiently probing? The Fascism of the autarky period introduced new developments that neither the Comintern's analysis of a "reactionary mass regime" nor Togliatti's own *Lezioni* fully appreciated. So, too, the Gramscian analysis of the "hegemonic bloc" was itself inadequate (or incomplete) as a guide for postwar development. Given the ramifications of the Marshall Plan and the related Atlantic "integration" of Western Europe, a *modernized* hegemonic bloc could be reconstituted (i.e. the Christian Democratic Party's role as so ably analyzed by Mariuccia Salvati) and could accept parts, if not all, of the politics of productivity. Rather than protectionism, the new dominant coalition could engage in export competition and use the new constraints of world-market prices (and currency stabilization) to keep a ceiling on domestic labor costs. The result would be to move from a centralized state regulated labor market to a discipline imposed systemically by world prices as enforced at the factory or sectoral level: the regime that the CGL — partially understanding the mechanism — would call "*supersfruttamento.*"

Moreover, it would take on a more complex class coalitional character. The new component of the bloc would be the *cadres* or what Marxist called the "technical intelligentsia" and what John Kenneth Galbraith later termed the techno-structure. In Italy's case the decisive component was often the managerial elite that had emerged within the parastatal agencies of the 1930's. Given the late-Fascist incubation of the new managers, the complexity of post-war economic strategies on the part of the recast elites (who moved from autarky to export competition), and their surprising capacity for modernization, Togliatti's concepts, I believe, did not adequately envisage the DC's capacity for long-term exclusion of the working class. Alas, as often before, the left underestimated the canniness and resilience of the conservatives.

In sum, Professor Vacca presents us with a Togliatti who a) desperately seeks to avoid the rupture between the wartime allies, b) aspires to a would-be reformist or "New Deal" program, and c) seeks economic modernization on the basis of a policy of growth — Professor Vacca generously borrows my concept of the "politics of productivity." Now certainly Togliatti is appealing in many ways. The Italian Communist Party has enjoyed three intellectually subtle and compelling figures in its almost seventy-year history: Gramsci, Togliatti, and Berlinguer. Each of these leaders obviously tried to think through politics seriously — if only to reconcile in an intellectually coherent way principles and tactics. This effort to bring tactics and premises together is a demand that the political culture of Italy, with the importance of continued press and journal debate and constant programmatic revision and refinement, makes mandatory, at least on the left, whereas it is a requirement that hardly exists in American politics. Thus when Americans encounter the Italian effort, it usually seems an impressive one.

Nevertheless, as I have sought to point out, grave difficulties were inherent in Togliatti's strategy and analysis. Was a "New Deal" concept realistic for Italy, and was this socio-economic model really possible for a country that was to be integrated into an American-dominated Western economy? Perhaps only the U.S. itself could enjoy a high-wage equilibrium. I am not sure the economic basis for Togliatti's progressive course was really at hand. Professor Vacca suggests in his conclusion that the middle course in the early Cold War was impossible: that alignment with the Soviets was the only alternative to a pro-Western stance that would have been neither possible nor useful. But if Togliatti really held "progressive democratic" views, was it not preferable to carve out an independent left course in 1948 after the Czech coup? Italian party leaders of the 1970's managed to contemplate such strategies as the "compromesso storico" or the "alternativa di sinistra" without awaiting the dissolution of the blocs. Did one have to wait thirty years for these reconceptualizations of the role of a national Communist party? Professor Vacca suggests Togliatti tried to a degree to forge a path against the constraints of bipolarity. Perhaps though, after Spain, the exile in Moscow, and the Second World War, Togliatti actually did see Communism without Soviet power as impossible. Perhaps he really was a Communist? This is not to deny him the subtlety and yearnings that Professor Vacca ascribes, but merely to say that he remained within the inculcated Third International loyalty to the Soviet Union that was so marked a hallmark of this political commitment now vanishing.

Notes

1 Franco Sbarberi, *I comunisti italiani e lo stato 1929-1956*, Milan: Feltrinelli, 1980, p. 204.

IX

Le Forze Laiche: The Cultural and Political Contributions of Lay Intellectuals and Journals in the Making of the Republic

Guido Verucci

There can be little doubt that historical analyses of post-war Italy and of the years 1945-1965 have paid much more attention to the Catholic world and party on the one hand, and to the parties and organizations of a Marxist inspiration on the other, than to the *forze laiche*, the lay forces.[1] Although these forces were present in Italian political life and culture, their parties, intellectuals and journals have been consistently understudied.[2] The principal reason for this allocation of interest clearly lies in the fact that the Catholics and Marxists, in their long held roles of majority and opposition, emerged as the dominant political and ideological forces of the country. They formed mass parties and organizations which rooted themselves deeply into Italian society in the years following the war, becoming the real protagonists of political conflict and, in different ways, the true architects of national reconstruction.

At a historiographical level it must be observed that the *forze laiche* do not make up a particularly homogeneous object of study. Not only did they consist of different political parties — initially the Action Party, the Republican Party, the Liberal Party, the Democratic Labor Party, to which were subsequently added other parties and groupings — but they were also composed of different political approaches and cultural traditions. Futhermore, neither in the immediate post-war years nor afterwards was the cultural world of the *forze laiche* organically linked to the lay political world and its parties. It retained, rather, a general autonomy and separateness of its own. Moreover, the lay forces were distinguished from the Catholic and Marxist areas in cultural terms and by their liberal democratic values, rather than being distinguished from the Catholic area at a political level and in terms of attitudes towards the state. The term *laico* had important historical roots in precisely this last mentioned context. During the nineteenth century, and in the first fifteen years of the twentieth, the term implied a position of the defense of the independence of the state against undue religious influences and a guarantee of the liberty and equality of different faiths and ideas. This position gave rise to sharp conflicts between Church and State and between anticlericals and Catholics. But during the period which followed the Second World War this position was not a dominant feature of the physiognomy of the *forze laiche* – not least because at the outset, for a variety of reasons, the years of anticlerical-Catholic conflict seemed far distant. If, therefore, the term *laico* expresses, rather, a collection of general principles, it should nevertheless be emphasized that to a certain extent these general principles were present in other political forces and cultural areas, both Catholic and Marxist.

Within these limits the overall contribution made by the lay forces, or to use more recent terminology 'liberal-democratic' forces, to the construction and development of the Italian democratic system appears undoubtedly most relevant — more relevant at a cultural and political level than at the level of the actual activities of the parties and other organizations. Indeed, much more relevant than has hitherto been shown to be the case by the few studies that exist. These studies, notwithstanding a wealth of memoirs, speeches, writing, propaganda, journalistic articles and other such material, have nonetheless proved to be fragmentary and inadequate.

The most studied period is that which runs from the end of the war into the first years of peace, when there was a veritable flowering of numerous journals in the liberal-democratic world. Most of these had a brief life and only a few were to last, but they developed an intense debate about the character of the new state.[3] This flowering, as Nicola Matteucci and others have pointed out,[4] was a sign of a strong and almost preeminent intellectual presence. Even though further investigations should be made into the cultural origins of this flowering, a number of principal factors clearly lay behind it. These include the contribution of the Rationalism of the Enlightenment, which Italian culture and historiography had begun to reacquire in the last years of Fascism, and above all else of Crocean historicism. There was also an increased appreciation of the radical democratic and federal tendency present in the *Risorgimento* headed by Cattaneo and Ferrari; the influence of the Concretism of Gaetano Salvemini and of the first attempt on the part of Piero Gobetti to unite Liberal thinking with the Socialist movement; meridionalism, which had its most recent exponent in Guido Dorso; and, as Delzell in particular has emphasized,[5] the rethinking, the alterations in mentality. Also influential were the changes of generation which had manifested themselves in all the anti-Fascist political formations from the first moment of Fascist triumph — prominent amongst these must be placed the revisionist tendencies of the Marxism of Carlo Rosselli, of Justice and Liberty, and of Liberal-Socialism; the awareness, at the time of the economic crisis of 1929, of negative consequences revealed by a form of almost unregulated capitalist development, and the desire to consider them within the framework of political economy, which introduced into the debates of the liberal-democratic journals an interest for the thought of Röpke, the analyses of Schumpeter, the theories of Keynes, and the assumptions of the Beveridge report. Finally, the conviction emerged that it was necessary to reconsider and to modernize the workings of the modern state which, in turn, encouraged a receptivity towards the new instruments of investigation offered by the Anglo-Saxon social sciences.

These are the heterogeneous elements which lie behind the effervescent activity of Adolfo Omodeo's *Acropoli*, Giovanni Conti's *La Costituente*, Luigi Salvatorelli's *La Nuova Europa*, Mario Paggi's *Lo Stato Moderno*, Piero Calamandrei's *Il Ponte*, Adriano Olivetti's *Communità*, and many other such publications. Salvatorelli was an early proponent of ideas about structures above the national level. These ideas developed into the project of European federation which in turn gained wide currency amongst the lay forces. These elements are to be found in different degrees and with different influence in each of the journals. With regard to the task of achieving a profound change in economic and political institutions along liberal-democratic lines the last two of this list were not very effective. The influence exercised by Crocean historicism and its conception of Liberalism proved greater. This conception helped, to a certain extent, to keep the debate in the journals at the level of principles and thus to encourage the divisions between the different groups. This it did because contemporary thought paid more attention to matters of theoretical philosophy than to institutions, and because of its tendency to emphasize the differences between Liberalism and democracy, Liberalism and Socialism, and Liberalism and non-Marxist Socialism, rather than the possibilities of reconciling them.

In reality the world of the liberal-democratic intellectuals and journals was characterized by diversities which reflected the notable divergences between and within their parties. This diversity expressed itself in projects for the renewal of the state which began their life in the first years of the Resistance. In these projects some groups displayed a liberal-democratic orientation while others evinced a democratic-socialist approach. These are positions which in some aspects were exemplified by two of the most incisive intellectuals of the time — Mario Paggi and Piero Calamandrei — and by the two journals they respectively edited — *Lo Stato Moderno* and *Il Ponte*.

In Calamandrei and *Il Ponte*,[6] and this bears witness to the influence of Rationalism, there was the conviction that with the fall of Fascism there had taken place a profound break with the legal and political traditions of the old state and that the Committees of National Liberation and the constituent assembly were the fundamental instruments for the establishment of a new democratic order. We find the proposal to construct a state which promotes the transformation of society through a recognition of social rights beyond individual rights. But on the other hand, in *Lo Stato Moderno*, there was a refusal to recognize a revolutionary break with the past and a distinct adherence to the idea of continuity in the state. There was a project for the state which was based predominantly on the mechanisms of government. Inside the same liberal-democratic area the tension between the anti-statist approach rooted in the experience of anti-Fascism, and the tendency to allocate to the state new tasks and roles, remained unresolved. There was not a sufficient homogeneity to allow common proposals in the direction of a more powerful executive balanced by an autonomist structure, or of a state which would promote social reforms, or, as Adriano Olivetti and his journal *Comunità* in particular propounded, of new structures which were different from traditional political representation and parliament.

The historical debate about the possible outcomes of the political struggles in Italy in the transitional years from the fall of Fascism to the creation of the democratic state is far from closed. A debate is still open concerning the component parts of the 'institutional compromise' which led to the creation of the republican constitution. With regard to the liberal-democratic area a number of factors led to the defeat of the most innovative proposals — some of which were common to other political forces. Prominent among these factors were the profound divisions within the lay area. Above all, the results of the general elections for the constituent assembly demonstrated that the cultural hegemony of the liberal-democratic area did not correspond to an adequate political backing producing instead overwhelming support for the three principal parties. Nevertheless, as numerous scholars such as Enzo Cheli have observed,[7] it was precisely at the level of rights and the relationship between the powers of the state — the key areas of the Constitution — that the liberal-democratic forces exercised their greatest weight. But it was from these forces — or rather from a part of these forces, the Republicans and Actionists — that the notable contribution of the regional provisions came, even though these provisions lacked the context the Actionists envisaged. The Constitutional Court, which was strongly supported by Calamandrei, was another contribution even though it provoked liberal-democratic divisions. The majority of the exponents of the *forze laiche* also contributed to the defense of the lay character of the state with regard to marriage, schooling, and the general relationship of Church and State.

However the inability of the lay forces to go beyond certain limits in impinging on the physiognomy of the republican state was more a testimony to the failure of the tentative and uncertain attempts to mark out a 'third way,' even though this possibility had been envisaged in theoretical terms from the outset. There was a failure to establish the bases for a 'third force' between the

Catholic and Marxist parties: a failure to construct a great democratic party, such as Ugo La Malfa had conceived of in and after
1941, which would consist of the Action Party, the Republican
Party, the Democratic Labor Party, the Liberal Party, and later the
Italian Socialist Workers' Party. This project was discussed much
more by the intellectuals and in the pages of the journals than by
the parties themselves, not only in the aftermath of the war but
also in succeeding years. This project, while always remaining open
to historical speculation, could only remain illusory.[8] A variety of
factors contributed to this reality: internal and international circumstances, especially after the outbreak of the Cold War, which
helped to determine the clear success of the great mass parties; the
already discussed cultural divisions between the parties of the liberal-democratic area – which reflected in its variegation the different parts of Italy's multiform society; the strong competition
between these parties; but above all else the unavailability of those
middling sections of the middle classes which these parties considered the essential social base of the nascent third force. Probably,
and once again because of the ascendancy of outmoded Crocean
categories over appropriate criteria for a modern social-historical
analysis, very few of the exponents of the liberal-democratic parties
realized that the ranks of the educated middle class of a European
level had been further thinned during Fascism, and that their
potential for social influence had waned, to the advantage of other
social groups – partly because of bureaucratic expansion. Very
few realized that a large part of the middle classes had gathered
under the banner of the Christian Democrats, as Leo Valiani had
noticed as early as 1945.

After 1948 the propulsive thrust of the *forze laiche* seemed to
weaken. In part this was because there was one party less by 1947.
Indeed it was around this Action Party that in the preceding years
the debate about the problems of the state had been most intense.
But in part it was also because after the relatively harmonious theoretical preparation of the constituent assembly there followed a
phase which became increasingly conditioned by the choices and
contra-positions linked to the economic and political reconstruction of the country. After the fertile period of the journals there
was a partial increase in the divergence between the orientations of
the lay parties and the orientations of the groups of intellectuals

and some of the journals. Nevertheless, the years which take in the years of centrism and the beginnings of the Center-Left and go up to the early 1960's reveal the *forze laiche* to have had a general influence on Italian political events. This period, although it has been the subject of intense political and historical discussion, is once again conspicuously lacking in analytical studies, not least with regard to the liberal-democratic parties, intellectuals and journals.

Without evaluating the role of the Republican, Liberal, and Italian Socialist Workers' parties in their adherence to the formula of Centrism; their more-or-less continuous participation in the governments of the first and second legislatures and in those immediately preceding the 'opening to the Left'; or even the role of the independent figures of the liberal-democratic area in De Gasperi's Fourth Ministry of May 1947 onwards, some important contributions must nevertheless be brought into consideration. First, the much discussed liberal economic policy initiated by Luigi Einaudi in 1947 and then continued by other ministers. This was a policy which was not strictly in line with some of the social-Catholic tendencies present in the majority party. Second, the activity of Carlo Sforza, the Foreign Secretary from 1947 to 1951, who committed Italy to the Atlantic Treaty in 1949 and in so doing overcame reservations and apprehensions which were present even in the Catholic world. Sforza also was an initiator of the policy of European integration. Third, the initiative in 1951 of the Republican Ugo La Malfa, who was Minister of Foreign Trade in De Gasperi's sixth and seventh ministries, to liberalize international trade. The move contributed to the subsequent large-scale economic development of the country in and after the middle fifties. Fourth, the long and dedicated efforts made by La Malfa to prepare and promote the idea of the Center-Left. The lay parties, however, with regard to Catholic attempts during this period to Catholicize public life, offered scant resistance and appeared subordinate to the Christian Democrats.

But in this last area some liberal-democratic journals took issue, and thus in the context of the period the term *laico* regained its more traditional meaning, although it retained its other cultural and political connotations. Foremost was *Il Ponte* whose activities were inextricably linked with its founder and editor Calamandrei until the latter's death in 1956. Calamandrei's influence, however, continued after his demise. Norberto Bobbio and Alessandro Galante Garrone[9] have contributed the most to an understanding of this figure. Many elements are found in his personality: an Enlightenment faith in reason; a radical and Mazzinian tradition derived from family connections; and the influence of Salvemini and of Carlo Rosselli's Liberal-Socialism. All these elements were sustained by a deeply held lay religiosity rooted in Christian beliefs. His political ideals gave rise to a Socialism which was rooted in an impulse towards justice and equality and strictly linked to political democracy. They also led to his support for European federation, which seemed the only way of ensuring peace at a time of sharply opposing power blocs and the Cold War. Calamandrei pursued these objectives with great independence, given the formations to which he belonged, during the first legislature from 1948 to 1951, first as a deputy of Socialist Unity and then of the Italian Democratic Socialist Party. After 1953 he continued to fight for his aims with articles and speeches. He always used *Il Ponte*, which became a focal point for many of the most representative figures of the Italian intellectual Left.

The central intention of the journal was the defense of the moral and political values of the Resistance and of the unity which they guaranteed. The journal and its editor fought a hard battle against Centrism's approach to politics in the name of these values and this unity. This approach, while keeping many bodies and laws of the Fascist period in operation, violated and failed to apply the constitution — the constitution being the most important legacy of the Resistance. From this position came a drawing of attention to the transgression, and the danger that an informal anti-democratic constitution could replace the formal constitution. The journal demanded that the constitution be brought into operation through such entities as those discharging regional tasks, the Supreme Judicial Council, the referendum, and above all else the Constitutional Court, which Calamandrei was able to see constituted in 1956.[10] These concerns did a great deal to prepare the ground for the social and civil transformations of the late fifties and sixties. *Il Ponte*, through its special editions, drew public attention not only to the grave and still unresolved problems of the country but also to the new developments in European and extra-European countries, from Great Britain to China, and in Kennedy's America. Calamandrei and *Il Ponte* took English Laborism as their model. After the hopes placed in a third force which would have had the Social-Democratic party as its building block, the journal adopted the Center-Left strategy. This latter approach adopted the Italian Socialist Party as its chief agent in the political world and in government. It did not, however, exclude the Communist Party, allocating to it a partial role.

Another political-cultural pressure group, which has been the subject of certain written reminiscences and the object of a comprehensive study by Paolo Bonetti[11] was that which surrounded *Il Mondo* from 1949 to 1966. This group was perhaps more significant than the *Il Ponte* group because of the quality and quantity of its intellectual input and impact. The journal was edited by Mario Pannunzio, a journalist of the highest order and a great cultural organizer. It looked to the Liberal and lay tradition of the *Risorgimento*, the legacy of Giovanni Amendola and Gobetti, and had its principal points of reference in the teachings of Croce, Luigi Einaudi, and Salvemini.

Compared to *Il Ponte, Il Mondo* was more Crocean-Historicist, although it was certainly not untouched by Enlightenment influences. It was strongly anchored in Liberalism and Liberalism's Anglo-Saxon traditions, and had a deep and informed concern with economic problems. It was Europeanist in a sometimes insular and eurocentric way, and rigidly pro-Western. It was decidedly anti-Communist and anti-Fascist, and was rigorously lay in the religious sense of the term without, however, having anticlerical prejudices. The line taken looked to a modern, tolerant, European and civil Italy, but was based upon an intransigent attitude characteristic of an intellectual aristocracy. As has already been observed, this aristocracy was unable to comprehend many of the real facts of the difficult development of mass democratic rule. *Il Mondo*, which was the work of a group of left-wing Liberals who had founded the Liberal party during the underground period, had left it in 1947 because of its right-wing direction, and had then returned again in 1951, adopted a critical support of Centrism during the first period. It attacked clerical intrusion into the state, under government, the failure to put the constitution into practice, and repeatedly sought to unite the lay parties into a third force which would be able to

check the power of the Christian Democrats. At the same time the
economic stance of the journal followed, with some exceptions, a
rigid economic liberalism along the lines of Einaudi and Röpke,
and also encouraged Ernesto Rossi's attacks on monopolistic and
parasitical capitalism. Once the Liberal party had clearly returned
to the Right the *Il Mondo* group once again left the party and
founded the new Radical party in 1955. This party initially
presented itself as an alternative, in conjunction with the Socialist
party, to the Christian Democrats and the Communists, and
promoted a program based on the defense of the lay character of
the state, civil rights, the renewal of the public administration, and
the restructuring of the economy.[12] In the same years, under the
influence of Keynesian theories and echoes of the New Deal
experience, the economic policy of *Il Mondo* which began in 1955,
many of the most important contemporary problems of Italian
society were subjected to analysis: the stock exchange and monopolies; energy resources and building speculation; the press and
schools; Church-State relationships; and economic planning. Concrete proposals of reform were also advocated. While the political
situation evolved and the Radical party moved from a position of
constituting an alternative to that of seeking, like the other lay parties, to push the Christian Democrats into collaboration with the
Socialist party, *Il Mondo* became, as has already been observed, a
kind of 'ideological laboratory' for what would subsequently come
about, and what was envisaged, namely, the governing formula of
the Center-Left. But, even when confronted with the first signs of
crisis of the formula in 1963, the journal never addressed the question of which political forces could bring about the required
reforms, and it continued to reject any involvement of the Communist Party and to deceive itself into thinking that the lay parties
could take the place of the Christian Democrats.

Two other journals of the liberal-democratic stamp adopted sim-
ilar positions towards the Center-Left, and these are worthy of fur-
ther study. *Nord e Sud* was edited by Francesco Compagna;
Comunità was the work of Adriano Olivetti. In the first, as
Giuseppe Galasso has well demonstrated,[13] the lessons of Croce,
Nitti, and Salvemini; the outline by Dorso of a formation of a new
Southern directing class; and the most recent teaching of Manlio
Rossi Doria, all grafted onto the analyses and the studies of the

SVIMEZ to initiate a project of development for the *Mezzogiorno*, which had as its aim the latter's eventual industrialization. The second journal, as Giuseppe Berta has observed,[14] had become by the middle 1950's the carrier of a 'capitalist heresy.' This heresy began with the idea of the rationalized and democratic factory, expanded into a plan for the regularization and planning, in a Socialist sense, of capitalist development, and led to the notion of a reorganization of the state on the basis of local communities. It also hoped — in marked contrast to Centrism — for a rapid and strong association of Socialist forces.

In the early years of the nineteen-sixties, with the dissolution of the Radical party in 1962 and the rapid crisis of the Center-Left, something that has been called the Italian attempt at a New Deal surfaced and failed. The attempt to create a third force which would be an alternative to the Christian Democrats and the Communist party failed, as did the attempt of liberal-democratic intellectuals and journals to achieve their reforms. An epoch seemed to have ended with the closure of *Il Mondo* in 1966 and the situation in which the other journals survived, while at the same time the government returned to a marked immobilism and the new and different social and cultural phenomena which were to mark the nineteen-sixties began to express themselves. But in this epoch the lay intellectual forces nonetheless left clearly visible signs — signs belonging to great Italian cultural traditions, bearing important foreign influences, and reflecting an honest public commitment and a critical attitude.

Notes

1 Although fully aware of the conventional meaning of the English term 'lay' I have nevertheless used the phrase 'lay forces' to translate the Italian *'forze laiche.'* The meaning of this latter phrase is set out in the text. The term *'forze liberal-democratiche,'* which may be translated into the English 'liberal democratic forces,' is partially synonymous with *'forze laiche.'* It was not, however, commonly used in the period under consideration.

2 The most important works of synthesis of relevance to this paper are: N. Kogan, *L'Italia del dopoguerra. Storia Politica dal 1945 al 1966.* It tr., 3rd edition, (Bari; 1972), G. Mammarella. *L'Italia Contemporanea (1943-1985),* (Bologna, 1985); E. Ragionieri, 'La Storia Politica e sociale' in *Storia d'Italia,* 4, III, *Dall'Unità a oggi,* (Turin, 1976); C. Pinzani, "L'Italia repubblicana," ibid. I should also cite the intelligent work of P. Ginsborg, *Storia d'Italia dal dopoguerra a oggi,* 2 vols., (Turin, 1989). Also to be consulted are AA.VV., *Dieci anni dopo, 1945-1955, Saggi sulla vita democratica italiana,* (Bari, 1955); A. Gambino, *Storia del dopoguerra. Dalla liberazione al potere DC;* (Bari, 1975); E. Piscitelli, *Da Parri a De Gasperi. Storia del dopoguerra, 1945-1948,* (Milan, 1975), and AA.VV., *L'Italia Contemporanea, 1945-1975,* edited by V. Castronovo (Turin, 1976). A variety of information and commentary on the lay forces is present in the works of G. Spadolini, *L'Italia della Ragione. Lotta politica e cultura nel Novecento,* (Florence, 1978) and *L'Italia dei laici. Lotta politica e cultura dal 1925 al 1980,* (Florence, 1980). In the following pages I have given only an essential and therefore limited set of bibliographical references. Much relevant information is contained in the journals considered in the text, and in others, which have been consulted.

3 The most important essays here are: N. Matteucci, "Introduzione;" L. Ornaghi, "I Progetti di stato (1945-1948)," and M. Fantechi "Fra terza via e conservatorismo" in R. Ruffilli, (ed.), *Cultura politica e partiti nell'età della Costituente, tome 1, L'area liberal-democratica. Il Mondo Cattolico e la Democrazia Cristiana,* (Bologna, 1979). "L'area liberal-democratica," pp. 31-44; see also the extensive bibliography. Reference is made in this paper to these studies.

4 Matteucci, "Introduzione," pp. 33-8.

5 *Cf.,* F. Delzell, *I nemici di Mussolini,* It. tr., (Turin, 1966), *passim.*

6 In addition to the first years of *Il Ponte* I have used P. Calamandrei, *Scritti e discorsi politici,* edited by N. Bobbio, vol. 1, *Storia di dodici anni,* 2 tomes, vol. 2; *Discorsi parlamentari e politica costituzionale,* (Florence, 1966).

7   E. Cheli, *Costituzione e sviluppo delle istituzioni in Italia*, (Bologna, 1978) p. 43.

8   A large number of newspaper and academic articles have appeared on the project and the events of the 'third force'. But a serious and comprehensive work of historical analysis is still lacking. The reader, however, may consult the essays of L. Valiani in *La Sinistra democratica in Italia*, (Rome, 1977), with a preface by G. Ferrara, and the recent publication of a part of the acts of a conference held on this question in Milan in April 1948 – *Sulla Terza forza*, edited and with an introduction by L. Mercuri, (Rome, 1985). Also of value are the observations of A. Asor Rosa, 'La Cultura' in *Storia d'Italia*, vol. 4, *Dall'Unità a Oggi*, 2 (Turin, 1975), pp. 1590-2 and *passim*, and E. Galli della Loggia, *Ideologie, classi e costume*, in AA. VV., *L'Italia Contemporanea, 1945-1975*, cit., pp. 379-434, and especially p. 407ff.

9   See N. Bobbio's long introduction to Calamandrei, *Scritti e discorsi politici*, cit., vol 1, tome 1, pp. XI-LVI, and A. Galante Garrone, *Calamandrei. Il profilo biografico intellettuale e morale di un grande protagonista della nostra storia*, (Milan, 1987). See also M. Cappelletti, *In Memoria di Piero Calamandrei*, (Padua, 1957.)

10 See G. D'Orazio, *La genesi della corte costituzionale*, (Milan, 1981.)

11 In addition to P. Bonetti, *'Il Mondo,' 1949-66. Ragione e illusione borghese*, (Bari, 1975), with a preface by V. Gorresio, the following should be consulted. AA. VV., *'I 30 anni del Mondo. Le battaglie economiche,'* edited and with an introduction by P. Bonetti which is to be found in the supplement no. 20 of *Il Mondo* of May 7, 1978; G. Spadolini, *La stagione del Mondo, 1949-1966*, (Milan, 1983), and the two books by the same author cited in note 1; V. Frosini, *Il Mondo e l'eredità del Risorgimento*, (Acireale, 1987); R. Sani, *'Il Mondo' e la questione scolastica*, (Brescia, 1987). At the outset *Il Mondo* was published by Mazzocchi. This publisher had to resist pressure from the Christian Democrats and from the government. When the Radical Party was founded Count Nicolo' Carandini and Arrigo Olivetti purchased the journal. They also financed the Radical Party. The circulation of this weekly seems to have been around thirty thousand, but the readership was necessarily larger. I am grateful to Dr. Manlio Del Bosco for this information.

12 I am referring here to M. Del Bosco, *I radicali e 'Il Mondo,'* (Turin, 1979), with a preface by R. Romeo.

13 G. Galasso, *Passato e presente del meridionalismo*, 2 vols.: 1, *Genesi e sviluppi*; 2, *Cronache discontinue degli anni settanta*, (Naples, 1978), see especially vol. 1, pp. 61-2 and *passim*.

14 Cf. G. Berta. *Le idee al potere. Adriano Olivetti tra la fabbrica e la Comunità*, (Milan, 1980), especially the first chapter.

X

The Action Party and the *Azionisti* Before and After 1946

Lamberto Mercuri

The years 1942-1947 constitute for the Action Party the temporal field which encompasses the story of this movement's political action. But perhaps not even this interval faithfully reflects the chronological arch in which one of the most significant experiences of recent Italian history makes its appearance and vanishes. Historical phenomena, like men, are given dates of birth and the formative phase of the movement can be traced to the fall and winter of 1943. As was the case with the other political parties (and with the one under consideration), the disastrous course of the war had accelerated the process of formation and renewal.

In reality, in the second half of 1942 the reconstitution, or the constitution, of the Italian political parties was still in an embryonic state, and behind this lay not only the omnipresent watchfulness of the police, but also a series of objective difficulties. We are talking about small nuclei, scattered throughout the country, and not connected with one another in a systematic way. The representatives of the old political class, liberal-democratic in orientation and defeated by Fascism, were gathered in the principal Italian cities, and among them there existed not a few personal grudges and bad feelings, due among other things, to varying attitudes held during the twenty years of Mussolini.

Actually, compared with the on-going reconstitution of the political parties, in large part along traditional lines, the Action Party had no precise tradition to refer to. What this "new" party was, and what goals it set for itself, has been the object of numerous writings and accounts, including those by Riccardo Bauer, Tristano Codignola, Guido Dorso, Aldo Garosci, Giuliano Pischel, Carlo L. Ragghianti, Mario Paggi, Leo Valiani, Franco Venturi and others as well. But let us proceed in orderly fashion. The events involving the Action Party can be broken down into periods rather easily. Certain phases are clearly identifiable. We made brief mention of the birth of the movement; the second phase corresponds to the struggle for National Liberation (1943-1945); the third the Parri government (June-November 1945); then the "diaspora" (the first National Congress, in February 1946) and finally, the Second National Congress (April 1947) and the "legal death" of the Party.

The war of National Liberation represented a decisive element in the history of the Party, especially during the German occupation of Italy and the re-formed Fascism of Salò. The war entailed a bitter struggle constantly sustained by acute moral tension, which involved the entire Party; a struggle which exacted high costs in human life and which was waged with the deep awareness that the Resistance was to represent a project of radical innovation. After the definitive defeat of Fascism, the Action Party won the Presidency of the Council as Ferruccio Parri became Prime Minister.

In the new cycle of Italian history, and particularly in the field of ideas, behind the young party lay the preaching of Carlo Rosselli, the teachings of Gobetti, Giovanni Amendola, Benedetto Croce, the liberal-socialism of Calogero, the democratic veterans movement ("combattentismo") of the First World War (Salvemini, Parri, Bauer and others) and, in certain respects, a tradition with roots embedded in the Risorgimento.

"The Action Party," it has been noted, "during the years of Fascism, represented a fundamental cultural nucleus," and, as regards its liberal, socialist and republican strains in the immediate postwar period, expressed its vitality in: 1) the organization of the democratic and parliamentary state in connection with the problem of the purges; 2) the return to the freedom of association and the safeguarding of the civil and political rights canceled by Fascism; 3) the uniting of democratic political principles with the richest and most varied liberal-socialist culture which existed in Italy, and which — known by the symbols of [the partisan group] Justice and Freedom — seemed to best reflect the function most appropriate to the intellectual in his relationship with the new society.

The intellectuals of liberal-socialist origin were in a condition similar to that of the Enlightenment intellectuals of the second half of the 18th century in Southern Italy, who considered themselves as irreplaceable elements in the plan to construct a modern state which would cast-off the remains of feudal society thus reawakening the democratic and popular consciousness which had been dulled by absolutism. (Piromalli)

At the First National Congress (Rome, February 4-8, 1946), the Party split. At the beginning of 1946, after De Gasperi had already replaced Parri at the helm of the government, the major political parties, including the Action Party, held their congresses. This gives us an interesting overview of the political situation as it was evolving at the time and of the outlooks with which the various political forces faced the institutional "referendum" and the elections for the Constituent Assembly. The Committee of National Liberation, and its historical and "revolutionary" function, was scarcely a point of discussion, although it had been at the center of a heated debate, stimulated in particular by the Action Party.

The general assembly of the Party was of particular interest, as it was a party which, as I have mentioned, had made a considerable contribution to antifascist activities prior to September 1943 and to the partisan war. For Party activists, it was the first opportunity to clarify, at a broader, national level, its political function, its responsibilities and its relationship with the other parties. Since its foundation, in fact, the party had held two meetings: the semi-clandestine conference in Florence on the eve of September 8, 1943 and the Congress of Cosenza (August 1944).

Practically all the plans, "cadres," and forces available to the young Party were absorbed by the twenty months of underground, armed struggle. The Resistance had interrupted (or "misled") the development of ideological positions, specificity and identity of the various branches and above all the sense of illusion and reality. Already in the summer of 1945, in fact, despite the euphoria stemming from the "wind from the North" and from the Parri government, the influence of the Party had diminished and a sense of failure was widely felt on the eve of the crisis in November 1945.

The wound from February 1946 was never healed. Some convinced "third-force" activists, led by Parri and La Malfa, as well as a numerous and prestigious group of intellectuals, formed the

"Republican Democratic Concentration" in hopes of recuperating the Party's orthodoxy, only to join the Italian Republican Party almost immediately. The majority, who remained under the Action Party roof a while longer, enlisted in the party of Nenni and the Socialism of Saragat. Still others joined small formations, and a very few went into the Italian Communist Party.

For better or worse, it was the political parties which, for various reasons, constituted the new and symptomatic element of the Italian situation. Out of the structure of the Committee of National Liberation, the Resistance had evolved, laboriously and gradually, from its tumultuous and original framework into somewhat more solid and less precarious structures. The republicanism of the middle classes was rather more ambiguous, not unlike that of the Christian Democratic Party, which came out in support of the Republic only when, in 1946, with De Gasperi as Prime Minister and no longer in a "burning bush" situation, the Party was convinced that institutional change would not open the doors to revolution.

In the 1946 elections, the "Republican Democratic Concentration" garnered 97,650 votes (0.43%), and Parri and La Malfa were elected. The Action Party as such won 334,748 votes (1.46%) and received seven delegates. These nine delegates (7 from the Action Party plus Parri and La Malfa) maintained a continuity of positions, if not always in line with the theses of the Action Party in various circumstances; this actionist roots were ever present. Above all, the liberal-democratic culture was dominant. The lay parties, in general, were able to offer a much more significant contribution of ideas and solutions than their actual political weight would suggest; and this continued to be true of the vast majority of those who had been active in the AP, whether they joined the various political parties or retreated into private life or teaching.

Following the collapse of hopes for renewal contained in the Resistance program, and after the failure of the continuity of the state to rupture, after the failure of "total democracy," in other words, there is no doubt that the Party experienced a difficult setback, both at an internal and international level (the "cold war" and establishment of opposing blocks). Internally, a Stalinist mode of Communism quickly took shape which tended increasingly to engulf the socialists. On the opposing side stood the Christian Democrats, who were rebuilding their ranks with the support of the Church.

The Action Party soon came to feel like "outsiders" in this rigid political framework. This was due in part to an inability to comprehend the system of mass political parties, but also for other reasons: the weakness of its political hinterland, and the elements of heterogeneity among its militants and among a few charismatic leaders. The *ethos* of the individual seemed to set that select handful of intellectuals on a pedestal, but the mass circulation of ideas distanced them from that approach, which was becoming a kind of historical feeling. There were other tenets of the Actionist program which failed to excite the middle-level bourgeoisie. The purge of Fascists from the levers of power did not enjoy wide support. The nationalization of monopolistic industrial and financial complexes, to which many progressive intellectuals were not adverse, did not appeal to those involved in reconstruction, and so failed, or was made to fail. The Party, and the Italian left in general, was further weighed down by the conditioning of anti-Fascism as the *negation* of Fascism in its authoritarian quality, which was countered with the exaltation and acceptance of so-called free enterprise in which a marriage between the great interests and the administration of the state was realized.

At the Second National Party Congress (Rome, April 4, 1947), the political formation ceased to exist. The National Council, in a majority decision, proclaimed the dissolution of the Party and its adherence to the Italian Socialist Party. A few other "unshakables" gave life to "Action Justice and Liberty" and to a newspaper, *Italia socialista*, directed by Aldo Garosci (which lasted until the end of February, 1949), and "this small movement," writes Paolo Vittorelli, "served to prevent the formation of an all-red Italy, called on to substitute the all-black Italy of the preceding twenty years, but not to reconstruct a broad line-up of lay democracy." (At the elections for the first legislative assembly, on April 18, 1948, the formation "Socialist Unity" garnered 1,858,346 votes, or 7.09%). The words of Riccardo Lombardi, spoken at the conclusion of the second General Assembly of the Action Party, proved significant for what was to follow:

The prospects for our work which appear before us are varied: it may be that we will remain autonomous, but let us remember that whatever our destiny as a party may be ... we will never have an easy life. I am not saying that we will make life difficult for others; but we will have a hard task, because wherever the men of the Action Party go, they carry with them a well-spring of ideas, a yearning and an inquietude, which compels them to search for more precise pathways, new pathways along which to move.

The hypothesis of "third-force-ism," which would recur often over the course of practically the entire forty years of the Republic, was ever-present and maintained as a point of reference the experiences of the Action Party and the culture of this political movement. The lay world fought to distinguish itself from the Catholic and Communist "duopoly" which seemed to characterize Italian public and political life. For these reasons, the protagonists of these battles included men who came from the dissolved Action Party as well as others from the lay tradition (both from outside and within the parties) whose aim it was to prevent the Italian political system from being reduced to Christian Democratic hegemony over the area of the government or Communist hegemony over the area of the opposition. It was not a matter of vague formulas or occasional positions, but of convergence on a certain number of problems.

Naturally, the democratic socialist components appeared important in these designs. It was also necessary to contend with the small movements, and in the larger parties to compete with a vivid knowledge of the various negative aspects of Italian life. Those who considered themselves as a "third force," then, included the Socialists as well as the Republicans, the Liberals and other groups of lay democracy. These were certainly minorities, and when we speak of democratic and enlightened minorities in Italy and in more recent history, thoughts run, once again, not only to the experiences or ideas of the Action Party but more generally to those forces which strongly felt the need for real reform. These experiences found expression, rather than in a genuine, organized party, in an entire current of politics and ideals.

The constant, almost desperate, dedication of Ugo La Malfa to the triumph of a "third force" democratic perspective, to break through the "formula of April 18," as he himself called it, cannot go without emphasis.

The results of 1948, as is known, had in fact frustrated any possibility of intermediary autonomous political life. The Christian Democrats created equilibriums destined to last. Communists and Socialists seemed prisoners of their unitary myth. The heaviest toll was paid by the Socialists of Nenni who, with their different tradition of more open sensitivity toward the values of democracy, of civil liberties, etc., bore the weight of considering, with greater realism, the demystification of the "frontist" formula.

Uncertainties, perplexities and disconcertedness were especially present in the lay camp. Now their force, both in the centrist parties and in the small formations, appeared rather weak, also due to questions of international politics. And this could not be explained merely by the strength of the Church, the support of the Americans and the errors of the Socialist-Communist alliance. All accidents are subject to causes, and not to "cynical and swindling" chance, as was maintained.

Our discussion would be incomplete if we did not mention so-called centrist policy (1948-1953) which indeed experienced a certain dynamism, and in certain respects produced positive signs and several important anticipations of economic modernity and of a social nature. The policy of De Gasperi was far-sighted, in that context; he could have done without the lay parties (and certain eminent "technical" personalities from the non-Catholic area), but he did not want to deprive himself of their important collaboration.

But the "Cold War" stands out over everything; it begins not in 1947, as is generally held, but immediately as the second world conflict ends and Europe remains the epicenter of the interests and clashes between the great powers in conflict. The opposing blocs are formed. This split is characterized by the birth in 1947 of the Cominform, that is the rebirth "mutato nomine" of the Comintern, dissolved by Stalin in 1943, and with this rebirth re-explode contrasts and crises which the world of the 1920's had already known. Stalin's reborn organism spares no one: not even the reformist socialists of the West. The all-out challenge is directed principally against the United States, which assumed the leadership of the West and possessed the atomic bomb.

As regards Italy's opting for the West, it is not exaggerated to state that it was the lay forces which undertook a more "positive" role (allied with the Christian Democrats), as they clearly recognized the need to repair the cracks caused by the war, and worked to rejoin Italy to the productive system into which it had to be integrated and from which it could not have separated itself if not at the cost of political choices which were impractical or unlikely in the climate of the period.

It should be briefly recalled here, going back a few years, that it was La Malfa who, in a series of articles published in the Action Party's newspaper *Italia libera* (at the beginning of 1945), proposed an alliance between the Action Party, the Italian Republican Party and Nenni's Party which might impose a democratic shift to the left on the Christian Democrats, whereas the alliance between Socialists and Communists would be condemned, in La Malfa's words, "to immobilism and impotence."

The inquietude, uncertainty and impatience as well as the various splits which characterized "azionismo" did, nonetheless, produce some positive results. Ugo La Malfa and Francesco De Martino directed at length two parties which were central to Italian democracy, a story significant in itself.

Certainly, there existed a general cause which helped these small groups, mini-parties, etc., as they were called depending on intentions and circumstances, to testify to a presence and the irreplaceable function of a cultural activity. An ethical, political patrimony which survived splits, disassembling, errors, schematisms; that those reasons would, in large part, be appropriated in a different context by Socialists and Communists, is a question which lies beyond the confines of these notes.

The "Movement of Popular Unity" was formed between the end of 1952 and the beginning of 1953 from the union of different groups, most of which had left the minor lay parties: the "Movement of Socialist Autonomy" (Calamandrei, Vittorelli, Codignola) from the Italian Social Democratic Party; Republican dissidents led by Parri and Zuccarini; a small group of former Actionists from Tuscany including Carlo Cassola and Luciano Bianciardi which had reassumed the old name of "Justice and Liberty". These were joined by a handful of prestigious personalities including Carlo Arturo Jemolo, Tullio Ascarelli, Edoardo Volterra, Diego Valeri, Giacomo Noventa, Carlo Levi and Bruno Zevi. The occasion for unity and the principal terrain of battle for the Movement (which also had a periodical, *Nuova Repubblica*, and a more modest publication directed by Ferruccio Parri, *Lettera ai compagni di Unità Popolare*) was the "legge truffa," or "swindle law," the electoral law passed by Christian Democracy in view of the political elections of June 1953, a law which was supported by several parties of the centrist coalition and accepted by many lay intellectuals, including Gaetano Salvemini, Ernesto Rossi, Ugo La Malfa and the entire group of *Il Mondo*.

The battle against the "legge truffa," as it was called, was crowned with success. The Movement ran with its own lists and garnered a rather scanty number of votes (171,000), not enough to elect even one of its candidates. But the result was significant and greater than that which the government line-up lacked to set the majority mechanism in motion. And the votes were drawn, in all probability, directly from the parties allied with Christian Democracy.

In reality, the elections of 1953 (which represented the decline of De Gasperi), were held in a climate of fiery passions, and defeated the majority law by a slim margin. The law had been presented late, toward the end of the legislature, which had to approve it hurriedly. It was too favorable to the parties of the governing coalition, which could seek alliances amongst themselves in order to benefit from the expected prize for the majority, while the forces of opposition, de facto, could ally themselves neither on the right nor on the left, obviously, and not even between Socialists and Communists, since the Italian Socialist Party had decided not to repeat the unhappy experience of the "Democratic Popular Front." If, in the end, the law had been pushed through, Christian Democracy would have gained, or rather recovered, the absolute majority in Parliament which it had won in 1948, but which, in the following five years, it had visibly lost in the country.

After the elections, the "Movement of Popular Unity" continued its activities for a few years longer. But lacking an objective of struggle comparable to that for which it had been established, and submitting, on the other hand, to the attraction of new, external poles of reference (the Italian Socialist Party on the road to autonomy and, to a lesser extent, the newly-born Radical Party), the Movement experienced a problematic and provisional life, almost as if awaiting the dissolution which came about in the fall of 1957.

The majority of its militants joined the Italian Socialist Party, where they assumed not a minor role in favoring the process of autonomy with respect to the Italian Communist Party (. . . "our action," wrote Codignola, "is not that of a party among parties, but of a ferment valid for all parties . . . ") and the experience of the first center-left government.

The experience of "Popular Unity" is without doubt eloquent, and symbolic of the path of non-marxist intellectuals in the fifties. In the experience of this small movement, the connection with the Action Party is evident, from which "Popular Unity" had drawn, in large part, leaders, "cadres" and fundamental ideology, and even the internal debate between the *socialist and democratic* components.

In the search for forerunners, one can go further back to Salvemini, Gobetti, Giovanni Amendola or to democratic interventionism; indeed, even further, as Max Salvadori, who belonged to Popular Unity, has reported: "Justice and Liberty, the Mazzini Society, Popular Unity were for a quarter of a century manifestations of what, among Italians, as a way of thinking, dated back to the coteries established here and there from the mid-eighteenth century. . . . " All the movements which we have cited were characterized by a strong drive toward new solutions in the sphere of democracy, by the absolute preeminence of the cultured element. From this point of view, "Popular Unity" represented, perhaps, the last act of fifty years of history: that of the attempts, always unlucky, which the Italian intellectual and progressive bourgeoisie made to create its own party.

For the sake of completeness, we must direct our attention, in concluding, to yet another attempt of this kind which does not lack in heterogeneity of tendencies, intentions and designs of time-honored inspiration. It is a case of the intertwining of the old and the new, of the attempt to group scattered and variously engaged nuclei to achieve a union of the entire Italian democratic left in view of the new Italian political order: the meeting of Catholics and Socialists.

Through his review *Criterio*, Carlo Lodovico Ragghianti assumed the role of promoter of the Convention "Liberty and Society" (Rome, November 30-December 1, 1957), together with other cultural reviews: *Comunità, Itinerari, Il Ponte, Tempi Moderni*, and

Opinione. The former exponent of the Action party raised the call to "men of the Action party, of Socialist split-offs, of liberal demands" for the "new" political task, thinking to find a pivot in the recently formed Radical Party, to which he had adhered.

We will not speak of the variety of opinions and different tones of the speakers: the center-left was around the corner, and the attention of the participants was directed toward the coming elections and the long-term choices which involved not only the democratic left but also Italian democracy: intentions and tendencies which, for better or worse, represented for Italy and Europe the general premises which it would have been difficult to ignore in the elaboration of programs of a stronger democratic left in the government.

Among the speakers at the Convention were Guido Calogero, Riccardo Lombardi, Altiero Spinelli, Franco Ferrarotti, Antonio Giolitti, Leopardo Piccardi and others. It was a passionate debate, at the conclusion of which Calogero made the essential point: " . . . I think that the debate between liberals and socialists (giving these two expressions the broadest and most comprehensive sense, and therefore also the most approximate) is particularly useful."

In the confrontation, at times harsh, which was ignited among the participants, and especially between Riccardo Lombardi and Ragghianti, once again the "irreconcilability" between the two spirits of "azionismo" was confirmed, which had been at the heart of the discussion and the basis of the "diaspora" sanctioned in the first general assembly of the Party in distant 1946.

Select Bibliography

1 Giuliano Pischel, *Che cosa e' il Partito d'Azione?* Milano, 1945.

2 Giovanni De Luna, *Storia del Partito d'Azione 1942-1947*, Feltrinelli, 1982.

3 Giancarlo Tartaglia (a cura di), *I Congressi del Partito d'Azione 1944/1946/1947*, prefazione di Leo Valiani, Ed. Archivio Trimestrale, Roma, 1984.

4 AA. VV. (C.L. Ragghianti, Leo Valiani, Ruggero Ranieri, Dino Cofrancesco, Lamberto Mercuri, Aldo Garosci, Arturo Colombo, Marina Tesoro, Aldo A. Mola, Giovanni De Luna, Stefano Vitali, Vittorio Telmon, Vincenzo Cicognani, Giovanni Spadolini, Enrico Serra, Fulvio Mazza, Giancarlo Tartaglia, A. Maria Cittadini Ciprì, Marina A. Saba, Antonio Alosco, Enzo E. Agnoletti, Giancarla Codrignani, Bruno Zevi, Gigliola Ventury, Leone Bortone, Michele Cifarelli, Raimondo Craveri, Pietro Crocioni, Pasquale Schiano, Vittore Fiore, Franco Andreani, Guilio Butticci, Agostino Zanon dal Bo, Joyce Lussu Salvadori), *Il Partito D'Azione dalle origini all'inizio della Resistenza armata*, prefazione di Giuseppe Galasso (a cura di Lamberto Mercuri e Giancarlo Tartaglia), Roma, 1985.

5 AA. VV. (Antonio Piromalli, Antonio Varsori, Leone Fedeli, Max Salvadori, Vittorio Foa, A. Maria Cittadini Ciprì, Paolo Vittorelli, Giancarlo Tartaglia, Joyce Lussu, Michele Cifarelli, Romeo Aureli, Arialdo Banfi, Giovanni Spadolini, Tiziana Borgogni, Carlo Pinzani,, Leo Valiani), *L'Azionismo nella storia d'Italia 1946-1953*, presentazione di Lamberto Mercuri, Ancona, 1988.

6 NAW *(National Archives of Washington) Records of the Foreign Service, Posts of the Department of State*, RG 84, Box 5.

XI

A Commentary on the Essays of Guido Verucci and Lamberto Mercuri

Charles F. Delzell

It is a pleasure to comment on the very informative papers presented by Guido Verucci and Lamberto Mercuri. Their papers have stirred up numerous recollections that I cherish of Italy during the early years after the liberation.

I was in Bari in the U.S. Army from November 1943 until December 1945. An agent in the Criminal Investigations Division (C.I.D.), I was attached to the headquarters of our Fifteenth Air Force. Fortunately, I was able to live with an Italian family and to begin to learn the language. As one who had grown up in Franklin D. Roosevelt's era of the New Deal, I quickly became interested in the efforts of a determined minority of Italians in the South to eradicate the remnants of the dictatorship and to lay the groundwork for a truly democratic system of government.

I recall, for example, the excitement that surrounded the Congress of Anti-fascist parties which met in Bari in January 1944. Representatives of the parties in the Committees of National Liberation debated vigorously how they could force King Victor Emmanuel III to abdicate in order to make it possible for Italians to cooperate more effectively in the liberation of the North. The parties on the Left looked forward to the election of a constituent assembly that would decide which kind of political institution – a republic or a monarchy – should prevail. The issue continued to be hotly debated for the next two years until the victory for the republic in the referendum of June 2, 1946.

I was able to visit Rome and the North after they were liberated. I was impressed by how much more politically conscious the people in this "other" Italy were in comparison to most people in the Mezzogiorno.

In December 1945, my military tour of duty came to an end. Happily, I was able to return to Italy in March 1946, this time as a civilian. I represented the Hoover Library on War, Revolution and Peace, located at Stanford University where I was to become a candidate for the Ph.D. degree in modern European history. As luck would have it, I flew to Europe with the library's founder, former President Herbert Hoover. President Truman had asked Mr. Hoover to head a mission to survey the food needs of war-torn Europe and Asia and to report back to him what the United States could do to alleviate famine conditions. After the Hoover Mission arrived in Rome in mid-March, I stayed in Italy until mid-summer, collecting materials for the Library. I sought all kinds of documentation pertaining to the Fascist era, the Resistance, and the postwar reconstruction. I was assisted by Fedor Nemirovsky, a young Jewish refugee from Yugoslavia who had been one of our C.I.D. interpreters in Bari during the previous two years. He was fluent in Italian, held a law degree, and had fought in Tito's Partisan forces, though he himself was never a Communist.

The spring of 1946 was an exciting time to be in Italy. The country was preparing for a referendum on June 2 to decide the fate of the monarchy and to elect a constituent assembly. My friend, Fedor, and I hoped very much that the republic would win. In our collecting work for the Hoover Library, we made an effort to meet and seek the help of as many of the political and intellectual leaders as we could. Our contacts were numerous among the laic parties, and especially so in the Partito d'Azione. I recall that in Rome we talked to Guido De Ruggiero, Luigi Salvatorelli, Guido Calogero, Alberto Cianca, Alba De Cespedes, and Vittorio Gabrieli — all of whom were then identified with the Action Party. We also met major figures in other laic parties — for example, Carlo Sforza and Ivanoe Bonomi. In addition, we conferred with the Socialists, Ignazio Silone and Mario Berlinguer; with Mario Alicata, the Communist editor of *L'Unità.* Among the Christian Democrats, we talked to Guido Gonella, editor of *Il Popolo,* and with others. We had a jeep at our disposal, so we could travel to other cities, too. At the University of Florence we talked to Piero Calamandrei. At Porto San Giorgio we visited Emilio Lussu. At the University of Bologna, Edoardo Volterra. In Turin, Alessandro Galante Garrone, Ada Gobetti, and Giorgio Vaccarino. In Milan, we met a number of people who had fought in the Resistance. In Naples, we talked to the liberal, Benedetto Croce. In Bari, Tommaso Fiore. On subsequent trips to Italy I became acquainted with Aldo Garosci, Ferruccio Parri, Altiero Spinelli, Leo Valiani, and others. In 1948-49, I was fortunate to receive a scholarship to Croce's new Istituto per gli Studi Storici in Naples. Its director, Federico Chabod, helped me start my research on *Mussolini's Enemies: The Italian anti-Fascist Resistance.* – so you can appreciate why the presentations by Professors Verucci and Mercuri this afternoon have been particularly interesting to me.

Let me now make a few comments about Professor Verucci's very informative and carefully nuanced paper on the complexities of the "Lay forces: The Cultural and Political Contributions of Intellectuals and Journals." Incidentally, I like his occasional use of the alternative label, "liberal-democratic" cultural forces, as an English-language substitute for the Italian *forze laiche* – a locution which is rather difficult to translate without going into considerable explanation.

Professor Verucci correctly underscores the influence on the postwar political system of such laic currents as Benedetto Croce's historicism, Gaetano Salvemini's radicalism, Piero Gobetti's *rivoluzione liberale*, Carlo Rosselli's *socialismo-liberale*, and Guido Calogero's *liberal-socialismo*.

Professor Verucci also makes the interesting point that there was much less friction between anticlerical and Catholics in the post-World War II period than was the case in the pre-1914 period. No doubt the common battlefield experiences of Catholics and anticlerical during two wars help to explain this. Another factor, it seems to me, was the signing of the Lateran Pacts in 1929, which brought an end, at least in considerable measure, to the preceding sixty years of *dissidio* between Church and State.

The first postwar elections in June 1946 revealed that the democratic-liberal parties were weak, in contrast to the Christian Democratic and Marxist parties. Verucci is no doubt correct in observing that the nascent Cold War worked to the advantage of the Catholic and Marxist *partiti di massa*. Many voters were inclined to cast their ballots for one of the strongest parties, in order not to "waste" their votes. It is also true that the laic political currents were not able to attract as many of the erstwhile fascistic middle class as they had hoped. Many of these middle-class people found it easier to shift their allegiance to the new and relatively conservative Christian Democratic party. It must also be noted, with regret, that Italy's liberal-democratic forces never could surmount their own rivalries and consolidate themselves into one or two parties in the way that Ugo La Malfa had hoped they could. But in spite of the fact that the laic currents obtained only limited support at the polls in 1946, some of them — and most notably the Republicans and Azionisti — were to be quite successful in persuading the Constituent Assembly to include in the new Constitution guarantees of civil liberties and provisions for a Constitutional Court and for a system of regional governments.

Although the Partito d'Azione disappeared in 1947, a variety of other "laic" forces were to continue to be influential during the ensuing years of Centrist governments. In coalition with the Christian Democrats, several of these laic leaders promoted liberalized economic policies in foreign trade, encouraged European integration, and supported Italy's entry into the North Atlantic Treaty Organization.

Professor Verucci has also reminded us of the significant roles played by such "laic" journals as *Il Ponte*, a monthly review of politics and literature that Piero Calamandrei started in Florence soon after that city's liberation. *Il Ponte* sought to defend the role of the CLN's in the Resistenza and to serve as an intellectual and political "bridge" for discussion of problems of the postwar era. Salvatorelli's publication, *La Nuova Europa*, focused on the need for European federation — a theme which found considerable support among laic currents in Italy. *Nord e Sud*, edited by Francesco Compagna after 1953, explored the socioeconomic problems confronting the backward Mezzogiorno. The journal, *Comunità*, launched by Adriano Olivetti in Piedmont, sought to explain his ideas for socioeconomic reform to be implemented at the level of local communities and factories. Most influential of all was the widely circulated *Il Mondo*, a weekly launched in Rome in 1949 by Mario Pannunzio.

With respect *Il Mondo*, let me call attention to a recent essay by Giovanni Spadolini in *L'Azionismo nella storia d'Italia, 1946-1953*, a collection of papers presented at a *convegno* in Porto San Giorgio in March 1986. Spadolini makes two important points, it seems to me: (1) that if it had not been for the utopian idealism of Mario Pannunzio, Italy would today be less laic and less European; and (2) that although the Partito D'Azione and other Enlightenment-minded forces were never more than small minority currents in Italian life, they succeeded in conditioning almost all the political movements in Italy over the past forty years.

Professor Verucci reminds us that in 1955 *Il Mondo* shifted toward the new Radical Party, and he declares that the closing of *Il Mondo* in 1966 symbolized the end of an epoch. Italy was about to enter several years of turbulence — not all of which was senseless terrorism, however. Significant changes in Italy's social and cultural life, as well as restructuring of the political left, were to emerge from this difficult era.

To the list of influential "laic" journals that Verucci has mentioned, let me suggest a few others that were of at least some influence in the early postwar years. In Rome, there was *Mercurio*. Founded by Alba De Cespedes, this was a monthly in the field of politics, arts and science; it survived for a few years. *Belfagor*, a review in the humanities, was edited by the literary critics, Luigi and Carlo Russo. *Itinerari*, a bimonthly journal of history and literature, was published in Genoa by Francesco Cesare Rossi after 1952. *L'Espresso*, started in 1955 by Livio Zanetti, also deserves mention. And in Milan, *Il Movimento di Liberazione in Italia: Rassegna di Studi e Documenti* was launched by Ferruccio Parri and others in 1949 to clarify and defend the anti-Fascist struggle. In addition, we should not overlook the influential role played by such laic book publishers as Laterza, La Nuova Italia, Einaudi, and others.

Let me now turn briefly to Professor Mercuri's paper on the Action Party. Mercuri is one of our best-informed historians of this subject. He has explained clearly how, from the beginning, the Partito d'Azione and its precursor, Giustizia e Libertà, epitomized the vague but widespread desire that postfascist Italy should be "purer" than the Italy of tradition. It never was quite clear, however, just what sort of revolution, a slow process of socialization with scrupulous preservation of civil liberties? Or would it be a more sudden change? And how would the Partito d'Azione relate to the Communist Party, which was the strongest element in Italian anti-Fascism and — during those years, at any rate — the known enemy of free institutions? The moderates in the Action Party espoused a liberal-democratic program with a mixed economy, whereas the party's left wing favored a much closer relationship with Nenni's Socialists. And some wanted to go further and have a close link to Togliatti's Communist Party. It is not surprising that the divergent factions within the Action Party could find ready agreement only on such issues as the need for a republic and for separation of Church and State. This intractable division led eventually to the dissolution of the Action Party in 1947.

Some of the most interesting points in Mercuri's paper, it seems to me, had to do with the activities of various ex-Azionisti after 1947: for example, the small minority group, Azione Giustizia e Libertà, which under the editorship of Aldo Garosci, published the newspaper *L'Italia Socialista* in Rome until February 1949. Mercuri points out that although this enterprise helped keep Italy's journalism from being dominated by the Social-Communists, it was not able to rebuild a liberal-democratic force. Mercuri rightly concedes that the Christian Democratic "centrist" coalition of 1948-53 did produce some economic modernization and certain benefits, thanks to De Gasperi's political astuteness in keeping the laic parties in his governing coalition. And he properly gives credit not only to the Christian Democrats but also to the laic forces in persuading Italy to identify itself with the Western democracies rather than with the Soviet camp in the late 1940's.

The fight in 1953 against the *legge truffa* (i.e., the "swindle law" that called for replacing pure proportional representation with a bonus provision for the bloc that gained a plurality) caused a split in the ranks of the laic forces. On the one hand, the Movimento di Unità Popolare — backed by Calamandrei, Parri, and others — fought the proposed "bonus" law. On the other hand, Ugo La Malfa and *Il Mondo* supported the provision. I didn't find in Mercuri's paper, however, a clear explanation of the reasons for La Malfa's stand. I wonder if he would agree with Norman Kogan, who has written that La Malfa feared that if the laic parties failed to cooperate with the Christian Democrats on this issue, the DC might instead form a coalition with the extreme Right after the election?

The *legge truffa* was enacted in 1953, but the Christian Democrats failed to win the magic figure of 50% of the vote in the parliamentary elections of that year. The outcome of that election brought the 8-year-long De Gasperi era to an end. In 1954 the *legge truffa* was repealed. Thus, the laic parties could take some modest comfort from their campaign.

For a few more years, the Movimento di Unità Popolare lingered on, but there were no more big issues. The Movimento experienced the same kind of schism between its liberal-democratic and socialist elements that had plagued the Partito d'Azione and Giustizia e Libertà. Some of the members sought to align themselves with the new Radical Party, while others joined Nenni's Socialist Party. Thus, by the end of the 1950's, the tensions between Italy's advocates of liberal-democracy and the proponents of socialism remained as insoluble as they had been in 1946-47.

Let me congratulate again our two well-informed panelists on their probing analyses of some of the controversies and contributions of the laic political and intellectual currents in Italy during the exiting early postwar years.

PART THREE

INSTITUTIONAL ISSUES IN POST WORLD WAR II ITALY

XII

Raffaele Mattioli and the Banca Commerciale Italiana in the Reconstruction of Postwar Italy

Piero Treves

The story of the Banca Commerciale Italiana's contribution to the reconstruction of post-war Italy begins in November 1944; and it suitably begins in Washington, D.C., with the arrival of the economic Mission of which the Bank's general manager, Dr. Raffaele Mattioli, was a member. The Mission's aims were officially described as "explorative and informative," but, in organizing its trip to America, the Italian government aimed at something practical and immediate. As Mattioli put it at the very first meeting, their aim was not to discuss relief problems but try to find out how Italy can be put to work again.

The legal and the *de facto* position of Italy were somehow anomalous and certainly contradictory. Italy was a defeated country which had unconditionally surrendered on September 8th, 1943, and was bound by the harsh clauses of an Armistice which put all its resources and financial means at the disposal of the Allied armies. Yet hardly a month after signing the Armistice Italy had declare war on Nazi Germany and had been admitted as a cobelligerent with the United Nations which were committed to a radical revision of its status and of the Armistice terms if — in Churchill's words — the Italians would be able to work their passage home. It was precisely to this end, that is to make Italy better able to join in the common war effort against the common enemy, that the Mission had come to Washington — to ask first and foremost that Italy should be allowed to resume financial responsibility and that its institutional powers should be returned to its Central Bank. The paramount problem was therefore the problem of the so-called am-lire, their issuance and their exchangeability into dollars.

Am-lire were being used and issued by the Allied military authorities in Italy for troops pay as well as for supplies and services. Mattioli said it was a question primarily of bookkeeping and in his customary phrase: "We must make accounts." No one knew how many am-lire had been issued, let alone how many by the Allied Commission without the knowledge of the Bank of Italy, and without any coverage — so that the first meetings of the Mission were chiefly devoted to try to determine the approximate amount eventually assessed at one and a half billion lire a month merely for troop pay. Neither was it easy to evaluate the potentialities of the industrial plants in liberated South and Central Italy, partly on account of war damage partly because whatever plant was still usable or immediately repairable had been promptly requisitioned by the Allied military authorities.

In the circumstances Mattioli's request for a reciprocal aid agreement between Italy and the United States could be met neither *de facto* nor *de jure*, the U.S. government refusing to enter into any agreement with Italy without the consent of other powers in the United Nations. Mattioli's insistence on a reciprocal agreement (though I doubt that he may have harbored the belief that the Mission could arrive at such an agreement or "arrangement") was more political and psychological than strictly speaking financial and economic. It would have provided a boost to Italian morale, and certainly it would have been of the utmost importance for both sides to reach some sort of "arrangement" before the day the success of the Allied armies in Italy and France led to the liberation of northern, industrial, Italy. The Italian Mission and Government feared that the war destruction was heavier than was actually the case; hence the justified dread of political and social convulsions which would have retarded, or even made impossible the work of rehabilitation of freed and reunited Italy. Hence the long-drawn-out discussions in Washington till March 6th, 1945 in the search for concrete results. Mattioli declared himself dissatisfied for nothing concrete and immediate was mentioned in the final American memorandum which moreover made everything dependent upon Allied war needs, their difficulties with transport, shipping, etc.

Yet, it provided for a notable victory, for the American government became fully aware of Italy's will to live and work, to produce and export. It represented a major concession on the moral and psychological plane. The announcement of the forthcoming reestablishment of full diplomatic relations between the two countries and the re-opening of their embassies in Rome and in Washington signalled that Italy was reverting to the status of a sovereign state.

The Mission was back in Rome a couple of weeks before the liberation of the country. Mattioli who hitherto had operated from the Bank's Rome branch, had long planned what to do as soon as he was able to resume control in Milan. In August 1944, jointly with his friend Signor Cuccia, who was also a member of the Mission to America, he had devised what he thought was best for the resumption of the orderly activity of the Banca Commerciale and the Italian bank system in general. Mattioli would have liked to call the new concern "Unionbanca," since it consisted of a consortium of the three banks of national interest, Banca Commerciale Italiana, Credito Italiano and Banco di Roma, plus several banks and companies, Italian and foreign. The name chosen was "Mediobanca," and it was more indicative of the purpose of the new concern. In its very name "Mediobanca" indicated Mattioli's aim of guaranteeing the granting Italian firms and industries medium term credits for no longer than five years. Mediobanca would help, as it did, to avoid the risk or temptation for ordinary credit banks, let alone for the banks of national interest, to revert to the pre-war status of mixed banks or *banques d'affaires*, from which Mattioli had saved *his* Bank in the 1930's. As early as 1931 a memorandum of his, which his current "boss" Toeplitz submitted to Mussolini, advocated a mixed economy for Italy, not ruling out State intervention in governing the economic life of the country, but (as Mattioli always stressed) without expropriations and without nationalizations. When a wind of indiscriminate liberalism blew over Italy in the wake of Leftism and Liberation and most people wanted to do away with I.R.I., the Institute for Industrial Reconstruction, which had become, in keeping with the so-called Bank Law in 1936, the biggest single shareholder of the three banks of national interest, Mattioli stood firm, in spite of, or because of, his Leftist propensities, for the maintenance of I.R.I.

And in agreement with the I.R.I. authorities he succeeded in sweeping away the hesitations of the Governor of the Bank of Italy, Professor Einaudi, the future president of the Italian Republic. It took, as Cuccia humorously remarked, "nineteen months of gestation" for Mediobanca to come into being, but it did come into being on April 10th, 1946, with two 35% quotas taken up by Comit & Credito Italiano and one 30% quota taken up by Banco di Roma, thereby assuring the banks of national interest the absolute majority within Mediobanca, while leaving the door open to foreign participation, which however occurred only ten years later, in 1956, Lazard & Lehman taking a quota equal to 10% of Mediobanca's capital. On Mattioli's death Mediobanca's chairman wrote that, apart from *his* bank, Mediobanca was Mattioli's favorite child, the creation he loved best. It was in fact the perfect outcome of Mattioli's leading ideas on banks and banking since he was at the helm of Comit and totally in keeping with the principles according to which Italy's bank system ought to be governed. He always took justifiable pride in maintaining (and emphasizing in most of the chairman's addresses to the annual shareholders' meetings) that Comit was the bank of the small or medium investor. Less than 1% of the Bank's clients asked for and got credits exceeding 20 million lire, whereas most clients were in the 10 million lire echelon. Mattioli had suffered too much from the Bank's immobilization and lack of liquidity in the 1930's not to preach and practice, especially in the immediate post-war years, a policy of utmost liquidity and speed of credits turnover, against the double menace of inflation and stagnation.

It was this policy which enabled him to ask for credit, i.e. trust, for the capitalists on the part of the workers, rightly maintaining that such a trust had the double advantage of enabling the industrialists to realize bigger profits and the workers to secure correspondingly fatter pay packets. Precisely because he was a good "boss," universally beloved by his staff, he was determined to stand no nonsense, for example when pay claims were being discussed. Once, on receiving a workers' representative committee, whose spokesman uttered that members of his union were earning, if I remember rightly, no more than 200,000 lire a month, Mattioli quickly cut him short with a pertinent, or impertinent question:

"How many months?" (people employed in Italian banks collect from 13 to 16 monthly installments per annum).

Nothing more helped to keep the Bank's vessel on the right keel than Mattioli's ability to deal equally with rich and poor, with big industrialists and the lowest ranks. He never concealed, for instance, his boundless admiration for the Bank's head chauffeur, to whom he once confessed he wished he were able to do his job as well. He had faith in man, he granted his confidence to anyone with vision and courage, attracted as he was by new ideas. Hence he and his Bank were responsible for the best part of the so called "Italian miracle." When a former leader of Christian-Democratic partisans, signor Enrico Mattei, asked to be supported financially in his plan for the prospection and exploitation of Italy's methane gas resources, which might prove a useful substitute for coal and oil, both of which Italy lacked, Mattioli unhesitatingly lent him one billion lire, the foundation stone on which the six-legged dog were to lie ever since, the now world-famous and omnipresent Agip, out of which a State concern of such dimensions as E.N.I. was to grow. But here Mattioli, much as he had approved of Mattei's pioneering activities, was bound to disapprove. He disliked, or came to dislike, nationalizations, at least in Italy, not so much *per se*, as in the form and because of the consequences that State mammoths like E.N.I. or E.N.E.L. imported into Italy's life. They became gigantic agencies for the financing of political parties, newspapers and politicians, thus furthering corruption and poisoning Italy by fouling the very principles upon which the Italian Republic was founded.

Not through these channels had the so-called, and miscalled, Italian "miracle" come about. Mattioli rightly denied it was a miracle at all and resented the feigned enthusiasm of foreign pressmen and experts marveling at the allegedly incredible fact of the Italians ever being able to achieve such an advancement. Profiting from the favorable international conjuncture, the Italians had worked hard, as they have been traditionally accustomed to, in order to assure a better future. Coming from a rather poor region of the Center-South, Mattioli knew in his bones what it meant to emerge, to come up in the world through sheer work, and it was but a reflection of his humanity and generosity that he should visualize as every Italian's lot what had been *his* lot, his share in and contribution to the common weal.

What is good for the nation is good for the Bank, was his motto in all the years he was at the helm and watched the forward march of his land, its progressive transformation from an agricultural to an industrialized country with all the advantages and all the ills of such a process. But the development of Italy in the aftermath of a war fought on its soil could not be merely economic or financial. Italy was a late comer into the comity of modern nations, but it had a long tradition of achievements and for centuries had powerfully contributed to European civilization, to the opening up of the human mind. A treasure hidden in the blood, memory and conscience of each of its inhabitants, which it was sheer and treasonable madness to do away with, as if it were merely the ashes from a past long dead. Hence Mattioli's activity, both within and without his Bank, conspiring towards the same goal of reconstruction through Italy's return to civilization, the one pursuit being inconceivable without the other.

There are *not two* Mattiolis, the banker and the humanist, nor even a Janus-like Mattioli. There is a man working for his country's future — and no future can exist if it is not born out of the past, unless it brings forth and to fruition what was sown in the past, unless past and present merge and mingle in a common stream.

To that end you must have an adequate, mature ruling class, the lack or tardiness of which Mattioli always regarded as the main drawback of Italy. Hence his constant ambition to train men within his staff and through the Bank's *kindergarten*, through books, schools, appropriate institutions and cultural devices. What his training gave to Italy's reconstruction and its political life is clearly attested by the life-work of two of his friends, Senator Giovanni Malagodi, the Liberal, and the late Republican leader Ugo La Malfa. But all the young men of promise he tried to win over, to associate them with the various trends of his activities, chiefly as a publisher and as a man consorting with all that was best in post-war Italy. It suffices to recall Montale, the Nobel-prize winner poet, Gavazzeni the conductor, Manzù the sculptor, Longhi the art-historian, Guttuso the painter, not to mention a historian like Chabod, and economists like Sraffa and Lord Kahn. If you had a scholarly book or paper to publish, you just turned to Mattioli who was always willing to help and care for publication, i.e. for the fact that the book was available, far more than for its sale or commercial success. Everything was welcome to him provided it fitted into the puzzle of the history and tradition of our country, provided it contributed to make it better known and interpreted in the light of current needs and problems, which he felt could be solved only by a plunge into the past and by emphasizing the connection of the past with the present. This too applied both within and without the Bank.

When its fiftieth anniversary approached (to be celebrated, though war prevented any celebration in 1944), he decided to refrain from commissioning any customary commemorative book, the Bank's history being part and parcel, inseparably, of the economic and industrial history of Italy. The latter should therefore be the only appropriate subject, the story of the transformation of the states of the Peninsula from the morrow of the French Revolution to the independence and unification of the country in 1870 and their slow merging into a single progressively industrialized unity which became strong enough and European enough to participate in and win the First World War. It represented a pioneer history of the origins of today's Italy, of its perennial problems: overpopulation, unemployment, administrative deadlocks, etc. Over twenty volumes are already out, a few more will follow shortly. A sort of companion history, under the bank's aegis, to the history of the Italian literature which Mattioli started as editor and publisher in the 1940's. It should have run into 75 volumes: *La letteratura italiana. Storia e testi*, the inaugural volume being a selection, or self-anthology, from Croce's writings, prepared by Croce himself and seen through the press by one of Mattioli's oldest and truest friends, the head of the Bank's economic research department, Dr. Antonello Gerbi, with whose name students of American history have long been familiar. The "Ricciardiana," as the collection is currently called, has by now run into over 80 volumes and it is still far from completion.

It is the best instrument to date for the study of Italy and its culture through the medium of its literary achievements, historians, economists, etc., not merely poets and novelists. There are far too many professional *littérateur* in the history of Italian literature — and they are deservedly dead and buried. But there are many figures who faced the problems of their time: history, economics, law, foreign affairs, travels and memoirs; which goes to prove that Italy's European vocation is not a novelty of the present century, in spite of the heavy parochialism which still plagues us today. At a time when men of the Right indulged in nationalistic chauvinism and men of the Left preached the destruction of our Classics *en bloc et en détail*, maintaining that Italian literature was old fashioned, dull, dusty and illegible, Mattioli gave the post-war generations a tool, a new root for their patriotism, a new feeling of belonging to an entity which was not born yesterday and which is therefore entitled to a future — provided the Italians are willing to build it up with their work.

Most of the editors of the single volumes of the "Ricciardiana" are, or were, young people, mostly belonging to the post-war vintage. Thanks to Mattioli's initiative they have proved their worth through their work, and have succeeded in doing away with the temptation of anarchy, with the withering away of our past and historical traditions. Everybody is now happily convinced that you cannot build a house from the roof, oblivious of the foundation.

Mattioli was always alive to the necessity of building the foundation, whether of his Bank (since he became its general manager in 1933) or of his country or of our culture. It is the application, in all fields he turned to, of his watchword: "We must make accounts." Our accounts with economics, is the Bank and its manifold aspects, activities and problems. Our accounts with culture, includes the study of the history, origins and structure of our country, or the prerequisites for the building of a ruling class.

It is with this aim in view that Mattioli helped Croce bring into being what the philosopher regarded as his major legacy. The Italian Institute for Historical Studies, of which Mattioli was chairman in 1955 (a chairmanship which on his death passed on to his son Maurizio) provides yearly hospitality in Naples to a limited number of young scholars, Italian and foreign, who are interested in research in the methodology of historiography. The results of their work are consigned both to the Institute's *Annals* and to a series of monographs covering every field of ancient and modern history. It has been possible even to do away with the traditional one sidedness of our historical writing, a bad inheritance from Livy and Tacitus, the neglect of European and extra-European affairs, to study only what happened within the wide and narrow margins of the Peninsula. From the Naples Institute as well as from the volumes of the Ricciardiana there have sprung the new masters, the new chair-holders, the members of the new ruling class. Just as the best pupils of the Commercial University Luigi Bocconi in Milan, where Mattioli taught before entering the Bank, of whose board of governors he was a member for many years (and to which his son bequeathed his library) are most often the new recruits of the Bank's staff.

Italy's post-war reconstruction was pursued by Mattioli, and the Bank over which he ruled with such authority and such a success for some 40 years, at different but convergent levels with the single purpose of rehabilitation and Europeanization, the different trends mingling harmoniously into one whole, as Mattioli's mind was one whole because of, rather than in spite of, the variety of interest, all grounded on the love of life. No truer summary of the man and his work was ever given than in the Latin words engraved on the house where he was born. *Vitam locupletavit*. He enriched life.

XIII

Commentary on Piero Treves' Essay on "Raffaele Mattioli and the Banca Commerciale Italiana in the Reconstruction of Postwar Italy"

Max Salvadori

"Vitam locupletavit" — this is how Professor Piero Treves ends his perceptive and informative essay on Raffaele Mattioli, one of post-World War II's outstanding Italian personalities. He encompassed in multiple activities the material and the spiritual. He contributed to the reconstruction of an economy first damaged by two decades of a totalitarian, visionary New Order (the Corporative State), then shattered by two years of war and civil war fought from Sicily to the Alps; and to the revival of a culture stifled by the repressive and suppressive obscurantism of the Fascist regime. As the capable head of COMIT (Banca Commerciale Italiana) all doors were open to him. Not only because of his financial expertise, but also — I would say primarily — because of his moral rectitude, lofty intellect, and what was known of his political past, all parties governing the democratic Italian Republic (or might have governed it, if successful in the 1948 general elections) would have like to number him among their own supporters and would have entrusted him with high level functions and responsibilities.

"Nos locupletavit" I add with reference to the author of the essay, who in the few pages allotted by the organizers of the meeting has been able to draw a portrait of Mattioli in simple masterful strokes. It wasn't easy to summarize the character, mind and achievements since his arrival in Washington at the end of 1944, of a unique, more than rare, businessman, the brilliant General Manager of a major financial institution, deeply concerned with the all-important precise accounting to which centuries ago Italian bankers, industrialists and traders too numerous to list, owed the success of their enterprises in Milan, Venice, Florence and Genoa.

Mattioli exemplified the humanist belief that correctly trained intelligence is more important for the creation of wealth than natural resources (of which Italy had few), capital (scantier in Italy after the war), favorable conjunctures and other factors listed in manuals. "The opening of the human mind" (Professor Treves' words) has been the primary factor in the Italian economy's post-WW II "great leap forward", has recently been the subject of an article by a foremost American columnist. Professor Treves rightly gives as much space to Mattioli the humanist as he does to Mattioli the banker.

Not a popular figure in the sense that statesmen and politicians are, Mattioli belonged to the relatively small sector of the national élite that had survived Fascism without having been tainted by it. *Rara avis*, together with Parri, Salvemini and other Resistance leaders, he was also deeply committed to the moral resurgence ("Insorgere, Risorgere" had been the appropriate slogan of a major underground organization he had helped) of a nation cut off for twenty years from the North Atlantic mainstream of modern progressive civilization.

Pre-World War II and wartime events being outside the theme of the meeting, Professor Treves limits himself to a couple of flashbacks for that period. But to understand Mattioli, his post-war influence, and the ambiance in which he operated, an American audience needs to be informed about an all-important aspect of Mattioli's activities: the help he gave to antifascists for whom a job in the Ufficio Studi of the Banca Commerciale meant the difference between going hungry much of the time (in Fascist Italy it was difficult for people suspected of antifascism to make a living) and to have enough to eat. Mattioli was not the only businessman who helped Mussolini's opponents: several other names come to mind (and I could list episodes with which I became acquainted during my conspiratorial years). But there was a very important difference: most of those I know about, whatever their inner convictions, were primarily — in the clandestine jargon of the time — *fiancheggiatori doppiogiochisti*, acting publicly as enthusiastic Fascists and serving the regime in various capacities. Mattioli was instead a genuine enemy of the dictatorship and of what made an Italian or a foreigner — a Fascist (nationalistic frenzy, corporative visionarism, rejection of reason, exaltation of violence, *ducismo*, hierarchism, statolatry). He never went beyond his duties as General Manager of an institution included in the economic structure controlled by the state. A question arises: did the OVRA (the secret political police) know of what was going on in the Ufficio Studi? Probably: it is most unlikely that among members of Mattioli's staff, there wasn't one, or more, of the myriad informers who for a pittance reported regularly to the police. However, the police chief, Senator Bocchini, an efficient bureaucrat loyal to whatever government was in power, did not bother Mussolini with details concerning antifascists as long as there wasn't evidence of militancy (La Malfa, just to mention the best-known name, had enough experience to 'mimetize' himself when engaging in clandestine activities). Bocchini's successor, a friend of an antifascist uncle of mine, while doing his bureaucratic duty was concerned about post-Fascism and aimed at giving it direction.

Another point. Professor Treves makes it clear that Mattioli, as an economist entrusted with a responsible position (and — it must be added — listened to by the post-Fascist political leadership) was no callous *libériste* (Manchesterian or other), indifferent to the suffering caused by the economy, relying myopically on market forces to put things straight, as were most Italian academic economists, nor was he a collectivist affected by Marxist visionary utopianism. Using a term once popular in France, he was a *dirigiste* (close to British Keynesianism and to American New Dealism), committed to a good dose of state intervention in a mixed economy in which medium and small enterprises deserved special attention and, in the words of Eleanor Roosevelt, there is "public responsibility for the general welfare of all people." However, in a nation in which distorting dialectics was then fashionable among the non traditionalist sectors of the intelligentsia, there was room, economically, only for 'capitalism' (*liberismo*) and its antithesis 'socialism.' In antifascist circles, briefly dominant politically at war's end and intellectually for a longer period, Mattioli was considered close enough to socialism to be entrusted with financial-economic responsibilities should the political conjuncture put the Popular Front coalition in power. Actually, in relation to the majoritarian orthodox socialism of the time Mattioli was no more socialist than Professor Galbraith, whom I have heard describe himself at times as a New Deal liberal and at times as a socialist.

The third point I wish to make concerns the Italian economy during the crucial immediate post-war period. For several years after the armistice of September 3rd (announced on the 8th) Italy's history is the history of a nation, not that of a state which functioned sporadically here and there, and at times, in most fields, did not function at all. What went on in Brindisi, Salerno and Rome, or in Salò on the other side of the battle-front, was of little interest to most of the nation. The economic 'leap forward' expected after 1860 had not materialized; it began to get going decades later but was interrupted by World War I, Fascist histrionics and World War II. It took shape from 1944 on. People did in a crucial period lasting several years what state and formal institutions, including most banks (but not the Comit) were not in a position to do.

State and provinces had disintegrated. There remained the local (municipal) structure. During the second half of 1944, from southern Abruzzi to northern Tuscany, roads had to be repaired, minefields cleared, schools, hospitals, *preture*, etc. re-opened, water, sewers, electricity reactivated. This was done on a scale large enough to make a real difference. People worked, somehow; ingenuity, initiative and imagination helped. The same happened in 1945/46 in northern Italy. There was no central government, Italian or foreign (AMG), to give instructions and to provide funds. The local community, at times dating within approximately its present boundaries from Roman *municipia*, came back into its own. Data can sometimes be found in municipal archives.

In Milan during the last months of the war, I witnessed another phenomenon, as unexpected as the vitality and cohesion of local communities. Industrialists, small, medium and big, inventing all kinds of pretexts, had slowed down their operations. (I was told that later some prided themselves on having produced only 1% of their normal output during the German occupation.) Banks had helped, providing cash for paying wages (redundant workers had not been dismissed). Production was down to a minimum, but I saw warehouses full of everything needed to get plants going again. Other warehouses were full of goods ready for sale. Supplies would not last long but there was enough for a start. There had been no instructions, no orders, but from Turin to Trieste most industrialists had done the same. It helped that among industrialists there was fear that Stalinists would take over (as Tito's Partisans did in most of Julian Venetia) as soon as the Allies left. One had to work fast and efficiently to use the supplies, to produce and sell goods, to make a profit. Under the stress of war, relations between employers and employees — united in their hatred of Germans if not of Fascism — had improved. As soon as the Germans surrendered and Fascists disappeared, there was a surge of activity, not everywhere, not uninterruptedly, but enough to start industry again. The Stalinist take-over did not materialize. The surge continued — it continues.

In the immediate post-World War II period there was also a wider and more far-reaching development than the initiative of municipal communities and the reawakening of dormant industrial activities. Ingenuity, imagination and initiative compensating for the paucity of resources and other handicaps, in various parts of North-Central Italy and even in Bari, Naples and Pescara — in the Center-South. One case can be multiplied thousands of times. In a hill village of central Italy artisans had for generations made substandard slippers for local winter use. When Germans withdrew early in the summer of 1944 some of the artisans — who hadn't made slippers for a year and only a few during the previous three years, and had successfully hidden their supplies of leather, heavy cloth, etc. — had the idea of making shoes. Passing Allied troops were acquiring, with fast depreciating am-lire, wine and other local products from peasants needing shoes, and middlemen looking for anything to buy and sell. Soon there were hundreds of imitators setting up themselves as small, minuscule entrepreneurs. . . . In a few years intelligent hard work — the source of wealth — transformed an economically backward rural area into a prosperous intensively industrialized one. The ten million lire or less mentioned by Professor Treves, borrowed from local savings banks and from branches of national banks, starting with Mattioli's Banca Commerciale, helped considerably.

Slowly at first, the Italian economy got going. When Marshall Plan funds became available, there was an expanding dynamic entrepreneurial class able to use them effectively. Mattioli and Professor Treves are right: there was no economic 'miracle', only the tenacious and intelligent hard work of millions of Italians, spurred by sound financial policies in an ambiance made secure by the constitutionalism on which Mattioli and his friend La Malfa insisted.

Although he had friends in all parties, although he was undoubtedly a man of the Left and was constantly invited to join a party, and to play a major role in the political life of the country, Mattioli steadily turned down any such invitation and all his life remained a man *super partes*. He was however suspected of, or admired for, his Communist sympathies. Some went so far as to describe him as a crypto-Communist. For instance, a friend of mine, the late Editor of a social-democratic periodical, perhaps because he had been refused financial support from the Bank, once said to me, without mincing his words, that Mattioli was a *bolscevizzante*, i.e. pro-Bolshevik. In point of fact, ludicrous as it may seem in the light of subsequent or present events, he never disguised his admiration for Stalin, chiefly, of course, for the leader of Russian resistance who had a decisive part in winning the Second World War.

But where is the evidence for calling Mattioli a Communist sympathizer — or even a crypto-Communist? It is true that his best friend, Dr. Piero Sraffa, a Fellow of King's and later of Trinity College at Cambridge was a militant Communist. It is equally true that both Sraffa and Mattioli had been in their youth, in the years immediately following World War I, under the influence of the Communist leader Antonio Gramsci, and remained faithful to him. It is above all true that Mattioli managed to salvage and preserve Gramsci's note-books by concealing them immediately after his death in 1937 in the safe vaults of the Bank from where they were eventually transferred abroad until their posthumous publication in post-war Italy. It is true that the Communists hoped to enroll Mattioli in their ranks and that whenever a general election occurred in Republican Italy the Communist leadership invited Mattioli to stand as a candidate for the Senate in a safe seat under the label of Independent in the list of Communist candidates. But Mattioli wisely turned down any such invitation, the result of which would have made his position at the Bank untenable. The gain, if any, of the Communist Party would have resulted in a grievous loss for the nation. Mattioli always sought the good of the nation, and he maintained that the good of the nation was also the good of the Italian Communist Party. This is the theme of Mattioli's letter to the Communist leader Togliatti of May 28th, 1947. Here Mattioli sketches a plan for the rehabilitation of Italy, to stem inflation, to stop the steadily declining productivity and purchasing power of the country. Italy was in urgent need of foreign help, which could come only from the United States. The rehabilitation of the country — Mattioli emphasized — was a special interest of the masses, of the poorer classes from which the Communists and the Left at large were deriving their maximum support. Hence, Mattioli implied, it was the Left, it was the parties of the working classes that should force a policy of economic planning on the moderate Government and press for a policy of collaboration with the Western democracies, chiefly with the U.S.

Togliatti did not answer Mattioli nor heed his advice. He led his party into violent opposition to the Marshall Plan and the beginnings of the economic unity of Western Europe. Mattioli's advice was sound, but Togliatti must have realized it was not the advice of a Communist. Mattioli was a member of no party, for he wanted, first of all, "to make accounts" and think, clearly, with his head.

References

The best introduction to Dr. Mattioli's thoughts and comments on the Italian situation in the post-war years is supplied by the B.C.I. (Banca Commerciale Italiana) Chairman's addresses to the annual shareholders meetings from 1945 to Dr. Mattioli's retirement in 1972. They were collected and edited in book form (3 vols., an English edition available). Some important essays and addresses on literary and economic topics are collected in the memorial volume *Raffaele Mattioli (27 luglio-27 agosto 1973)*, Milano, B.C.I., 1973, pp. 195 ff. Two major writings, his memorandum for a new settlement of Italian economy (1931) and Mattioli's letter to Togliatti (1947) form two appendices to G. Malagodi, *Profilo di RM.* Milano-Napoli, Ricciardi, 1974, pp. 67 ff. Obituaries on M. are collected in the above quoted book edited by the Banca Commerciale Italiana. Memorial addresses, besides the already quoted *Profilo* by G. Malagodi, are numerous. Among the most important, G. Stammati (Mattioli's successor as Chairman of B.C.I.) (Milan, 1973) and R. Bacchelli (Naples, Istituto Italiano per gli studi Storici, 1973). Several conventions were held in Milan, Florence and his native Vasto to commemorate Mattioli. The proceedings in the following volumes: *Ricordo di R.M.* (Milano, Casa della Cultura, 1975); *Ricordo di R.M.* (Firenze, Le Lettere, 1987) (here, pp. 11 ff., Signor Cuccia's address on the origins of Mediobanca); *La figura e l'opera di R.M.* (the Vasto conference, 1988). A general study by G. Rodano, *Il credito all'economia. R.M. alla Banca Commerciale Italiana*, Milano-Napoli, Ricciardi, 1983. On the mission to Washington, cfr. also E. Ortona, *Anni d'America*, I (*La ricostruzione*), Bologna, Il Mulino, 1984, pp. 16 ff.

XIV

Trends and Issues in Postwar Italo-American Relations: The Role of Alberto Tarchiani, Ambassador in Washington

Ilaria Poggiolini

In discussing post-war Italo-American relations there are, of course, a number of issues and three major trends. These trends are all related to Italy's effort to improve her status and to the American plan to stabilize the country after the end of World War II. Thus, these trends can be seen as long-term interactions between expectations, on the one side; and planning, or the lack of it, on the other.

Between Italy's surrender in 1943 and the signing of the Peace Treaty in 1947, the major trend in Italo-American relations was that of "working Italy's passage" from ex-enemy to ally. During the second period, from 1947 to 1949, bilateral relations focussed on the difficulties of achieving both security and reconstruction. Finally, the third trend, from 1949 to 1954, was characterized by a deterioration of Italo-American relations in the context of rearmament plans and slow revision of the Italian Peace Treaty. While looking in details at these three trends, I shall also discuss a number of the most relevant issues which arose during the period 1943 to 1954. In that context I will discuss the role played by Alberto Tarchiani at the Italian Embassy in Washington.

During the years of Italy's defeat, following 1943 and preceding the signing of the Peace Treaty in 1947, the Italians felt that what they had achieved with the "cobelligerency" was nothing but ambiguity and all their efforts were aimed at receiving allied status or, at least, at relieving themselves of the burden of the armistice. But what they did not seem to take sufficiently into account was the fundamental change in international relations brought about by the war. In this context the debate over Italy's occupation and future tested interallied relations, because no change in her status was possible without international consequences.[1]

This was clearly demonstrated by Soviet recognition of the Italian government in March 1944, when both Italy's diplomacy, albeit subject to rigid limitation under the armistice, and the Soviet diplomacy itself — almost completely excluded from the occupation policy — succeeded in the initiative. The event is well known and much discussed, but important in this context are Italy's motivations and British-American reactions. From the Italian side this was an attempt to soften the Soviet attitude towards Italy during future peace negotiations, and to exploit the existing tension between the occupying powers and between them and the Soviet Union. However, the result was that of bringing Allied policy into line — at least official — with the elaboration of the "New Deal for Italy" at the end of the year.[2]

Even if the affair of Soviet recognition did not put an end both to Italian illusions regarding their freedom of action in the game of international diplomacy or the British-American antagonism over the future of the peninsula, it was definitely a turning point in Italo-American relations. From that time onward the problem of the "Communist threat" became directly interrelated with the debate over Italy's settlement.[3]

In the meantime the internal political situation in the peninsula had evolved resulting in the formation of the second Bonomi government with De Gasperi as Foreign Minister, in December 1944. By the first half of 1945 Italy had to face a concerned and indecisive America and the slow British retreat from direct involvement in Italy's affairs.

From the point of view of international relations, the post-Yalta situation saw Italy pursuing the rather illusory goal of depriving the inevitable peace treaty of any punitive intent. This ambition lay between facts and perceptions. Italy's peculiar status and the British-American concern of keeping her within the Western sphere of influence, were certainly facts. As for perceptions, the overwhelming majority of Italian politicians and diplomats did not seem to realize how narrow was their maneuvering capacity and overestimated the importance of Italy in the post-war international scenario.

Among the few leading personalities in the field of foreign affairs who immediately grasped the meaning of the change which had taken place, and saw the risk of reviving a tricks attitude in Italian foreign policy, there were certainly Carlo Sforza and Alberto Tarchiani. Their previous experience in the United States during Fascism made them even more aware of such change than De Gasperi himself, notwithstanding his parallel experience as a refugee in the Vatican. Before Sforza became Foreign Minister on January 1947, Tarchiani was perhaps in the best position to warn Rome about misplaced ambitions.[4]

The choice of Tarchiani as the first ambassador of democratic Italy in the U.S. was made not only on the basis of his twenty year anti-Fascist record and his experience in the United States, where he collaborated with Sforza in the movement "Italia Libera," but also because from the Vatican and Roosevelt's representative there had been clear signals that he would be welcome in Washington.

As the ambassador wrote in his memoirs, Myron Taylor was Roosevelt's "eyes and ears" in Rome.[5] Accordingly, his positive opinion about the appointment of the Italian ambassador would be crucial in achieving Washington's place. Writing to Roosevelt in February 1945, Myron Taylor actually agreed with the advisability of Tarchiani's appointment and his opinion was soon to be shared by the American President.[6]

In March 1945, soon after the arrival of the new ambassador, the Italian Embassy in Washington reopened and was confronted by the most urgent economic needs and by the threat posed by Yugoslavia's occupation of Trieste. Then came an attempt by Rome to negotiate Italy's declaration of war on Japan and to play a role in the peace negotiations at the end of 1945.[7] It must be pointed out that Rome's hesitations about the timing of the declaration of war on Japan and its hope of receiving something in return, were again based on misconceptions of Italy's international position. The long delayed Italian technical "cobelligerency" in Asia, in fact, was to last only one month and did not have any relevant repercussion on Italy's status at Potsdam or in subsequent negotiations.

The American government kept promising support and a "just peace" for Italy, but it became rather clear — at least at the Italian Embassy in Washington — that "just" did not have the same meaning in Rome and in Washington. Furthermore, the very same concept of "just" regarding the Italian settlement, was questioned in London and rejected by the victims of Fascist expansionism.[8]

Both the Italian government and Tarchiani shared a feeling of deep disappointment but the latter quickly realized that even Washington, the most sympathetic of the Western governments, would never understand or tolerate a nationalistic line of reasoning. From the American point of view, there was a need to refuse the imposition of huge reparations on Italy and to defend her territory from mutilations. This was "just" and reasonable, based on their previous efforts not to treat the country as an enemy and was planned as a first step towards rehabilitation.

But the Italians were expecting more, including keeping their colonies and preserving their frontiers. Therefore, they were not in a position to face subsequent events, when the discussions over the Italian settlement turned into one of the most striking examples of post-war East-West confrontations.[9] In that context the debate over Italy's status became irrelevant. As the American delegation at the peace negotiations noted in 1946, rearranging the well known tune from the movie Casablanca, "a country can be an enemy and still be an ally. This no one can deny. The issues are all still the same as time goes by."[10] What was only worth writing lyrics about during endless and hopeless peace negotiations, did not cease to foster the dialogue between Rome and Washington through the mediation of the Italian Embassy.

In Italy the signing of the Peace Treaty in February 1947, blew away any illusion of regaining the status of equality through traditional diplomatic means and placed relations with the United States in a rather different perspective. Disappointment over the Trieste issue echoed Italian feelings towards the problem of Fiume after 1919 but, unlike the inter-war period, from 1947 onwards the Italian government was in a position to pursue its revisionist policy without offering any threat whatsoever to the new international order.[11]

Signed only a month before the formulation of the Truman Doc-trine, the Italian treaty would need to be reconciled with the new role taken by the United States in promoting the stabilization of Western Europe. Therefore as soon as the final attempt to keep alive post-war Soviet-American collaboration was over, the U.S. government revived its interest in the numerous problems left open by the Peace Treaty and aimed at obtaining Italy's signature and ratification of the Treaty as a precondition for starting the process of revision.[12]

Soon after the war Italo-American relations had been based on the assumption that Italian expectations and American promises would not be matched the one against the other. However, during the years 1946 and 1947, Italy's difficulties in reshaping her foreign policy and the progressive failure of American hopes of granting a "just peace," had shaken belief in the undertaking. The cumulative effect of De Gasperi's first visit to the United States in January 1947, the appointment of Carlo Sforza as Minister of Foreign Affairs in the third De Gasperi cabinet soon afterwards, another government crisis which led to the dismissal of the leftist parties and, finally, the announcement of the Marshall plan in June and Italy's ratification of the Peace Treaty in July, all suggested a read-justment in Italo-American relations.[13]

The new course of U.S. policy offered Italy concrete straightfor-ward political and economic guarantees. But in spite of all the promises and the prospect of a revision of the treaty, Italy's security was still a remote achievement and the insecurity of her Eastern frontier a daily issue.[14] Given this situation, it is no wonder that the Italian government and its ambassador in Washington played on the "Communist threat" in relations with the United States. After the economic collapse of the previous winter, the Yugosla-vian attempt to lead her troops back to Trieste and the break-up of the anti-Fascist coalition, Tarchiani had been instructed to request immediate aid to avert the political consequences of further reduc-tion of bread and coal rations. "Of course" − the ambassador wrote − "De Gasperi was playing on the 'Communist threat'" but the reality was actually very tough.[15] In the United States the eco-nomic and political instability of the peninsula, as well as the uncer-tainty of her Eastern border, were seen as threats to the global plan of stabilization. Finally, during the early months of 1948, the Truman administration focused on the approaching Italian general elections. American plans for European reconstruction together with the Tripartite Proposal of March 20, 1948 were among the crucial elements which helped the Christian Democratic Party in winning the election.[16]

Only three months afterwards, however, Tito broke with the Cominform. The move of the Cold War frontiers towards the East not only frustrated Italian expectations regarding Trieste, but also made more difficult the integration of Italy's security needs with those of the other Western Powers. The attitude of the Italian government towards the developing Western security system was based, once again, on one fact and one perception. The obvious fact was the peculiar economic and strategic position in which Italy found herself. The perception was actually an over-estimation of the role Italy could have in Western defense strategy. Italy was slow in realizing that her participation in the Atlantic Pact allowed no room for negotiations and that neutrality would only mean total isolation.[17]

From Washington, the need for a clear Western choice was strongly advocated by Tarchiani whose messages aimed at making clear that Italy was not in a position to negotiate, and that the country would not be included in any defensive plan until a clear choice in favor of the Western military alliance were made.[18] Tarchiani's commitment in achieving Italy's participation in the Atlantic alliance did not easily dispel doubts or the leaning towards neutrality among Italian politicians and diplomats. Furthermore, as soon as Rome finally put forward her consent, an invitation to join the alliance was dispatched rather reluctantly and at the very last moment.

From the point of view of the countries discussing the Atlantic alliance, the inclusion of Italy would mean binding themselves to the defense of the Southern Mediterranean as well as granting the revision of the Italian Peace Treaty in order to put Italy in a position to meet her obligations under the alliance. It is well known that the role of France and her interests in North Africa were crucial in broadening the original Atlantic idea and in supporting Italy's invitation.[19] Tarchiani's untiring activism was also extremely important in overcoming U.S. Senate opposition against growing military and financial involvement. In the course of a meeting with

Senator Connally, Tarchiani went so far as to argue that the Mediterranean is an Atlantic gulf like the gulf of Mexico or the Hudson Bay. As Tarchiani himself wrote afterwards, Connally did not attempt to question such a desperate dialectic effort.[20]

But extreme as it may sound, Tarchiani's argument was based on the belief that the American strategic interests in the Mediterranean would work in favor of Italy's adherence to the pact. Italy's final admission to the Western military block seemed to confirm the analysis but it had no effect on military provisions, or on any other provision of the Italian Peace Treaty.[21]

For a few months after the signature of the Atlantic Pact disappointment alternated with hope in many Italian diplomatic quarters. Only Tarchiani was firm in advocating definite Italian support for the U.S. plan of European rearmament through the Military Assistance Program.[22] However the Roman policy of "low profile" was neither an answer to Tarchiani's appeals nor a successful internal strategy confronting public dissatisfaction with the policy of the government regarding Trieste. It also played a part in creating difficulties in relations with the United States. During the last months of 1950 Italo-American relations were "at their lowest ebb since World War II." This was due, according to the Director of the Office of Western European Affairs at the State Department, to "a tendency of the Italian people and government to seek substantive positions in international organizations as a matter of prestige rather than from a clear ability and intention to contribute substantially to the work of the organization concerned."[23]

Zoppi, Secretary General at Palazzo Chigi, was fully aware of American criticism as well as of the ambiguity of Italy's policy. He warned "we shall comply with American wishes . . . but we shall do that among so many doubts, hesitations and proofs of technical inefficiency and with such sluggishness that we shall lose any benefit . . . ".[24] Such was indeed the case during the first year after the outbreak of the Korean war. Finally, the Seventh Session of the North Atlantic Council in Ottawa, followed by the second visit of Prime Minister De Gasperi to the United States, offered new opportunities for Italian diplomacy. Meanwhile at San Francisco a "peace of reconciliation" was concluded with Japan.

In the face of such a turning point in post-war international relations, the U.S. government, together with the British and French government, all agreed that Italy had a strong case on military, political and equitable grounds for definite revision of the Peace Treaty. By the end of 1951, the preamble of the Treaty and the political clauses had been canceled while the military clauses were declared no longer "consistent with Italy's position as an equal member of a democratic and freedom-loving family of nations."[25] Nonetheless, agreement over the partition of the Free Territory of Trieste was still far off. Only in October 1954, did the U.S. and British governments succeed in convincing the two parties to agree on a solution: the so called Memorandum of Understanding. Trieste was handed over to Italy and the partition of the free territory of Trieste agreed upon.[26]

The achievement marked the end of a period of uncertainty in Italy. In particular, during the months after the Italian general election of June 1953 — which proved a major disaster for the Christian Democratic Party and for De Gasperi — mutual confidence had been at stake. Italy had feared the Western interest in keeping Yugoslavia outside the Soviet bloc as well as the strengthening of the Balkan Pact composed of Yugoslavia, Greece and Turkey. Thus, during the first half of 1954, Tarchiani's efforts had been directed at avoiding conversion of the Balkan Pact into a military alliance until after the Trieste negotiations had reached a more conclusive stage.

The rejection of the European Defense Community Treaty and the final partition of the Free Territory of Trieste in the course of the following months were events which marked the end of Italy's illusions regarding the Trieste area and her own role in promoting European political integration. These events also gave rise to a deep sense of insecurity in the Italian government. Italy reacted by clinging more closely than before to the policy of collaboration with the United States.[27] Once again, Tarchiani contributed by reaffirming Italy's Western choice even if the question of where to direct the major emphasis of NATO's strategy would soon be reopened by the Italian demands to strengthen the Southern flank of the Alliance.[28]

Within this context, Tarchiani had been the best able to decode and to interpret with a remarkable degree of independence the intentions of the Italian government. For about ten crucial years his untiring efforts to mediate between Rome and Washington were based on the belief that only the United States could become the source of an Italian military and political resurgence. This belief and his contribution helped to avoid a serious deterioration of Italo-American relations in the early 1950's.

Notes

1 E. Collotti, "La collocazione internazionale dell'Italia dall'armistizio alle premesse dell'Alleanza Atlantica," in: *L'Italia dalla liberazone alla repubblica* (Milan, 1977).

2 E. Di Nolfo, "La svolta di Salerno come problema internazionale" in: *Storia delle Relazioni Internazionali*, I/1 (1985), 5-28; B. Arcidiacono, *Le 'précédent Italie' et les origines de la guerre froide. Les Alliés et l'occupation de l'Italie, 1943-1944*, (Bruxelles, 1984); D. Ellwood, *Italy 1943-1945*, (Leicester University Press, 1985), 113-15.

3 B. Arcidiacono. "La Gran Bretagna e il 'pericolo comunista': gestazione, nascita e primo sviluppo di una percezione (1943-1944)" in: *Storia delle Relazioni Internazionali*, I/1 (1985), 29-65; I/2 (1985), 239-266.

4 E. Di Nolfo, "The Shaping of Italian Foreign Policy during the Formation of the East-West Blocs. Italy between the Superpowers," in: *Power in Europe? Great Britain, France, Italy and Germany in a Post-War World 1945-1950*, 487.

5 E. Di Nolfo, *Vaticano e Stati Uniti 1939-1952. Dalle carte di Myron C. Taylor*, (Milan, 1978), 9-10.

6 Ibid, 419-420; 431-432.

7 A. Tarchiani. *Dieci anni tra Roma e Washington*, (Milan, 1955), 29-78.

8 Ibid, 78-126.

9 I. Poggiolini, "Una pace di transizione. Gli alleati e il problema del trattato italiano: 1945-1947," Ph.D. Thesis (Florence, 1988).

10 P. Dawson Ward, *The Threat of Peace: James F. Byrnes and the Council of Foreign Ministers, 1945-1946* (The Kent State University Press, 1979), 87.

11 I. Poggiolini, "Italian Revisionism after World War II: Status and Security Problems (1947-1956)," in: *Proceedings of the Conference on: "Problems of West-European Security 1918-1957,"* Nunham Park-Oxford, 9-13 November, 1988, (Oxford University Press), (forthcoming).

12 Ibid.

13 J. E. Miller, *The United States and Italy* (University of North Carolina Press, 1986), 213-271.

14 P. Pastorelli, "L'entrata in vigore del trattato di pace e il problema della sicurezza", P. Pastorelli, *La politica estera italiana del dopoguerra* (Bologna, 1987), 107-122.

15 A. Tarchiani, *Dieci anni tra Roma e Washington*, cit., 138.

16 J. E. Miller, "L'ERP come fattore determinante nelle elezioni italiane del 1948" in: E. Aga Rossi (edited by), *Il Piano Marshall e l'Europa*, (Rome, 1983), 139-147.

17 E. Di Nolfo, "The Shaping of Italian Foreign Policy during the Formation of East-West Blocs," cit., 499.

18 A Tarchiani, *Dieci anni tra Roma e Washington*, cit., 155.

19 On Italy's adherence to the Atlantic Pact see: M. Toscano, "Appunti sui negoziate per la partecipazione dell'Italia al Patto Atlantico," M. Toscano, *Pagine di Storia Diplomatica Contemporanea. Origini e vicende della seconda guerra mondiale*, (Milan, 1963), 455-519; P. Pastorelli, *La politica estera italiana del dopoguerra*, cit.; E. Di Nolfo, "Motivi ispiratori e genesi diplomatica del Patto Atlantico," *Trenta anni di Alleanza Atlantica* (Rome, 1979), 4-42; A. Varsori, "La scelta occidentale dell'Italia," *Storia delle Relazioni Internazionali*, I/1, 2 (1985), 95-159, 303-363; B. Vigezzi, "La politica estera italiana e le premesse della scelta atlantica. Governo, diplomatici, militari e le discussioni dell'estate 1948," B. Vigezzi (edited by), *La dimensione atlantica e le relazioni internazionali nel dopoguerra*, (Milan, 1987), 1-190; T. H. Smith, "The Fear of Subversion: The United States and the Inclusion of Italy in the North Atlantic Treaty," *Diplomatic History*, 7 (1983), 139, 155.

20 A. Tarchiani, *Dieci anni tra Roma e Washington*, cit. 168.

21 I. Poggiolini, "Italian Revisionism after World War II: Status and Security Problems (1943-1956)", cit.

22 A Varsori, "Italian Diplomacy and Contrasting Perceptions of American Policy after World War II (1947-1950)." *Storia Nordamericana*, III/2 (1986), 86-87.

23 From Byington (WE) to Perkins (EUR), Relations between Italy and the U.S., November 16, 1950, in National Archives Washington (NAW), R.G. 59, 765 00/91150.

24 A. Varsori, "Italian Diplomacy and Contrasting Perceptions of American Policy after World War II (1947-50)," cit., 90.

25 The Acting Secretary of State to certain diplomatic Offices, December 10, 1951, in Foreign Relations of the United States (FRUS), 1951, vol IV, 749-750.

26 Department of State Bulletin, October 18, 1954.

27 EUR/WE, September 9, 1954, in: NAW, Lot File 58D357, Subject Files Relating to Italian Affairs 1944-1956, box 10.

28 Memorandum of Conversation (The vice-President, His Excellency Paolo E. Taviani, Ambassador Manlio Brosio), December 5, 1955, in NAW, R.G. 59, Lot File 57D577/58D71, Miscellaneous Lot. Files, box 6.

XV

Commentary on Ilaria Poggiolini's "Trends and Issues in Postwar Italo-American Relations"

James Miller

Upon observing the title of this paper, my first reaction was a double take. Outlining the trends and issues in Italo-American relations during the postwar decade is quite an undertaking and when an analysis of Alberto Tarchiani's specific role is added, we are presumably talking about a very long book. Given this enormous task, Dr. Poggiolini has succeeded in providing a succinct summary that manages to touch all the bases. She provides us with a periodization of the most complex decade in the postwar history of both nations, touches on most of the major diplomatic issues, and stresses the realism that marked Tarchiani's mission to Washington.

I think that she is particularly on the mark in underlining the air of unreality that marked much Italian diplomacy in the post-surrender and immediate postwar era. This lack of realism was rooted in an understandable human inability to completely adjust to a total military defeat, foreign occupation, economic chaos, and the uncertainties of the nation's postwar future. Lacking economic, political, or military muscle, Italians found themselves reduced to the role of interested bystanders who observed each move by London, Moscow and Washington — particularly Washington — with passionate concern and tended to put the most optimistic shading on every declaration coming from the capital of one of the major occupying powers. Powerlessness and an understandable self-absorbtion also led the Italian government and press to overestimate the importance of their nation in the calculations of the victor powers. The result was that moments of high expectation were the prelude to months of deep disillusion. The "New Deal" policy, the Yalta Conference, the peace treaty process, and the Venezia Giulia settlement of 1946-57 were all examples of Italy's dashed expectations.

Adjusting to the realities of the postwar world was a painful process for Italy and here Dr. Poggiolini usefully underlines the role of Alberto Tarchiani, Italy's man in Washington, in stressing the need for realism in Italian diplomacy. Given the reluctance of Italy's leaders not simply to join NATO, but later to actively participate in the U.S. inspired rearmament program, Tarchiani was a critical voice for acceptance of both programs and for a larger objective: the abandonment of Italy's longstanding dreams of great power status and colonial empire for the more realistic role of an ally and partner of the United States. After some hesitation, Italian leaders came to agree with Tarchiani that the achievement of the nation's most pressing goals — security, internal stability, reintegration into Europe, and escaping from the peace treaty's restrictions — could only be achieved by participating in the U.S.-led Western alliance.

At the heart of all Italy's problems was the peace treaty. Indeed, Dr. Poggiolini's three-fold periodization of Italian policy could as easily be described as Italian efforts to secure Allied commitments to a non-punitive treaty, and, after its September 1947 ratification, Italian attempts to break free from treaty restrictions. The United States was, from the Italian perspective, the key to all three of these objectives. Italy's frustration with U.S. policy lay, at least in part, in the terminology each nation's leaders used to describe the treaty. Italian officials, seizing upon wartime U.S. rhetoric, insisted on a "just" treaty. U.S. diplomats, particularly Secretary of State James Byrnes, actively pursued a "non-punitive" agreement that would limit damage to Italy's industrial capacity and territorial integrity. Anti-Fascist Italian leaders, again citing wartime Allied rhetoric ("One man and one man only"), rejected any war responsibility for their nation, and foisted it upon Mussolini, his henchmen, and the former King. U.S. leaders had to accept the reality that the injured victims of Fascist aggression would demand their pound of flesh from a defeated Italy and sought to limit the damage to Italy's interests. The remarkable thing about the peace making process was how limited a punishment the victors imposed on Italy and how quickly Italy, with U.S. and West European assistance, was able to throw off the treaty's restrictions.

Thus, I find that Dr. Poggiolini's references to "endless and hopeless" peace negotiations a bit off the mark. From a temporal standpoint, the four powers operating in the Council of Foreign Ministers managed to put together not one but five peace agreements in less than 16 months. Moreover, measured by any reasonable scale, the impositions were limited. Compromise, albeit a hard won compromise, was the mark of the peace negotiations of 1945-46.

Finally, I would like to suggest that one issue needs further development in this paper. Anti-Communism blossomed among both the U.S. and Italian leadership during the postwar era. More than any other element, anti-Communism provided the glue for the U.S.-Italian alliance. Tarchiani, the realist, was by far the most consistent prophet of anti-Communism. From the first days of his mission to the United States, he attempted to arouse U.S. anti-Communism. The ambassador was acting from profound conviction but also from a shrewd calculation of the latent potential of this issue. Initially, Tarchiani's frequently shrill anti-Communist rhetoric undercut his effectiveness. After 1946, however, U.S. leaders came to accept a great part of his analysis, particularly his emphasis on the threat posed by the Italian Communist Party both to Italy's independence and to U.S. interests in Europe. Paradoxically, this anti-Communism ultimately undercut Tarchiani's viability as ambassador. Following De Gasperi's 1953 election defeat, the Christian Democratic Party began a slow, careful reapproachment with the forces of the left in the form of Nenni's Socialist Party. Washington, now under Republican leadership, resisted any accommodation, branding Nenni's party a "Trojan Horse" for the Italian Communist Party. Rome needed a diplomat of greater subtlety and, one might add, "realism" to explain the reasons for this policy change to a skeptical U.S. Government.

Tarchiani's departure from Washington helps to mark the end of one era in postwar U.S.-Italian relations. While the United States remained the undisputed leader of the West, a new Italy was emerging: a nation with a restored economy, a strongly implanted democracy, and a foreign policy proportioned to its power and needs. Tarchiani, together with De Gasperi and Sforza, stands as one of the creators of this foreign policy.

XVI

Organized Labor in the Postwar Reconstruction

Tiziano Treu

The reconstruction of labor unions and their role in postwar Italy remain less extensively analyzed than other aspects of Italian history. This, in part, reflects the traditional inclination of historians to consider labor relations as an aspect of relatively minor interest to political and social relations. However research has developed to correct if not to reverse this opinion, and to contradict its most extreme implication namely, the interpretation of labor relations as a sort of "necessary" consequence and variable of "external" events (political even more than economic).

The protagonists of Italian reconstruction had a clear view that the labor movements and labor relations were highly controversial "areas" open to possibly different developments, and that the outcome of the struggle over the labor movement organization and governance was to be decisive for the future of the nation. The factors influencing the possible outcomes and the very terms of the alternatives open to the Italian labor movement are still debated, which confirms the depth and relevance of the controversy[1].

In the process of labor union reconstruction some features are commonly identified as most relevant since its beginning and believed to influence Italian labor relations well beyond the immediate postwar period (until the late 1950's which mark a new phase in the usual periodization of the matter).

A first feature is the profound difference of the reconstruction process in northern and southern Italy. This difference reflects but also reinforces the heterogeneity of the labor force and of working conditions which characterized the "two Italies" for the whole postwar period, emphasizing the historical cleavages between industrial development and agricultural stagnation, between private development and public inefficiencies. In northern Italy the practice of anti-nazi resistance contributed to forge both a significant group of highly politicized activists and a strong network of organized institutions in the major industries acting with multiple roles: center of political activity, defense and representation of economic interests of the workers and in the most critical moments direct contribution to production (with consequent claims of co-determination to last for several years). Such an experience — the "Northern wind" — was totally absent in southern Italy where the reorganization of labor unions was a chaotic top-down process more exclusively influenced by a restricted number of political leaders, by the allied military government initiatives and for some time framed within the institutions of the Fascist regime[2].

The institutional and organizational continuity with the immediate past is a second feature usually mentioned of the reconstruction process. Some distinctions seem important as to the meaning of this continuity. The basic structure of the labor unions — double line of organization, i.e. vertical (by industry) and horizontal (by territory) with the predominance of the latter; absence of occupational unionism; key role of the central confederation — was too rooted not only in tradition, but in the weak structure of Italian economy, to be reasonably altered. Some "products" of Fascist unionism — in this respect quite different from the Nazi — were also to be used: the over-complex but not irrelevant bargaining practice (around 10,000 small collective agreements)[3]; the union participation in public bodies (particularly public placement offices, and social security institutions); and some aspects of protective labor legislation.

The centralization of union and bargaining structure is a more ambivalent aspect. It is greatly influenced by past practice, not only of unionism but of Italian public tradition. It is reinforced by the continuity of the apparatus of labor administration, overstaffed by bureaucrats: some of it remained interchangeable with union officers particularly in agricultural and public sector unions. Centralization was grounded both on objective and subjective considerations: on one hand the heterogeneity and weakness of the Italian labor market[4], on the other the widely shared decision of the union leadership to represent the "general" interest of the working class and to provide a minimum uniform level of protection and income distribution in the difficult environment of the 1940's. Both reasons were reinforced by the overall need of "national solidarity" in the reconstruction which was the basis not only of political life but also of the Pact of Rome of 1944.

There is controversy concerning how compelling these reasons were in bringing about the "extreme" degree of centralization predominant in all aspects of labor relations and even more so in maintaining it for over 15 years. Some have questioned whether the control of basic bargaining policies implied the total abolishing of the bargaining autonomy of the national union federations and of plant representatives; not to mention the compression of the most radical forms of collective action at plant level.

Commentators of different orientations[5] converge in claiming that while an overall control was necessary the consequence was hardly inevitable. On strictly union grounds it brought to a net loss: i.e., to a wage dynamic far below the level allowed by economic resources[6]; at the same time, it did not guarantee a stable income and normative harmonization among different sectors and areas of the country.

The interconfederal agreement on the escalator clause (1947) appeared to be ambivalent and possibly more significant for the social peace and control over the enterprise which it guaranteed to employers, than for the actual wage benefits it provided to the working class. The doubts were to grow in the following years when the continued reliance on the escalator clause contributed to prevent all kinds of decentralized bargaining practice. The matter of decentralized bargaining soon became a major area of controversy between the Communist CGIL and the other components of the labor movement (CISL and UIL) because it implied a basic divergence on the content and objectives of trade union action vis-a-vis economic growth and income distribution.

The terms and balance of the trade-off implied in the decision to keep industrial relations strictly centralized were questioned. The trade-off between Italian income distribution-wage restraint on one side, and job security protection on the other, were well grounded in the Italian trade union tradition; but it deteriorated after the agreement of 1947 which fully restored the Italian employers' freedom to discharge workers[7].

The political and organizational reasons for centralization prevailed within the CGIL. Centralization was also necessary in order to guarantee to the major components the respect of the reciprocal balance of power. Outside the CGIL the interest of the Communist militants of CGIL and of the Communist Party was to confirm through the central handling of wage bargaining their capacity to control the labor movement, their maturity in collaborating to the reconstruction of the economy[8], while emphasizing the need for political "guidance" in labor relations.

In fact the clearest aspect of this political use of centralization was the choice explicit in the CP leadership to exclude the full use of conflictual capacity of organized labor particularly at plant level[9] as a pledge for Communist participation in government and of a politics of social reforms to be brought about by party action. The pledge continued to be "offered" in different forms for a considerable time after the CP exclusion from government (1947); it indicated the inclination (or need) of the Communists to use the CGIL and possibly the union movement as an instrument to experiment with forms of collaboration, while participation was precluded at the political level.

Politicization is certainly the most widely acknowledged feature of Italian labor relations in those years. It implies at least two different meanings relevant to our theme[10]. First, the political allegiance diffused among large sections of the Italian working class, within and outside organized labor. Second, the close connection or identification of union with party leaders particularly in the Communist movement and consequently the strict response of the former to party decisions. It accounts for the strong militancy of the Italian labor movement which will cause recurrent tensions with party politics and also between rank and file and union bureaucracy. It also contributes to explain the relatively rapid aggregation of the population around the two major political/ideological poles: the Catholics and the Communists, more clearly than the Social-Democrats which traditionally lacked a similar mass allegiance.

The ideological reasons for mass unionization were not sufficient to build strong organizational links. In fact Italian unions have remained loose protest aggregates more than well organized structures well into the 1960's. But they provided a potential for union development far greater than in other nearby countries like France[11].

In the immediate postwar period the second aspect of politicization was predominant, beginning with the Pact of Rome of 1944 and ending with the breaking down of the unitary CGIL in 1948, which are both unanimously recognized as "political decisions." In the reconstruction of the Italian labor movement the influence of state and public institutions since the earliest stage, cannot be underestimated.

The continuity of public institutions with those of the past regime in spite of the innovative drive of the liberation movement has been widely demonstrated[12]. Some aspects of this continuity played a direct role in conditioning and containing union action and organization, well before the breaking down of the collaboration among the three major political parties at the top executive level and within the unitary CGIL. Already in 1945 the "freezing" of the CNL as new forms of public organization; then the immediate restoration of prefects as the most efficient control apparatus of the Italian state, and the remilitarization of police; the confirmation of the 1931 legislation on public order and security which proved equally efficient in repressing labor conflict[13]. The very reorganization of the Ministry of Interior, of the Ministry of Labor and peripheral labor offices inclined to become very active in controlling labor relations[14].

This institutional "sequence"[15] is paralleled by a consistent body of provisions which confirms the restrictive policy orientation in labor matters already of the first postwar governments. The abolition of all forms of union control on the labor market, was only partially compensated by the 1949 Act on Public Placement Service. A similar attitude with respect to the co-management committees (Consigli di Gestione, CDG) operated for a few years in most large firms of northern Italy cancelling any legislation on workers participation at the enterprise level[16]. There remained little public support for mass unemployment following the liberalizations of collective dismissals; and in general the restrictive budgetary and monetary policies pursued under the "liberalistic" guidance of the financial ministers.

The institutional continuity which prevailed since the first years of the reconstruction was favored by a certain undervaluation of the importance of state policies and by a weakness in institutional culture common not only in the labor movement but also in the tradition of the left-wing parties[17].

If the Italian labor movement had a clear perception that its initiative had to go beyond the economic sphere and extend to public institutions, such a perception did not materialize in adequate strategies and initiatives in the critical years between 1944 and 1949.

Conflicts over state policies among the political parties were enough to block a large part of the innovative proposals. They deprived the social and conflictual tensions diffused in the labor movement of a realistic institutional outcome and support[18].

Particular attention to state action was paradoxically devoted by the "social left" of the Christian Democrats and by the Catholic components most directly committed in the labor movement[19]. They denounced the emphasis on institutional continuity to the detriment of the reformistic objectives pursued by the liberation movement and were also among the most active in the constitutional assembly[20].

In the labor front they greatly contributed to elaborate the strategy of the Christian component of the CGIL, and then of the CISL, and to deprive both of the ancient confessional ascendancy of the social Catholic doctrine. But their influence was to remain marginal in the actual politics of the CD party. Their "frustration" contributed to shift both their commitment and their cultural interest toward a more marked voluntaristic and pluralist conception of social and union actions: precisely that developed by the CISL in the 1950's.

A similar analysis can be reproduced with respect to the directives of economic policy in that period. The "objective justification" of the liberalistic approach and its real impact on labor issues are open to discussion[21]. Nonetheless it became predominant during the coalition against a rather weak opposition within the major parties.

In fact it has been claimed that the political and labor components of the left were "themselves strongly influenced by economic liberalism"[22] and that they failed to insist on an economic policy based on public control of monetary aggregates through a Keynesian use of public expenditures (to sustain demand)[23].

Only after 1949, following criticism of the second American study on the use of Marshall plan funds by Italian authorities, the CGIL attempted to shape an economic policy alternative to that of De Gasperi governments. The 'Piano del Lavoro' which is the most elaborate outcome of the CGIL debate was bitterly criticized as being too dependent on traditional economic doctrine, and too willing to accept as necessary relations between increases of investment, wage freezes, and consumption control[24].

Alternative lines were also developed by the social left of the Christian Democrats; but these too remained "inactive" well into the 1950's due to the power relations within the CD.

Institutional continuity and restrictive labor and economic policies represent a further contradiction in this reconstruction of the Italian social and political system. The contradiction appears most evident with respect to the major reformist efforts of those years which brought to the Republican Constitution: the "last product of the Resistance and of that political unity of the mass political parties which had characterized the first postwar period"[25].

The constituent process was a major area of collaboration within the labor movement. This collaboration was one of the most important and natural consequences of that pledge of "national solidarity" which represented the basis and the only firm point of political and union action from 1944 to 1948. Organized labor directly contributed to the framing of the Constitution in close relationship with the most prestigious representatives of the three major political components of the Constituent Assembly; and the Assembly recognized labor as a founding factor of the social and political life in the new Republican order.

This central position of labor in the Constitution forms part of the institutional design which greatly revised the Italian tradition. It is supported by specific norms on the major aspects of labor relations: freedom of organization and collective bargaining (art. 39); right to strike (art. 40), workers participation in the enterprise (art. 46) and in the economic life (art. 99). These norms, even though themselves ambivalent, provide organized labor with instruments which could be used to play an important role not only in contractual relations, but also in "the social and economic organization of the Republic" according to the explicit directive of art 3, par. 2[26].

The constitutional process confirms that the potential for a reformist approach in labor as in institutional policy were still present and cut across all the major political components on the eve of the 1948 political and social confrontation. These potentials required support in a consistent social and political initiative. But such an initiative had in part been contradicted by earlier practices and was to become less and less likely in light of future events.

These antecedent and subsequent factors contributed to "reduce" to programmatic value significant parts of the constitutional design, first of all those pertaining to the labor relations system, to the point of "freezing" indefinitely the effectiveness of some constitutional norms. The analysis sketched so far confirms that the deterioration of labor relations and the increasing tensions among the different components of the labor movement in the years 1944-48 resulted from a complex set of factors both internal and external to the labor movement. Together, these factors caused a net decline in the chances for organized labor to contribute to the reconstruction process as a unitary actor fully participating in shaping the basic decisions.

The increasing polarization of the major components of the CGIL toward divergent "poles of attraction", which came to be symbolized by the "Communist" and the "western" world, has appeared to many commentators so strong as to exclude other possible "alignments" particularly of the Communists and Christian Democrats components. More questionable were the different "strategic choices" of these actors, particularly of the Communist CGIL and of the Communist Party in the bargaining policies, and in the institutional and economic matters indicated above. Some commentators are inclined to exclude this possibility and argue that the characters of centralization, political polarization of the labor movement were on the whole "consistent" with the economic and socio-political situation of the postwar Italy[27] and that a significant change would have been possible only a decade later, in the late 1950's following a transformation in the economic and political environment.

Others believe that aspects of instability and contradictions, not only external but internal to the labor relation system, and we have highlighted some, could have been exploited by the actors at least for some years to different ends: possibly to reduce the tensions among the different components of the CGIL, the gap between central decisions of the same components and the decentralized labor movement, and the drastic decline of organized labor influence in preparation for "better times"[28]. The controversy — whatever its merit and the belief in the "openness" of the labor scenario — necessarily includes an evaluation of the strategy of other actors directly influential on the labor movement such as at least the three major parties and the employers.

The breaking-down of the CGIL in 1948 is commonly cited as the turning point of labor relations after World War II, decisive for future development in the whole postwar period. The influence of political factors is also held responsible for the end of the fragile unity of the labor movement. Some specifics should be noted. The first relates to international factors. Their importance has been emphasized or minimized according to different opinions: not only the general impact of the Cold War, but direct USA pressures exerted both officially and unofficially through the active intervention of American union organizations.

A recent history of the relations between the United States and the European labor movements, which has been widely discussed in Italy, provides convincing arguments that "the breaking down of CGIL belongs to Italian history much more than to the relations between Italy and United States. Nonetheless, the American intervention in Italian labor affairs represented a relevant factor in light of the profound interaction between international polarization, and internal (Italian) social and political divisions. While the global influence of American politics was considerable, the capacity to direct specific Italian events and decision was rather scarce."[29] In this respect the very (subjective) directions of American intervention, particularly those coming from or passing through the union channels were to a considerable extent divergent.

The emphasis of some (among others those controlled by the AFL channels) was mainly or exclusively on the containment of the Communist influence in the Italian labor and political arena. Other interventions proved more determined to condition the necessary anticommunist containment supporting the modern participatory unionism of reformistic economic and labor policies of the Italian government and employers. The Marshall Plan in its various stages and institutions was committed to these ends[30].

The impact of these latter interventions was reduced by a certain degree of ambivalence in the model of labor relations "proposed" to the Italian counterparts by the various actors, reflecting different traditions within the American labor movement and society. These differences were emphasized when interpreted by the Italian recipients where the cleavages had much deeper roots and extreme implications. One might argue that the various proposals for social reform and union promotion which accompanied the Marshall Plan lacked in Italy the necessary support in political and union groups devoted to similar reform projects, and capable of implementing them. Furthermore, many of these proposals underevaluated or naively interpreted the specific traits of the Italian (and European) labor traditions, beginning with its politicization and the institutional links between state, unions, and employers' action.

A delicate cultural and social mediation was needed in order to make viable even the aspect of volontarism, of collective bargaining, and of union participation to economic growth and productivity which appeared most acceptable to the non-Communist components of the Italian labor movement. The ambivalence of the labor relations messages coming from overseas, and their discrepancy with the political and labor context then prevailing in Italy, account for the uneven effectiveness of the American intervention mentioned above. The success of the containment politics and later of the "productivity drive" for Italian and European industry was not immediately followed by the proposed growth of responsible unionism and industrial democracy.

A complex interaction can also be seen between political and social factors which go beyond the "events" of 1948. These events reflect the global conflict of interests and of ideologies opposing the major components of Italian society: not only the government coalition and the left-wing parties split in a dramatic political confrontation, but also the employers and the different components of the labor movement. "The unity of the labor movement has its own specificity", it has been justly said, which may be difficult, or even impossible to uproot with a sheer political manoeuver[31], and "the specificity consists of organizational and bargaining practices on one side, and of institutional practices and relations on the other."

In fact the breaking down of CGIL was also the consequence of a profound cleavage within the labor movement. The deterioration of the unitary bargaining practices and of the relations with public power was influenced by external (political) factors but found specific ground in the interaction between the different components of the labor movement, in their different social composition, and ideological traditions. These differences, influential since 1944, barely "covered" the common commitment to economic reconstruction and national solidarity sanctioned in the Pact of Rome. For these reasons the contradictory trends emerging before 1948 in the institutional and economic scenario cannot be underestimated.

Along this line one must explain why a major role in this cleavage and then in the breaking down of CGIL was played by the Catholic component, which had developed a coherent design of labor relations, and which could count on a solid social background supported by a tradition of relatively autonomous organized action and by the strong political and institutional reference of the CD and their governments. A much weaker and more hesitant initiative was taken by the other non-Communist components of the CGIL, of social democratic tradition. The weakness in their social and political background contrasted with an ideally key position which they shared with other European social-democratic labor movements and was not to be balanced by American support and by the initial preference showed in their respect by most American influences[32].

The complexity of factors accounting for the break-down of the CGIL in 1948 continued to operate afterwards. This suggests that while the "event" in itself was probably "inevitable" the evolution of labor relations was open to different alternatives. Indeed the immediate aftermath of 1948 seems to contradict this "openness." The prevailing scene indicates bitter global antagonism between the Communists and the "breakaway" Catholic and social-democratic components. Diffidence and divisions also existed, which foreclosed the formation of a "unitary democratic confederation" in spite of the pressures coming from the international political and union actors, the rapid fall in unionization and in industrial conflict as a combined result of anti-union action by employers, persisting high unemployment and drastic industrial reconversion.

The CISL was originally concentrated in some protected sector of the public service and/or "white" area of the country, which was enough to guarantee a necessary period of "incubation" but for several years not enough to challenge the CGIL on the core industrial sectors. Neither was the CISL component within the Christian Democratic Party influential enough for some years to reverse the prevailing political orientation which kept the economic and social scenario — to say the least — unfavorable to union growth and participation.

In this respect the structural conditions were to remain adverse to the emergence of any alternative to the prevailing pattern of weak, and ideological labor relations dominated by the Communists: namely the alternative of a "democratic" unionism which could challenge the Communist predominance on the ground of strong militant collective bargaining practices and effective participation in an expansionary economy[33]. The search in that direction, already present in the immediate postwar period, in the non-communist components of CGIL, was accelerated particularly by CISL; UIL was more pragmatically oriented[34]. This search resulted in a consistent model of labor relations not only as an alternative to the Communist one, but largely innovative with respect to the Italian tradition.

The CISL eliminated from its conception of unionism all elements of confessionalism present in the social Catholic tradition, which were in harmony with the conservative agrarian bloc represented in the Catholic movement but incompatible with the industrialization and modernization of Italy, which were the objectives of the new leadership of the CD, which the CISL shared and wanted to influence. The CISL envisaged a type of unionism politically "moderate" and integrated in the existing order but quite ambitious in its economic and social programs, both in the bargaining relations with the employers and vis-a-vis the economic government of the country[35].

These ambitions were clearly expressed in the various themes of the program elaborated with a considerable degree of sophistication in a relatively short period of time. It provides for promotion and articulation of collective bargaining at various levels, including a marked decentralization of plant level wage bargaining linked to productivity; contractual association instead of institutional partici-

pation directed to influence enterprise decision-making and productivity sharing; contractual participation in economic planning
and even in capital accumulation. At the center of this program
was a conception of union activity and organization which emphasized volunteerism and associative action to an extent quite alien to
Italian tradition. The proposed model of labor relations drew
many suggestions from the American liberal tradition and from the
practices of industrial unionism more than from sheer "trade
unionism," to the point of being labelled as a sort of
"neoinstitutionalism." These elements were originally combined
with others drawn and originally adopted from the social-democratic tradition of the European labor movement, particularly with
respect to the role of labor vis-a-vis the state and society.

During the same period the CGIL was occupied in the difficult
tasks of resistance and adaptation of its strategy which in the process of time opened a profound revision of its model and practice
of unionism[36].

Already in 1949 the Piano del Lavoro represented an attempt to
break CGIL isolation in the labor movement by opposing a positive
economic proposal to those elaborated by CISL and by the government. In the congress of the same year the top leaders of the
Confederation — the Communist Lama and the Socialist Santi —
clearly denounced the excessive centralization of the Confederation and the practice of political co-optation of CGIL leaders as
the two weakest points of the postwar experience: an early denun-
ciation which produced effects only in 1956 following CISL proposals and initiatives for decentralized bargaining. A parallel revision began in bargaining policies directed to elaborating new
approaches capable of competing with CISL proposals particularly
in the industrial areas of the North. These efforts indicated a
growing autonomy of the Communist component in the shaping of
its policies. This relative autonomy would put the CGIL in the
forefront not only of the collaboration efforts with future governments, but also in the "revisionism" and in the "westernization" of
Italian Communism.

The Socialist components of the CGIL, even though deprived of
a real initiative within the Confederation, contributed to this autonomous research to keep alive the aspiration of the CGIL for
unitary action[37]. The effects of this internal elaboration both in

the CISL and in the CGIL were limited in the early 1950's not only by the narrow margins allowed to union action by the prevailing economic and political climate, but also by the links of the two Confederations with the major political parties.

The theory of "cinghia di trasmissione" (conveyor belt) was denounced by Di Vittorio in 1949 precisely to exorcise a dependence on the Communist Party which was to remain for quite a few years the dominant reality for the daily life of the Confederation. The ambition of the CISL programs and the frequently asserted value of union autonomy could not cancel the fact that the Confederation was part of the Christian Democratic world: what has been called the "double soul" of the CISL[38]. Most of CISL proposals depended essentially on the Christian Democratic initiative and could not become "realistic" without a new pro-labor politics implemented at the governmental level: which the CISL championed from the beginning.

The illusion that progressive labor relations could develop spontaneously by way of economic growth[39] was shared not only by the CISL; but not to the point of cancelling the conscience of the strict correlation between union action, state policies and political action. This search for new strategies confirms that already in the early 1950's the Italian labor movement was reacting to the "shock" of 1947-48, and looking for a positive role in the second phase of the reconstruction which it had supported since the beginning. This reaction was to appear "voluntaristic" for quite some time in the light of the structural constraints; but when these were "softened," the Italian labor movement was prepared to use the elements of instability and the potentials existing in the labor relations system to experiment. In fact some of the first signs of a new social and economic climate came from the labor front; beginning with the experimentation of innovative decentralized collective bargaining at plant level unitarily supported by renewed unions presence and promoted through the reaffirmed role of public enterprises. These experiments proved to be solidly based in theory and practice and spurred a development of Italian labor relations, revealing a degree of effectiveness and maturity quite unique in the tradition of Latin countries.

Notes

1   Among the general analyses of Italian labor in the reconstruction, see: B. Beccalli, "La ricostruzione del sindacalismo italiano, 1943-50", in S. J. Woolf, (a cura di), *Italia 1943-50. La ricostruzione*, Bari, 1974, p. 330 ff.; the essays of B. Bezza, L. Pennacchi, E. Soave, A. Pepe, B. De Cesaris, in Accornero (a cura di), *Problemi del movimento sindacale in Italia 1943-73*, Annali Feltrinelli, Milano, 1976; S. Zaninelli, "Politica e organizzazione sindacale dal 1943 al 1948," in S. Zaninelli (a cura di), *Il sindacato nuovo*, Milano, 1981, p. 281; P. Craveri, *Sindacato e istituzioni nel dopoguerra*, Bologna, 1977; L. Lanzardo, *Classe operaia e partito comunista alla FIAT, 1945-48*, Torino, 1971; P. Rugafiori, F. Levi, S. Vento, *Il triangolo industriale fra ricostruzione e lotta di classe 1945-48*, Milano, 1975; V. Foa, *Sindacato e lotte operaie 1943-73*, Torino, 1975; A. Pepe, "La CGIL dalla ricostruzione all scissione", in *Storia contemporanea*, 1974, p. 635 ff.; S. Turone, *Storia del sindacato in Italia 1943-1969*, Bari, 1973; W. Tobagi, "Il sindacato nella ricostruzione 1949-50", *Il Mulino*, 236, nov.-dic. 1974, p. 944 ff.

2   See the essays by B. Beccalli and B. Bezza, quoted; and also C. De Marco, "La costituzione della confederazione generale del lavoro e la scissione di Montesanto 1943-44", in *Giovane critica*, 1971, 27, p. 52 ff.; D. Horowitz, *Storia del movimento sindacale in Italia*, Bologna, 1966.

3   See P. Roncato, in *Prospettiva Sindacale*, 1971, n. 6, p. 25 ff., and U. Romagnoli, T. Treu, *I sindacati in Italia dal 1945 a oggi: storia di una strategia*, 2a. ed., Bologna, 1981, p. 13.

4   As late as 1951 only 2 million workers were employed in large industrial firms out of 6 millions in the industrial sector, a minority of the working class; the large majority was active in agriculture until the mid 1950's: see P. Sylos Labini, "Sviluppo economico e classi sociali in Italia", in P. Farneti (a cura di), *Il sistema politico italiano*, Bologna, 1973.

5   B. Beccalli, "La ricostruzione etc.", p. 337 ff. P. Craveri, *Sindacato e istituzioni*, p. 52 ff. U. Romagnoli, T. Treu, *I sindacati in Italia* etc., p. 10 ff.

6   P. Merli Brandini, "Evoluzione del sistema contrattuale italiano del dopoguerra", in *Economia e Lavoro*, marzo-aprile 1967, p. 71.

7   See P. Craveri, *Sindacati e istituzioni*, p. 212 ff.

8   These elements of maturity and self-restraint are almost obsessively repeated in those years by the top leaders of the CP and CGIL — Togliatti and Di Vittorio. Furthermore the contribution to economic restoration and to produc-

tion was felt as a necessary fulfillment of the antifascist Resistance process and of democratic reconstruction. V. Foa, "La ricostruzione capitalistica del secondo dopoguerra", *Riv. Storia Contemporanea*, 1973, p. 445 ff.

9   See A. Accornero, *Gli anni '50 in fabbrica*, Bari, 1973, p. 13 ff.

10 See B. Beccalli, "La ricostruzione, etc", quoted, p. 324 e 351 ff.

11 In the immediate postwar the membership and mass presence of CGIL were more considerable than the objective labor market conditions would suggest. Even though the organization remained rather loose, in early 1947 CGIL membership was estimated around 6 million.

12 See P. Craveri, *Sindacati e istituzioni*, ch. I and III.

13 Balladore Pallieri, *La costituzione italiana nel decorso quinquennio*, Foro Pad. 1954, p. 31.

14 The active state intervention in this area is confirmed also by the budget distribution: in 1947-48 out of 1,694 billion, expenses for public order amounted to 103 billion and defense to 349. A. Pedone, "Il bilancio dello stato e lo sviluppo economico 1961-63", in *Roma Economia*, marzo-aprile 1967.

15 See for details P. Craveri, *Sindacati e istituzioni*, p. 209 ff. and T. Treu, "I governi centristi e la regolamentazione dell'attività sindacale", in A. Accornero, *Problemi del movimento sindacale*, quoted, p. 553 ff.

16 Research on this is quite extensive, see: P. Craveri, *Sindacati e istituzioni*, quoted, ch. II. L. Lanzardo, *Classe operaia*, quoted, and the documents in Confindustria, *I consigli di gestione*, Roma, 1948.

17 This has been considered "possibly the most serious limit of the left's politics during the Resistance", see Quazza, "Storia del fascismo e storia d'Italia", in AA.VV., *Fascismo e società italiana*, Torino, 1973, p. 37 ff.

18 U. Romagnoli and T. Treu, *I sindacati in Italia*, quoted, p. 16 and V. Foa, "La crisi della Resistenza prima della liberazione", in *Il Ponte*, nov.-dic. 1947, p. 982 ff.

19 See the remarks of L. Pennacchi, in A. Accornero, *Problemi* etc. p. 257.

20 See in particular the positions and contribution of G. Dossetti.

21 See M. De Cecco, "La politica economica durante la ricostruzione 1945-51", in Woolf, *Italia 1943-1950, etc*. For a less negative evaluation in this respect, G. Maione, *Tecnocrati e mercanti*, Milano, 1986; B. Bottiglieri, *La politica economica dell'Italia centrista*, Milano, 1984; on the American attitudes in this respect see J. Harper, *L'America e la ricostruzione dell'Italia*, Bologna, 1987; F. Romero, *Gli Stati Uniti e il sindacalismo europeo*, Ediz. Lavoro, Roma, 1989, chs. VI-VII.

22 V. Foa, "La ricostruzione capitalistica etc.", p. 453.

23 P. Craveri, *Sindacato e istituzioni*, quoted p. 209.

24 See G. Amendola in *Politica ed economia*, marzo-aprile 1962, p. 59 and the well known report by V. Foa, B. Trentin, "La CGIL di fronte alle trasformazioni tecnologiche", in *Lavoratori e sindacati di fronte alle trasformazioni del processo produttivo*, a cura di F. Momigliano, 1962, I, p. 161 ff.

25 V. Onida, *La costituzione nella storia della Repubblica in Italia 1945-1975*, Milano, 1975, p. 381, notices that the constitutional pact mainly resulted from the contribution of two sectors of political forces, marxists and social left of the Christian Democracy who appeared as losers in the immediately subsequent events.

26 On the constitutional framework of labor relations, see in general the already mentioned works by P. Craveri, U. Romagnoli, T. Treu, as well as F. Mancini, *Il lavoro nella costituzione in Italia 1945-75*, Milano, 1976, p. 490 ff.

27 See A. Pizzorno, "I sindacati nel sistema politico italiano: aspetti storici", in *Rivista Trimestrale Diritto Pubblico* 1971, p. 1510 ff. These characteristic features of Italian unionism have been considered necessary consequences of the economic underdevelopment of the country by the first American commentators: M. Neufeld, *Italy: School for Awakening Countries*, Ithaca, 1962.

28 See B. Beccalli, "La ricostruzione etc." p. 387 and P. Craveri, *Sindacati e istituzioni*, quoted.

29 F. Romero, *Gli Stati Uniti e il sindacalismo europeo*, p. 243.

30 See in particular F. Romero, *Gli Stati Uniti e il sindacalismo europeo*, chs. IV and VI.

31 P. Craveri, *Sindacato e istituzioni*, p. 237.

32 F. Romero, *Gli Stati Uniti e il sindacalismo europeo*, quoted.

33 As openly advocated by American union leaders like W. Reuther, see F. Romero, *Gli Stati Uniti*, etc. p. 297 ff.

34 P. Craveri, *Sindacato e istituzioni*, p. 295 ff.

35 The labor conception of CISL and its role have been extensively analyzed, which confirms the key role attributed to this Confederation in the postwar period. See in general T. Treu, "La CISL degli anni 50 e le ideologie giuridiche dominanti", in *Dottrine giuridiche e ideologie sindacali*, G. Tarello, ed, Bologna, 1973, III/2, p. 246 ff.; Ciafaloni, "Ideologie e prospettive del sindacalismo cattolico", *Quaderni Piacentini*, Marzo 1972, n. 46, p. 63; G. P. Cella, B. Manghi, P. Piva, *Un sindacato italiano negli anni settanta*, Bari, 1972; V. Saba, *Giulio Pastore. Sindacalista*, Roma, 1983 and several essays in *Analisi della CISL*, vol. I, G. Baglioni ed., Edizioni Lavoro, Roma, 1982.

36   In addition to the essays quoted in A. Accornero, "Problemi del movimento sindacale", quoted, see M. Ricciardi, "Appunti per una ricerca sulla politica della CGIL: gli anni 50", in G. Tarello, ed., *Dottrine giuridiche*, etc., p. 210 ff.; G. P. Cella, B. Manghi, *La concezione sindacale della CGIL: un sindacato per la classe*, Roma, 1969.

37   P. Craveri, *Sindacato e istituzioni*, quoted, p. 290.

38   P. Craveri, *Sindacato e istituzioni*, quoted, p. 308 referring precisely to the connections with the Christian Democratic Party and to the search for autonomy.

39   This illusion was widely shared during the 1950's and 1960's in the Labor movement in countries of the West and supported also by well known sociological and labor relations theories.

XVII

Commentary on Tiziano Treu's "Organized Labor in the Postwar Reconstruction"

Professor Treu's paper is a very effective, synthetic treatment of the subject. Unfortunately — for the sake of excitement — I find that I agree with most of what he says. Fortunately, his paper easily lends itself to use as a kind of vehicle for a brief discussion of several of the classic, general historiographical questions that go beyond the issue of labor *per se*, but that ought to be mentioned on a retrospective occasion such as this.

The first is the famous question of "la continuità dello stato", the continuity of the state. Treu says: "The continuity of public institutions with those of the past regimes in spite of the innovative drive of the liberation movement has been widely demonstrated." It is not at all surprising that much of the old regime survived. Italy, unlike Germany, had no "zero hour," when the clock of history stopped. The long term pattern of historical change in Italy is not one of sharp breaks with the past, but of layer built upon layer, of the new grafted upon the old, in short, of a hybrid structure. Sometimes the results are rather grotesque, as with the survival of the codice Rocco in the postwar liberal system. In other cases the results are rather ingenious, as with the survival of the Fascist state industrial sector in the open postwar economy. In general, historians have perhaps tended to underplay the novelty of the new system and of the accomplishments of the period 1944-1947, including the Constitution and its provisions on labor mentioned in Treu's paper. (By the way, the accomplishments of the period 1944-1947 were due to a kind of *consociativismo*, even if *consociativismo* has become one of the worst sins that anyone can be accused of in Italy today.) At the same time historians have perhaps tended too readily to assume that everything and everybody who survived from the old regime was bad. This is obviously nonsense if one thinks of IRI and AGIP (later ENI) and of the precious experience in running a modern mixed economy acquired during the 1930s by people like Oscar Sinigaglia, Pasquale Saraceno, Domenico Menichella and others who became so important after 1945. This is a tradition that degenerated in the sixties and seventies; it is also the tradition that produced Romano Prodi in the eighties. If you ask yourself what Italian figure of the last decade has accomplished the most against the highest odds, the answer can only be Prodi.

A second general question raised by Treu concerns the economic strategy of the reconstruction period, 1944-1955. Lurking in Treu's paper is the suggestion that a different set of economic policies — different, that is from the generally liberal (*liberista*) line of Corbino, Einaudi, and for that matter, Togliatti — more consistent with the interests of the working class, might have been adopted. Anyone who studies this period inevitably comes to grips with the issue of alternatives, of whether the period really did represent an "occasione mancata," a lost opportunity for addressing some of Italy's basic economic and social problems. Perhaps Treu's paper might have been more daring in tackling this question. For example, could Keynesian-type policies have provided for a more balanced, less wasteful and painful (in terms of unemployment) economic recovery? Personally I agree with Saraceno who in his lucid and rather poignant *Intervista sulla ricostruzione*[1] concluded that Keynesian policies were irrelevant and even dangerous, and that there was no choice but the Einaudi line by 1947. This is not to say that specific interventionist policies might not have worked in, say, 1945-1946. The currency conversion is one example. The problem was that the big parties including the PCI rejected economic reforms of this kind. As Andreotti recounts, Togliatti reached for his newspaper when Scoccimarro rose to discuss economic and financial issues like the *cambio della moneta*. His priorities were political — cultivating Catholics and the middle classes — and institutional — writing the new rules of the game — not economic, and the left paid a price for this after 1947.

The third general question raised in the paper is related to the other two: the question of how much autonomy the local actors enjoyed in order to shape the destiny of the new Italy. What was the role of political pressure, and in a more subtle way of the power of example, emanating from the United States? Here Treu and I agree with Federico Romero (*Gli Stati Uniti e il sindacalismo europeo*[2]) that while the Americans set the basic parameters to which everyone had to adapt, they were not very successful in actively intervening to shape parties and institutions in their own image. Thus, as Romero says, the split up of the CGIL has much more to do with Italian history than it does with the history of Italian-American relations. This was the same conclusion I came to several years ago in studying the US intervention in the Italian political economy in a more general sense and I would consider myself part of a recent trend in the historiography which has tended to stress, in contrast to earlier accounts, the latitude which the local forces enjoyed (including the latitude to do things they did not do) with respect to the US, and the skill with which they transformed the precariousness of their position into diplomatic strength. Treu's paper might have taken up the point — for which Romero was criticized in a very singular "afterward" attached to his own book — about the limited impact of the American model of apolitical collective bargaining. Certainly Romero's argument is questionable in the case of the CISL. On the other hand the CISL's real bargaining power emerged after the renewal of collaboration with the CGIL, something not foreseen by the CISL's American friends.

In any event, we should be grateful to Treu for a paper that covers the labor question with great thoroughness while stimulating us to think about more general issues: the continuity of the state, alternative economic strategies and the autonomy of the local forces.

Notes

1   P. Saraceno, *Intervista sulla ricostruzione*, Bari, Laterza 1977.

2   F. Romero, *Gli Stati Uniti e il Sindacalismo europeo*, Roma, Edizioni Lavoro 1989.

XVIII

The Impact of Women's Political and Social Activity in Postwar Italy

Paola Gaiotti de Biase

A feminine reading of the social and political processes that characterized postwar Italy automatically calls into play a number of factors relative to its social, cultural and religious history. A single report cannot deal exhaustively with all these areas. In fact, much remains to be clarified by historical women's studies, which, apart from a few isolated attempts in the sixties, have only really taken-off over the past ten years. Therefore, I'd like to concentrate on three issues, or rather three hypotheses, deliberately colored by a feminist 'bias,' considering the persistent lack of attention on the part of official Italian historiography.

The first issue deals with the social and cultural context surrounding women's access to the vote and to political citizenship. The second issue defines the ways in which women's franchise has affected the political balance of the Republic. The third, which cannot be fully developed given the time-frame of this conference, introduces some preliminary reflections on how women's active participation has affected the development of Italian society. This outline, which reflects some of the findings arrived at through extensive research, allows us to examine three distinct chronological phases: the first phase involves the months following liberation, the second deals with the earliest decisive election results in 1946 and 1948; and finally, the fifties which marked the beginning of true dynamic change.

The three hypotheses can be summarized as follows. First, the social and cultural context surrounding the January 1945 decree which sanctioned women's right to vote was characterized by a sense of necessity, a democratic obviousness. It exemplifies a cultural phenomenon typical of the times, which we have defined as "the myth of the easy conciliation between the traditional role of women and their new social duty." This presumed irrelevance has had a long lasting effect; not even the swing in electoral preference on the part of women since the seventies and the decisive influence they have had on the crucial issues which have swayed traditional political stability has brought about any visible, significant awareness.

Second: despite its limited scope, women's suffrage proved a determining factor in supporting the winning side and in defining the general character of Italian democracy as mass democracy as opposed to one of an elitist or jacobin nature. It is an established fact that the parties which played a key role in the history of the Republic, i.e. the Christian Democrats and the Communists, were those a) which opted for mass democracy, b) were alone in courting women's votes, c) relied on women's organizations within the party, as well as encouraging widespread involvement of women and, in the initial phases, even their candidacy.

Third: the dynamism of Italian society cannot be examined without taking into account its growing feminization and the phenomena which characterize it. In terms of civic awareness, we must not overlook the political commitment common to both Catholic and Left wing women's organizations and their struggle to obtain civil rights such as access to the professions, job legislation and full acknowledgement of the female role. Economically, the importance of the family business highlights the development of the role of women in the business world and the highly 'feminine' slant of "Made in Italy" manufacturing.

The Context of Women's Franchise

In Italy, on January 31st 1945, a presidential decree sanctioned women's access to full political rights.[1] The official reports of the two meetings of the Cabinet Council relative to the approval of the decree reveal that the matter aroused no significant debate. The few objections made were, on the whole, random and vague.[2] The date was determined by the urgent convocation of the National Council at which the absence of female nomination could have established a precedent.[3]

The "obvious" character of this achievement is also undoubtedly related to two previous attempts: a parliamentary vote in 1919,[4] which came to nothing due to the premature dissolution of the Chamber of Deputies and in 1925, during the Fascist regime, when some partial concessions were made, a Pyrrhic Victory, some were to call it.[5] But it is worth bearing in mind that the issue of women's franchise was far more intriguing than it would appear from the accounts of Italian historians.[6] In 1912 universal suffrage was granted to men but not women. This marked a serious defeat for women, and proved to have a disruptive effect on all women's movements.

The 1945 decree, without the backing of a political debate to give it meaning,[7] and dictated also by the necessity to conform to a consolidated European model,[8] was greeted by the press with neither reservations nor dissent,[9] the comments, save few exceptions[10] were rhetorical, belittling and condescending.

What were the reasons for this atmosphere, which though not uniquely Italian, revealed Italian characteristics? For women, the Fascist era represented a time of maximum regression both from an operative and a legal standpoint. However, despite the intentions of the regime, women's material position was being profoundly modified, in keeping with the trend of all industrialized societies, by the steady growth of the consumer market and the widening of social relations. In spite of Fascist polemics and restrictions, women's schooling increased; in spite of the regime's hostility, there was widespread acceptance of the growing number of women who joined the work force.[11] A large percentage of women worked in the field of education, in the face of explicit Fascist legislative opposition. However, unlike the women teachers at the beginning of the century who were highly motivated and intensely involved in the innovations of the times, those who joined the profession during the Fascist era seemed to have been prompted more by a desire for status and security typical of the petit bourgeois (which in itself was nevertheless an innovation).

Women's social condition was affected by increasing urbanization and the growing popularity of the radio and the cinema. Another factor was the relatively new issue of leisure time, the political repercussions of which the regime tried to keep in check,[12] to little effect however, where women were concerned.

Undoubtedly, the degree to which women were emerging was much greater with respect to 1922, not only in 1945, following the tragic experience of the war, but as early as 1940.

The passive nature of the feminization process was reinforced by what appears to have been the most significant anti-female characteristic of Fascist culture, and one which continued to exert a powerful influence in the early years of the Republic as well: by capitalizing on the frustration and weariness of the feminist movement which had achieved so little over so many long years of struggle, the Fascist culture was able to virtually cancel it from collective memory. In fact, what is most striking to historians is this very loss of historical memory regarding Italian feminism which has permeated debates within women's movements since 1944. One repeatedly encounters the statement that "feminism is not an Italian phenomenon." In a recent reconstruction of the history of the UDI (Italian Union of Women), we read that in early postwar years" . . . any reference to the history of the emancipation of Italian women is missing, there is no trace of any link with the issues raised at the beginning of the century, there is no echo whatsoever of the dramatic rifts which had undermined and weakened the various trends of Italian feminism."[13] This loss of memory, together with the failure to measure up to any of the social or political commitments which represent the fulfillment of feminist awareness, also exerted, as we will see, an extremely negative influence on the most important innovation of the Fascist era, the birth of a mass Catholic women's movement.

The Resistance Movement obliged all the political forces to take a critical stance with regard to Fascist anti-feminist culture. But all over the world, in the post-World War II period, the cultural trend was entirely family-oriented, as can be seen in the American sociological changes of the thirties and forties,[14] the changes in Russian family policy [15] and the French demographic and avant garde spiritual considerations.[16] Scientific studies carried out at the height of the war produced data which substantiated the indispensability of the mother in the formation of the child's personality.[17] This was quite a contrast to the period following World War I, which, even in terms of their image (cropped hair and short skirts) seemed to signify the freeing of women from the shackles of traditional sexual stereotypes.

However, we believe that this concern with a family-oriented society in the forties was in no sense reactionary, but was based on much deeper truths. It was very different from the crude, contradictory Fascist idea of the family[18] which preached both traditional values and adventure and subordinated the family to power politics. The worldwide 'civil' concept of the family confirmed the spontaneous and very real sense of family which had been felt throughout the war, the Resistance and the post-war reconstruction period. Social solidarity became an extension of family solidarity[19] and, while the reunited family and the newly reconstructed home were symbols of peace, any signs of breaches of conduct — "segnorine" and "sciuscià" (women in brothels and children put out onto the streets to work) — were seen in a negative light.

The very similar opinions on the matter expressed by Pope Pius XII, or Ferruccio Parri or Rita Montagnana are due to this common denominator rather than to strictly political reasons.[20] Umberto Calosso, a brilliant socialist, was perhaps the only exception. He paid dearly, however, and was in fact ostracized for constantly referring to the Scandinavian model of family relationships and for introducing issues such as divorce and free love into the political debate.

The intertwining of this growing feminization of society and its apparently painless, 'unthinking' nature conspired to give the impression of a nation of tranquil, reconciled women, untroubled by any rash or uncurbable wants or needs. It is this overall picture which shows how Italian society viewed the expansion of the electoral body as a purely quantitative phenomenon, without taking into account either the civil planning problems implicit in the inclusion of women in the modern system of civil liberties, or the qualitative problems relative to the political outcome of women's suffrage, with those exceptions which we shall be examining.

But the historical context surrounding women's franchise is not characterized solely by a state of passive continuity. Women brought to the reconstruction phase a complex set of experiences, an unprecedented degree of awareness of their responsibilities, a sense of complicity among themselves, all of which, openly or tacitly, called for solidarity.[21] The most obvious example of women's new found initiative was their presence in the Resistance. The interest centered on this participation has consisted both in acclaim and in the compiling of statistics (how many women were killed, how many received military honors, etc).[22] Meanwhile, critical research into its real significance is still being conducted in an almost clandestine fashion. How did the direct and indirect anti-fascist partisan experience serve as a model for the feminist elite?[23] What aspirations did it inspire? What disappointments did it bring about?[24]

The debate surrounding the more or less 'feminist' nature of women's role in the Resistance risks becoming nominalistic. On one hand, women's participation has been colored by the previously mentioned loss of historical memory and by the cultural context of the time, but what emerges quite clearly is their strong urge to take a leading role, to assume direct historical responsibilities and to live beyond the confines of domestic duty, even when the family remained a point of reference. Their experience in the Resistance affected women in many other ways: the influence of physical courage and mental endurance on character, the need to make often crucial decisions alone, the development of skills in unfamiliar fields, a growing sense of solidarity and a more active participation in collective class awareness and finally, a new way of experiencing Christian spirituality. All these are frequently recurring elements in the new self-awareness of the protagonists themselves.[25]

But in evaluating these effects on Italian society we shouldn't underestimate the new distances which separated the two parts of the country. While southern Italian soldiers (the men!) had substantial involvement due to their presence in the north on September 8th, 1943, southern women were completely left out of this experience.

Prior to becoming directly involved with the Resistance, women were active in mass Catholic organizations such as Gioventù Femminile (a branch of Azione Cattolica) which, particularly after the twenties, had spread even to the remotest outskirts. This fact is noteworthy both because women's involvement in the Resistance often sprang from their participation in the activities of the parish and other Catholic organizations which in turn had prepared women for assuming a wider range of responsibilities. Guided by Armida Barelli's lucid intuitions regarding the impact of the masses on history, the GF set up a network of solid, powerful parishes sensitive to matters of collective psychology, to extending the parochial network, and to establishing strong collective behavior within a very solid and powerful organizational framework.[26]

The first official Catholic women's organization Unione Donne, was formed in 1909, and as a reaction to the cautious accusations of modernism previously aimed at Catholic feminists, it took an explicitly anti-feminist stance. They were unable, however, to ignore the problems and transitions inherent in the ever-growing awareness of themselves as women.[27] The Gioventù Femminile (GF), which was formed in 1919 and developed during the early Fascist years, paid the price for its lack of involvement in the political and unionist front, apparently denying the problems modern women were facing and moving ahead in spite of them.[28] It is not, however, sufficient to see it from this perspective in order to understand what the GF meant for women.[29]

However, in retrospect, in contrast to the seemingly submissive position of women with regard to the Church, the GF was a hotbed of lay activity working within a contradictory framework: on one hand, the emphasis laid on the mystical and supernatural and the diffidence felt towards critical modern rationalist thought,[30] and on the other, the newfound efficiency at an organizational and economic level. In fact, in several parts of the country, in the south and in Sicily, the GF brought about a decided break with the traditional concept of women as being invisible. During the Fascist era, the GF was instrumental in helping women loosen the restrictions of home and Church, offering them the possibility of assuming a more active, responsible involvement in society. Conceptually associated with a conventional feminine model, they were able to bridge the gap between tradition and innovation, most effectively in the area of new job opportunities for women. Furthermore, these groups introduced a note of cultural solidarity between women from the north and women from the south, and laid the foundations for a possible homogeneity of customs through active interpersonal relations (in contrast to the standardization offered by the mass media and consumerism). In fact, participation in group activities provided women from the south with virtually the only opportunities for travel.[31]

The historical significance of Catholic women's movements with regard to women's entry into the political arena is twofold: on one hand they contributed to the approval of the suffrage for women by the more traditional factions, including Pope Pius XII himself, as a God-sent and controllable phenomenon: they also facilitated the acceptance of mass women's movements, including left-wing organizations. However, the most profound long term effect was on the cultural and spiritual evolution of Catholic organizations, as a result of the accretion of democratic processes which climaxed in 1948. We believe that it was through this accretion that the Catholic women's movements, which had a strong working class element, gained access to a new, democratic culture and to women's rights, thereby redeeming itself from its previous lack of assertiveness.[32] It would otherwise be inexplicable that such significant number of women within AC supported De Gasperi against the "Operazione Sturzo" in 1951.[33]

In considering the overall picture, it would be a mistake to get bogged-down in the question: was women's right to vote a victory or a concession? Formally speaking, the decree has all the characteristics of a concession,[34] but one which was the result of a chain of events. Its value is not diminished by a certain unconsidered inevitability; in fact it gains in strength by being part of a series of undeniable, compelling historical necessities.

The historiographic debate about the post war period has substantially ignored the effects of women's franchise, and continues to be tendentiously "sexist." We should at this point take a closer look at it. In fact the issue of the restoration must take into account the new dynamism introduced by women's franchise into Italian society, above and beyond its political structure; women's participation represents the biggest innovation in terms of entry of the masses into history; and it emphasizes the central role of the parties as mediators of the consensus.[35]

Women's franchise was a key element in the political upheaval of the period between 1945 and 1948, both for its electoral effects and especially for the profound influence it had on shaping the Republican experience. As we have already pointed out, women's franchise paved the way for a new democracy based on mass consensus as opposed to Jacobin democracy. The political choice was formally made later, during the Parri administration crisis and the choice of the referendum. However, the January 1945 decree, signed by De Gasperi and Togliatti and approved by a government which did not include the Socialist party and the 'Partito d'Azione,' summarizes (perhaps unwittingly) the intended character of the new state as representative of the real country rather than the monopoly of an enlightened minority, of a social vanguard.

"Thus, the parties who are fully aware of the importance of women's franchise and, consequently, the importance of the masses within the political framework of our country are the ones destined to play a more incisive role. The consensus of women and leadership in the country have become congruent."[36]

Three strategies were aimed at keeping women's franchise under control and giving it political direction.

Togliatti, who stood to lose most by the concession of women's franchise, was in fact the one to make the first move in an attempt to turn it to his own advantage, or at least to attenuate the possible damage. He had already shown keen interest in women's issues since his arrival in Salerno.[37] Women's franchise, which penalized the PCI, might objectively have weakened the political front for gaining power through consensus, at least in the eyes of the most impatient factions of the party. Togliatti, in his determination, succeeded in circumventing any such consequence.[38] His speech, in June 1945,[39] was the first addressed to women. He praised the progressive drive for change and transformation that women's franchise[40] brought to socialist ideals at grassroots level. The link that Togliatti established between citizenship and emancipation led to the relinquishing of "a concept of passivity in the face of authority", to the establishment of a new ruling class, and to overcoming the backwardness which characterized economic and civic dealings in the country at the time.[41]

The Communist Party's open acknowledgement of the challenge presented by women's franchise triggered off a concentrated effort in terms of image, political culture and organization which was to have its culmination in women's candidacy.[42]

The second strategy was that adopted by Pope Pius XII. Women's franchise severely frowned upon by his predecessor, Pius X, had become the subject of one of the major controversies among Catholic women at the beginning of the century; it symbolized the kind of relationship that existed between religious conscience and the modern world.[43] During the post World War II period, the Catholic movement came out in favor, in spite of all the traditional reservations,[44] and sided openly with the Partito Popolare. But the negative influence of 20 years of Fascism (as we have already mentioned) took its toll and Armida Barelli who, in 1920 had been in favor of votes for women, in 1945 felt it her duty to express her doubts to the Pope.[45]

Pius XII accepted the challenge boldly and, in fact, in his pontifical plan to win the masses back to the Church through democracy,[46] women's franchise was seen as leverage, an historical and providential help. So the new social duty was proposed to women as a religious mission, in line with the reconfirmed maternal role, as a defense of the family, as a struggle against any change in the traditional idea of women, even with a strong feeling of personal female dignity.

In this way the confident unreserved acceptance of democracy by the Holy See during the final years of the war can be most closely linked to the renewed confirmation of the supremacy of the Roman "Magistero." In fact the speech[47] addressed by the Pope in November 1945 to the women of the Catholic Center of Italian women (CIF) was perhaps the most severe in his judgement of the modern world, the world of capitalism, socialism and individualism, from which women were to be saved and from which, in turn, they were to save humanity.

The third strategy was that of De Gasperi, who was in favor of women's franchise and appeared to be favored by it; nevertheless he feared the consequences (and he was not the only one of his party to do so[48]), particularly the pressures which might have been exercised by a clerical right-wing, which would have found a secular outlet in Azione Cattolica. In his speech to the women of his party[49] his objective was to introduce the lay, autonomous awareness of political reality into the feminine religious conscience. He emphasized the importance of political organization, of freedom, of tolerance, of conciliation and respect for the outsider. He warned them against the deviations of civic and spiritual non-committal, the risks inherent in the reawakening of nationalism. Politics was presented to women as "the third phase" which followed the phase of social organization and the ethical-religious phase; it was the conquest of citizenship together with the acknowledgement of the value of civil rights in modern times. In this framework, however, De Gasperi made no reference to any specifically feminine issues beyond the usual rhetorical concessions.

In retrospect those strategies, however positive they were, now appear too closely related to the pursuit of consensus.

Togliatti channelled the newly awakened strength of the women's movement into a political front in Stalinist terms: although this measure didn't stunt the dynamism of the women, it did however limit the possibility of communication and inhibited its liberating function.

Pope Pius XII harnessed the novelty of women's franchise within a technical and instrumental conception of democracy. He proposed a model for reconciling the old with the new,[50] that didn't threaten the modern conception but in fact assumed a defensive stance with respect to it, thereby leaving women defenseless with respect to consumerism which was just around the corner. This is the most important element to keep in mind when looking at the reasons for the Church's final move in guiding the secularization process.

De Gasperi's influence on Christian Democratic women's political commitment was such that progress in women's issues was very slow, uncertain and difficult, the global vision of politics invariably taking precedence. However at different times history rewarded such initiatives. For example, that of Pope Pius XII, by instantly guaranteeing a strong Catholic presence in the country; that of De Gasperi by the ever-growing democratic conversion of the aforementioned women's groups; much later that of Togliatti when in the seventies the first real, as yet unresolved, shock to the Republican political balance was felt as a consequence of the women's cultural evolution.

It is an acknowledged fact in Socialist circles that . . . "the Socialist party failed to deal with women's issues in as committed and innovative a way as Togliatti did in 1945."[51] There is, however, no evidence of any link between this shortcoming and the vicissitudes of leftwing leadership. Socialist political strategies took different tacks: *L'Avanti*, the official socialist newspaper called upon women to become active in the party, but made no mention of franchise; the PSIUP campaign strategies were directed at creating "a Socialist Republic made up of factory workers, farmers, technicians, office workers and their superiors, of culture and of science"

... "bearing no relation to the old parliamentary democracy."[52] In this strongly class-oriented proposal, women aren't interesting.

There were undoubtedly differences of opinion and reservations among the Socialists, the Liberals[53] and members of the Partito d'Azione, but, as they were never publicly expressed, they are difficult for the historian to trace. It would be extremely interesting, from a historiographic point of view, to study the relationship between the rapid crumbling of hopes aroused by the Partito d'Azione, the political and electoral weakness of Italian liberal culture, and the way in which these groups underestimated or were indifferent[54] to women's entry into the political system.

The political debate, which should have taken place at the time of the decree, finally occurred within and around the Consulta Nazionale, which was to decide on making voting mandatory for all citizens, thus involving women's entry into the electoral body.[55] The legislative conclusion reached was a balance between reminding people of their civic responsibilities and a confirmation of citizenship as a political duty[56] rather than a right. It is within this context that Italy developed its extremely effective voting tradition. The percentage of voters increased dramatically; strict measures were taken against abstentionism; the electoral machine was very efficient (ample time to vote, polling stations conveniently distributed, well-run services).

The way in which these strategies concretely engaged women's consensus was by means of separate women's organizations within the parties[57] and formally autonomous mass organizations which in fact acted as support groups. Togliatti's approach, based on Lenin's line of thinking as the latter outlined it in an interview with Clara Zetkin, and on the experiences of the French Popular Front[58] led to the birth of "Unione Donne Italiane." At the same time, on the Catholic side, a federation of Catholic women organization, called the "Centro Italiano Femminile", was created. It was promoted by mons. Giovanni Battista Montini, Maria Rimoldi, Vittorino Veronese.[59]

The birth of these women's organizations was seen as a dramatic post-Resistance break with the past, "the first stage of a party split," when it ought to have been viewed as the inevitable setting for the practical expression of mass consensus.

Women's organizations in the immediate postwar period were seen mostly in terms of their limitations. Their weakness lay in their obvious dependence on the PCI and the Church initially, then later, on the PCI and the DC. Although this was true, we must bear in mind the overall phenomenon of the role that the political parties played in the formation of the new state and a democratic society. The direction and the new trends of the central parties tended to favor rather than limit women's desire for a more prominent position in society. Although there were attempts to keep this in check and to use women's voting power to serve their own ends, the central parties did help women to overcome many of the obstacles still firmly rooted in traditional beliefs. Later on, both the UDI and the CIF movements were to experience many limitations to their autonomy, but at this initial stage, there appeared to be no real conflict between party strategy and the spontaneity of women's organizations; in fact the parties stimulated and promoted this very spontaneity. The same situation was true of women's organizations within the parties.[60] "It is conceivable that it was precisely the fact of belonging to a separate organization that allowed Communist women, more than Socialist women, to assume rapidly a position of supremacy within the movement. Socialist women, generally speaking, opted for working in politics like the men and with the men of their party and considered their role as feminists as a secondary activity; this probably prevented them from playing a more incisive role in the movement and favored an elitist attitude among them."[61]

Italian electoral sociology consolidated from its origins, the thesis of the determining role of women's franchise in 1946, and even more significantly, in 1948.

As Mauro Dogan expressed it: " . . . without the presence of women, the PCI and the PSI would have been the major political forces in Italy."[62] He links the backwardness of the electoral body to political results: "Women voters included a large percentage of elderly widows and single women who were the least politically informed citizens and more susceptible to being used and influenced."

The tendency to equate women's franchise with political backwardness has remained a constant element.[63] Not even considering the risks of Stalinism in the 40's and 50's were women given credit for their contribution to maintaining democracy. Backwardness or not,[64] women's franchise can only be analyzed from the point of view of women's mobilization, their explicit and visible motivations, bearing in mind of course that, by doing so, one is examining a more active elite of women, those who were emerging as new leaders.

The mobilization of women's electoral forces was characterized predominantly by a strong sense of the existentialist value of the first vote. By all accounts, oral and written, it was a highly intense, emotional time. All things considered, it really is amazing how well-organized and widespread the propaganda network was, reaching every condominium and affecting every neighborhood. The effects of women's franchise go far beyond mere percentages of consensus of women; they modified the climate of mobilization, the means used to spread women's propaganda and the directions taken by the electoral organization.

One is aware of a significant dichotomy between the ways in which men and women approach politics. Women tended to favor pragmatic involvement in the day to day issues of life. We have already noted elsewhere[65] the various institutions set up by women's organizations in aid, for example, of veterans, of the homeless, and of orphaned children, all of which were a direct continuation of their support activities during the Resistance. Of their more active female comrades, the Communists would ask: "Are you a political leader or a 'Dama di San Vincenzo?'" (Lady bountiful)[66]. There is little doubt that women saw their participation in these institutions as a political commitment and, without falling into petty partiality, it seems pointless to attempt to determine the degree to which women spontaneously followed their own paths of political expression.

In Emilia and in Toscana, which were the areas where the PCI succeeded in overcoming the prevailing negative attitudes, the role of women's franchise — along with other general political elements[67], became a determining one. Women's mobilization was very strong, and here too, the candidacy of women increased substantially at the administrative level, for the Constituent Assembly and then for the first legislature.

Among Catholics, particularly among the more activist groups, women's franchise was highly motivated and widespread, thanks to the Pope's positive influence. The leaders of the Church were well aware of the contradictions that existed between the traditional ways and the new responsibilities that women were facing. In fact, a careful reading of newspaper files of that period shows how the Church set about emphasizing the importance of sacrifice and courage as components of women's new role, thus keeping it in line with the more traditional role of the past. In spite of this, the younger generation of Catholic women were strongly affected by the new experience. In 1946, the more active Catholic women were those more culturally open, who had political contacts through anti-Fascist and Resistance activities. In 1948, the political commitment was even more widespread, directly involving the Parishes, directly aimed at safeguarding the Church and with a strong anti-Communist feeling. The percentage of abstentionism at the polls was greatly reduced; assistance was provided for sick, elderly or invalid voters. As for preferences in the referendum, we can assume that the women of Azione Cattolica kept to the general position taken by the large majority of the ecclesiastical hierarchy[68] which in formal terms was meant to be neutral, but which was in fact Monarchical. Nevertheless, some areas particularly in the north, were strongly committed in favor of the Republic. To date, the relationship between women's vote and the Monarchical vote has yet to be analyzed. The only exception are a few pages by Maria Macciocchi,[69] in which she pokes fun at the situation in Naples, and the notes, referring the absence of a "feminist" republican platform.[70]

The Constitution represented the link between the innovations outlined in the January 1945 decree and the subsequent evolution of the condition of women in Italy.

The 21 women elected, 9 each for the DC and the PCI, one socialist, one rightwing, confirm the theory we have proposed.[71] The proposals made by feminine organizations, both Catholic and leftist, were very similar, except for differences in emphasis regarding family; Catholic women's proposals have been more progressive with reference to the family than those of other Catholic groups.[72]

Women's juridical equality in the Italian Constitution is sanctioned in the following articles: 29 (equality between spouses); 37 (equal rights and equal pay for working women); 51 (equal right to hold public office and be elected to power in full equality). These articles are based on the fundamental principles of equality of the Constitution, which represent the Italian equivalent of the Bill of Rights: art. 3 ("equality without any distinction of sex. . . . "); art. 2 ("the inalienable duties of social solidarity," and a reference to "social reality within which the personality develops.") Such a conception of human rights represents an even greater potential guarantee for women than an individualistic conception of rights.

By guaranteeing full access to citizenship to one and all, the Constitution was projecting toward the future, rather than reflecting contemporary attitudes. One of the reasons for this was the presence of women in the Assembly and their unity of purpose.[73] Another reason has to do with the nature of the political forces: whatever the individual cultural background of the constituents, whatever the undercurrents of deep rooted prejudice may have been, what counted was that, having publicly supported women's franchise, the major parties could not openly oppose the egalitarian principle regarding citizenship.

Is there or is there not a connection between the political reasoning behind the major parties' support — albeit reluctant and belittling — of women's franchise, and the "solidarismo" present in the Constitution? This link is obviously less plain than that with the legal guarantees now assured to women; but would the political balance in the Assembly have been such as to produce the same results without women's vote? There seems no doubt that the social contract which binds the Italian people shows the first flickerings of the presence of female negotiators.

A feminist historical review of the 1950's has recently discredited, on the basis of women's experiences, the theory, prevalent in the leftist historiography of the 70's, which presented the 50's as "an almost total halt in the processes of cultural renewal and social modernization." "The 1950's represented the first transition into concrete terms of a way of life that was being slowly but surely assimilated by the country's various vital centers ever since the end of the war." According to this thesis, several typical aspects of the changes that occurred twenty years later, "such as the growth of anti-authoritarian feeling, changes in the relations between the sexes, consumerism, the rupture of cultural transmission by way of accredited institutional hierarchies, cannot be explained if we do not place them at their proper point of origin, in that farther off decade, and if we do not trace their first manifestations hitherto unexplored."[74]

Although the processes of this period were not so overwhelmingly spectacular as those of the 1970's, they still represented strong changes in mores.[75]

According to the convincing analysis of Simonetta Piccone Stella, the change consisted primarily in an effort to reconcile the model of the "emancipated" woman — professionally active, sure of herself, ignoring and overcoming her traditional weaknesses — and the traditional figure of the woman as faithful to her proper duties. "The image of the emancipated woman had to include that of the traditional woman as well in harmonious balance." From texts of that epoch Piccone Stella reminds us of the image that the emancipated woman projected of herself by repeating such phrases as "nobody stood in my way" or "it wasn't at all difficult."[76] This is what I called at the time "the myth of easy reconciliation of the new and the traditional female roles."[77] "In the dialogue between emancipated women and those women who wanted to achieve emancipation there was no room for the fears, needs and desires connected with their bodies and their sexuality" . . . "The dragons of emancipation hid from themselves and others their being different by bearing its entire weight and not calling on men to pay the price even of the practical aspects of life. They turned themselves inside-out so that their emancipation would not upset the 'privacy' of their family life."[78]

The rejection of certain rites, certain types of consumption along with the acceptance of others, the use of a new freedom of choice (connected to work and professional activity, but also to the passion for political and civil issues and for travel) were innovations "that necessarily brought with them transgressions of the inculcated female role." Such a break with tradition did not occur in the male world. All of this, furthermore, often took place within the ambit of an emotional relationship and was almost always a question that regarded the couple rather than the woman alone. In effect, the young women of the upper-middle class, who were those most involved in this process of modified behavior, were involved more on generational grounds than on account of their being women. But the novelty lies in this very fact: for the first time women were participating in the adventures, the places, the activities of that generation which was confronting history. The growth of female scholarship, no longer running along separate lines, proved in the end to be the determining factor for future developments.[79]

Although in practice sexual mores were constantly changing, they were not as yet being radically challenged.[80] But the rituals that expressed and marked the passage of a woman from one age and from one "civil status" to another, such as certain ways of behaving, of dressing, and of occupying one's time, were quickly disappearing. A woman's body and her way of showing it acquired an entirely new dimension which was also favored by the photographs circulated by the media and by that mirror of life which is the cinema.[81] What the new publicized and mythicized professions for women (airline hostesses, fashion models, radio and TV announcers, beauticians), had in common was their visibility.

The change of models was not a phenomenon of the upper classes: this was the period marked by the flight of young women from the countryside in search of a city marriage or an independent income. This in turn led to the propagation of women doing piecework out of their own homes.[82] The number of working women was in constant growth and underwent a qualitative change: especially in the South, there was a supply of women workers wherever opportunities opened up. But above and beyond the explicit phenomena of "modernization" that can be documented, and the phenomena connected to political and social mobilization of which we will speak later, the dynamics of the rural world and of the life of the people in general, the life of women, must be investigated while keeping in mind Amalia Signorelli's above-mentioned criticism of the superficial equation "rural women-backwardness."[83] The desire to be a protagonist, to make decisions and to count for something which had characterized the immediate post-war period, persisted even though it expressed itself in other environments and in more private forms. In short, even if still unconsciously, women were beginning to express their desires and were becoming aware of having entered the libertarian system.

The signals indicating the change of models were certainly still uncertain and ambiguous, but the many surveys carried out at the time, with their complicated results, highlight prominently the variously experienced ambivalence and dilemmas, the restlessness and the changing points of reference rather than the solid certainties of the past.[84] The fact is that women's issues were beginning to get lots of press coverage, even if often it was simply for the sake of color and continued to present classical stereotypes even when a vague attempt was made to bring them up to date.[85]

In this context of cultural transformation, the censure on the Roman Catholic concept of women, disseminated by Catholic organizations, as "a sort of national female ideology destined to dominate from the end of the war until the 1960's" appears limited and misleading.[86] All evolution was also taking place within this concept with the growth of its transgressional aspects as opposed to socially consolidated stereotypes and their internal variables. And that too was indicative of the dynamic quality of the cultural models of the period. Recently more emphasis has been put, for the second half of the 1950's, on the crisis surrounding an "education based on models," one of the pillarstones of the G.F.'s educational projects. "Initially timid, there was an even more explicit affirmation of the importance of work in the development of the female personality, the right of young women to choose their work freely and autonomously on the basis of their interests and aptitudes, the definition of work as a vocation. All these elements contributed to the transition from an education based on models to an education which promoted autonomy, and the development of the personality not without misgivings and precautions on the part of leaders and above all the clergy."[87] Although still elitist, an important influence for the change in educational points of reference was exerted in the Roman Catholic world by the increasing influence of French spirituality that had a radical foothold in the Girl Scout movement along with the spirituality of the "route." The intense relationship with French Catholicism also favored a new conception of the couple and the first steps towards a culture of sexuality with the "Family Spirituality Groups."[88]

The basic historiographic question nevertheless remains to pinpoint the degree to which such dynamics were the passive and involuntary fruit of material changes still generally referred to as consumerism, and to what degree they were tied to cultural factors and to the mobilization of conscience due to the introduction of freedom.

The changes in consumerism dated, as we know, from the second half of the 1950's. Nevertheless we should not forget that prior to the great process of urbanization and industrialization at the turn of the decade,[89] the world of working class housewife sparked changes which apparently minimal, were in fact epoch-making. The availability of liquid gas, synthetic fibers, detergents[90] changed women's relationship with fire and dirt and opened up the previously unimaginable prospects for the reduction of work; the rapid spread of Lambretta and Vespa motorscooters also involved girls and popularized a highly unconventional image[91] that modified women's spatial relationship with the outer world. The further spread of the radio, even before television, the cinema habit, the end of isolation by the building of roads and the telephone, the improvement in sewage and plumbing services — all these processes familiarized women with the idea of improvement and the value of innovation. These first changes already brought about a break in the subservience to tradition and to the authority of the older generation. This had been a common fact for the young generation of males for over a century, but it represented an explosive new factor in the world of women,

The changes in consumerism and the material evolution of the country, would not have had the same development without the participation of the women's organizations, in spite of the contradictions and difficulties with which they were beset. The way in which they rooted themselves in the country's history can also be seen in their activities during the 1950's.[92]

After 1948 women's organizations were involved in political confrontations and they aligned themselves with the prominent political positions in the context of which most head-on clashes occurred. There was a strongly felt concept of UDI as "a trade mark designed to feminize the directives and undertakings of leftist party echelons." UDI's powerful commitment to the peace movement, and its activities in the battles on women's issues (from the laws regarding working mothers to the union battles of women sharecroppers, rice-pickers, against the lay off of workers) were rather "useful to the main objective: to direct women towards the leftist opposition."[93]

There was a growing refusal among Roman Catholic women to have any contact with women of the Left. This marked a decisive break from Resistance collaboration. Within the CIF, despite the organization's pushing for independence, there prevailed the ambitions of the women of AC not to lose ultimate control.[94] At the same time there was the risk that the central powers would use indirect methods and strawmen to gain their ends and would exert control through the administering of state funds for assistance.[95]

Nevertheless even then, women were forming ranks and taking a united stand along the battlefront. The laws to protect working mothers,[96] which put Italy in the forefront, is a continuation of the tendency to have women from both sides sign everything obtained through women's pressure groups, a tendency that began with the articles of the Constitution and lasted until the introduction of divorce. As has already been mentioned with reference to the Sturzo operation, Roman Catholic women closed ranks against any blocking moves made by the Right,[97] a result that would appear improbable on the basis of any flat analysis of the cultural origins of those organizations. In a word women contributed directly to keeping democracy alive along the historical lines that the Resistance and the Constitution had opened up.

But it was during that very period of hard-line "centrismo" that a maturing process began among the various female sectors and an important debate, even if shaped by ideologies, took off on the prospects opening up for women. Within the logical bounds of a "conveyor belt" concept of political deployment, the work of social assistance influenced the political idea of social services on the Left and so did the analysis of the need for solidarity among women and for cultural promotion among Roman Catholic women.[98] ACLI women and women unionists,[99] but above all UDI women were competitively involved in social struggles that "would see to it that even the most hidden aspects of female subordination would enter the collective conscience, centering around a few emblematic figures: the women rice-pickers, olive harvesters, sharecroppers and farm hands of the South."[100]

Before 1954 the reopening of a theoretical debate on the women's question in its own terms had become explicit and also went together with the rebirth of the National Council of Women in 1954.[101] At this time the main issue was that of women and work poised between ideological[102] and concrete questions. If the former often appeared as burning issues on the level of political confrontation, the latter were what strongly influenced the female conscience, customs, and through these Italian society's readiness for reform.[103] Urgent questions such as prohibiting the lay off of women when they got married,[104] granting women the access to the administration of justice,[105] establishing a female police force,[106] the abolition of the brothels, equal pay for equal work — were posed in the 1950's partially as a result of the long debate imposed by a backward political culture. They gained force from the essential consensus of women's groups and triggered a round of criticism of traditions and stereotypes that went beyond the aims of legislation in a strict sense and prepared the way for the equal rights' legislation of the 1950's and 1970's. From this point of view the latter two topics deserve a closer scrutiny.

The bill for the abolition of the brothels[107] had already been proposed by Angela Merlin in 1948 in tandem with the similar French proposal of Martha Richard. According to some, the long debate that it aroused "did not bear the mark of women; it did not appear as an exposé of male chauvinism" and it too is marked by the loss of memory of the historic battles waged by Italian feminism. When the bill was finally approved in 1958, it would appear to have resulted more from the need to conform to legislation and international conventions than from the women's struggle.[108] Such an interpretation seems distinctly pessimistic. Perhaps the world of women moved with a certain initial slowness in support of this proposal which, on the Left, reflected the diverging relevance that Communists and Socialists gave to sexual questions, and in the center, the reticence of Catholic groups. Neither was it a subject that could arouse the mass demonstrations that were typical of the mobilized Left-wing women. But women kept the debate going uninterruptedly,[109] and women found themselves to be the interlocutors between those women "directly involved" and the law and they helped them to confront the practical problems that subsequently arose. Above all they utilized, within the terms of the culture of that time, all the stimuli that they could to overcome the hypocrisies of the traditional double moral standard.

The question of equal pay came up in the second half of the 1950's in connection with the general problems of putting the Constitution into effect and in retaliation to commitments made on the international and European level; but even more so, thanks to the distinct evolution of the issue of women's work on both the concrete[110] and theoretical levels. The Italian unions claimed the right to manage directly such questions with the inter-confederational agreement,[111] but it still left room for pressure from women. With regard to equal pay the women's groups totally closed ranks. Nevertheless it was precisely on this issue that the anti-Communist prejudices of the Christian Democrats had a detrimental effect and allowed the Communists effective hegemony over the entire range of feminist groups. The National Council of Italian Women participated once again in the Italian debate over distinctly emancipatory prospects through and during an important conference where the Communists were represented in force by highly qualified delegates, and the Christian Democrats for that reason were absent.[112] The question of work and its central position in the emancipatory design eventually formed the terrain for left-wing hegemony.

A hegemony of this kind lent strength to women within the Communist Party as well. The Kruschev report, the Hungarian events, the beginnings of the center-left which created new problems for the co-existence of Socialists within the UDI, sparked courageous and critical reflection regarding the limits of the mass experience of women and their meager political autonomy.[113] In the years following the VIII Congress of the PCI Communist women were to work-out a relationship between the politics of emancipation and "the Italian road to socialism" that constituted one of the most original attempts at a synthesis between reform and revolution. If history writing were more attentive to the debates which went on within the women's movements, it would have documented long ago how they had anticipated the evolution of the Communist ideology and policies.[114]

Two aspects marked these legislative results: on the one hand, their slowness; but also the fact that when they were accepted they appeared to be practically ripe, uncontested and aroused no significant opposition or political reservations. But were these not perhaps the very characteristics of the longest revolution, destined to harvest visible successes when these were already consolidated in the common way of feeling and behaving? These are the reasons why one cannot speak of the 1950's as a "passive" interval. The 1950's are revealed as a period of slow incubation and transformation that wasn't simply materialistic, economic and consumeristic.

Italian society in the 1950's was still not a dynamic society and the dynamic quality of women was not yet visible. And yet even on the level of economic evolution women were already preparing for a leading role.

One of the most controversial issues of the period was the enormous development of piece-work done at home by women in the most varied fields of production. The Left saw this as yet another twofold form of exploitation: "evil" capitalism could profit both from the backwardness of the system and the increased earnings while avoiding social security payments; traditionalism kept women locked up at home, bound by the chains of servitude and a double workload. In the critical approach there prevailed "an ideological element — the factory as the focal point for the formation of class conscience and organization."[115] Decentralization of production appeared all the more negative when it happens in the long-established industrial areas such as the North. Just as weak is the cursory defense of those who saw there a form of conciliation among the various tasks of women — a conviction which was tempting to many Catholics and the subject of much controversy on the part of Catholic women. Today, however, it is not difficult to perceive in this widely diffused phenomenon a choice on the part of women, an attempt to make the inevitable changes in the organization of labor meet their needs and to put their mark on it.[116] During the 1950's piece work at home certainly bore all the signs of women's weakness, thus the necessary steps taken in order to set limits and promote legislative controls in order to reduce the problems it caused, were more than justified.[117] The result was a stronger sense of self, the further stimulation of initiative and the formation of women's cooperatives. But it also foresaw that need for self-determination in one's own work that, however ambiguous, marks the change in the culture of labor in the 1970's and 1980's.

The question that it posed, however, and that still remains unanswered, is the question of the role it played in the later development of a typical form of the Italian economy, the family business. All it takes is a quick look at the geographic areas (from Prato to

Emilia to the Veneto, the Marche, Apulia and Lombardy) and at the productive sectors (from knitted goods to clothing to small mechanical products and leather hides) where there is the greatest development, and we can see the connection which is confirmed by specific research such as that into the pressed-wood industry at Carpi.[118] But there has still not been sufficient emphasis put on the emergence of women entrepreneurs from the experience of free-lance piece work done in the home, along with direct relations to the market and the system of technological and productive conveniences.

Writing about the origins of entrepreneurial family strategies in Italy, one of the most acute observers of this phenomenon, Giuseppe De Rita, has discovered "three founts of strong entrepreneurial initiatives with strong family connotations: workers aiming at setting up on their own . . . artisans trying to enlarge the market for their technical and creative capacities . . . sharecropper families aiming at transposing to industry . . . that natural way of arriving at the division of labor that they had gathered from their experience in agricultural work." In his recent analysis, Giuseppe De Rita[119] never considers it necessary to mention women as protagonists in the strategies for utilizing resources, organizational adaptations and the explosion of economic vitality that marked the Italian family in the 1970's and 1980's (even though he cites as relevant the intermediate phases of work done at home). On the contrary, he actually sees the head of the family's firmly anchored "position of hegemony for the entire management of business affairs" as one of the "historical" reasons for the positive outcome of such a strategy that nevertheless produced "degrees of freedom supplementary to the choices of its own components, reducing the bonds of necessity."

Vice-versa, on the basis of the extensive knowledge already acquired as well as new research, it should not be hard to confirm the key role played by women, even when tacit, discrete, unpublicized, in the transition from the diffusion of the underground economy to the development of family businesses.[120]

To this we must add that the relationship of women to the growth of consumerism was not simply passive but was also able to influence tastes and trends, and reward innovations and originality so that the Italian woman consumer too, and not only the leading figures of the fashion and design industries, played a part in the creation of the "made in Italy" label that changed the image of our country abroad.

There is no question that the process of feminization made its mark on the society of the 1950's even before the explosion of the economic boom itself and beyond the controversial forms it took. The existence of strong collective aggregates, which promoted innovative ethical responsibilities with respect to the traditional roles, the central role assumed by the increased level of education among women (even with all its ambiguities), favored a transformation that cannot be reduced to fit within the schemes of a passive revolution. Material changes certainly played a central role here, at times supportive and at other times in opposition to conscious leadership on the part of women. However they did not represent the only dynamic factor involved.

The absence of women in political institutions was in drastic contrast to their growing presence in society. From the first to the third legislatures there was a constant drop in the number of women in Parliament — from 45 to 33 to 25 in the Chamber, from 4 to 1 to 3 in the Senate — whereas the number of seats increased as a result of population growth.[121] Was this a sign of women's reduced political tension after the innovation of 1945? This however favored the persistent lack of attention of the part of men, and the perennial assumption that the questions posed by transformation on a practical level were irrelevant and marginal. There was a double paradox here that cannot be overlooked: a country that after forty years of Christian Democratic political guidance was among the most backward for planning and activating policies for the family and for maternity assistance; a country marked by strong ideological presences and in which, vice versa, legislation in support of equal rights for women was entirely placed within a framework of a modernizing (and as such certainly worthwhile) pragmatic adjustment to the processes of transformation taking place.

In fact women's problems exemplify the contradiction between the maturing of Italian society (and within it women's experience) and the foot-dragging of political society and its limited representativeness. This is an expression of what is true about the "continuity" of the Italian political system. The historical function of the political parties in furthering democracy and the new state (also with regard to women) has been contradicted and blocked by the self-renewal of the political élites and the intertwining of local oligarchies and the central power. This too has kept women out and pushed aside their political demands. There has been a price to pay for this, and, absurdly, it has been higher in recent years: it has been the exasperation of ideological battles on the objectively disquieting and discriminatory issues relating to women, which has used them in a distorted way. Undoubtedly questions such as divorce and abortion, introduced into the Italian debate with the pressure from women, have played a determining part in upsetting the political picture, in slowing down the processes of renewal within the Christian Democratic Party, in the pragmatic and power drift of the system of political alliances. But they played this role all the more because they were used as weapons for political retaliation and employed within a male tradition of political action that categorized women as a marginal force, as a pressure group rather than as a governing force that included the new political emergencies, among which were the problems of maternity.

The fact is that there still have been no answers or resolutions to the epoch-making political provocation implied by women's entering in the system of freedom and political sovereignty and the way they have modified its coordinates and its sense. But this is not exclusively an Italian problem.

Notes

1 See my *La donna nella vita sociale e politica della Repubblica 1945-48*. In *Donne e Resistenza in Emilia-Romagna* Milan 1978, and *Questione femminile e femminismo nella vita della Repubblica*, Brescia 1979.

2 A report of the meeting of the Council of Ministers in G. Spataro's *I democratici cristiani dalla democrazia alla Repubblica*, Milan 1968, page 357. According to Spataro, the only minister expressing any uncertainty regarding his party's position was the Liberal Brosio who, however, took a more positive view the following day. He also mentions Togliatti's peculiar reaction which could be interpreted as a hope for further opposition to the vote (though this is firmly denied in other accounts of the meeting), which would have allowed the PCI to keep the flags of democracy flying without any immediate electoral costs to them. There was most certainly opposition within the PCI as was shown by the line of defense to the decision taken by the party's leader. There were, however, no significant political repercussions.

3 In fact, fourteen partisan women were nominated: Ada Marchesini Gobetti (Piero Gobetti's widow); Gisella Floreanini, who was a Communist and had been a minister in the Repubblica dell'Ossola; Marisa Musu, a Roman of the Left wing Christian movement; Laura Bianchini, a Christian Democrat from Brescia who had been head of FUCI; Communist women who had shared the experience of political exile such as Teresa Noce and Adele Bei who spent many terrible years in Fascist prisons; others such as Angelina Guidi Cingolani who picked up the threads of pre-Fascist women's union and political involvement. The nominations were made in March of the same year 1945.

4 The Chamber of Deputies had approved the law on women's suffrage on September 6th, 1919, but as the Senate failed to approve it before the end of their legislature, it all came to nothing.

5 This is the expression used by Maria Rimoldi at the time *a propos* of the approval of the Acerbo Law in 1925, which granted women the administrative vote, but, obviously, with no concrete effects during the Fascist regime; see Franca Pieroni Bertolotti's *Femminismo e Partiti Politici in Italia 1919 - 1926*, Rome 1978.

6 Between 1862 and 1888 (when Crispi's opposition put an end to a long series of unsuccessful attempts) the Chamber of Deputies was challenged on various occasions by legislative proposals put forward by the Ministers for the Interior themselves. In the unified State, in fact, the presentation of the issue of women's suffrage was not the romantic or subversive whim of some Radical deputy; it was supported, albeit in a purely administrative context, by

some of the most prominent names in our political history. Nevertheless, it failed. The first bill for women's suffrage was presented with amazing promptness by Benedetto Cairoli in February 1861, the day after the Kingdom of Italy was proclaimed. In 1863, in light of provincial and municipal elections, Peruzzi, the Minister for the Interior, introduced women's suffrage in the Cabinet. Of course, the women in question only included taxpayers and single women who were of age. The bill was turned down. More bills were introduced: by Lanza in 1864, by Peruzzi in 1865, again by Lanza in 1871 and by Nicotera in 1876. Then, with the swing to the left, things began to look more hopeful. In 1880, another Minister for the Interior, Depretis, introduced the administrative vote for women who were of age and paid at least 5 lire in taxes annually. The parliamentary committee responded with a flat "no." In 1881, the Cabinet discussed a law granting all citizens of age, men and women, the right to vote. Again, it was turned down. Depretis introduced another bill in 1882 and again in 1886 which failed owing to the opposition of Crispi. A. M. Galoppini, *Il lungo viaggio verso la parità. I diritti politici e civili delle donne dall'Unità ad oggi.* Bologna, 1986.

7   A pro-women's suffrage committee was constituted in an effort to persuade the Bonomi government to recognize women's right to vote in view of the approaching 1945 administrative elections. The committee had a multi-party base; members belonging to women's movements from all the parties in the CLN, the Pro-Women's Suffrage Association and FILDIS. M. Michetti, M. Repetto, L. Viviani, *UDI Laboratorio di Politica delle Donne,* Rome 1984. The committee did not encounter any particular difficulties, nor did it give rise to any significant debate. "An appeal to the women of occupied Italy" was broadcasted by the Committee on Radio Roma, on January 15th, 1945.

8   In the thirties women gained the right to vote in Ecuador, Mongolia, Brazil, Republican Spain, Chile, India, The Philippines and the Dominican Republic; in 1944 it was granted in France and in 1945 in Guatemala and Liberia.

9   From a survey of the daily newspapers on January 31st and February 1st, emerges the fact that, although all the papers carried headlines regarding the "hush-up" of votes for women, the actual column space dedicated to the issue is minimal compared to the rest of the news. The comments made are either banal or astounding. According to Panfilo Gentile, one of the most competent journalists of the time, it would " . . . not change the situation because women will vote like their men. Women have no interest in politics because they have no place in public life; if they had, things would be different because it is in only two fields that women have an inbred lack of creativity: philosophy and music." According to the Socialist paper *L'Avanti*: "Awaken in every woman her sense of responsibility towards her country which is, after all, nothing more than a sense of responsibility towards her family. Do not take her away from her home which is her kingdom, but persuade her that in order to defend her home she must take part in the struggle for democracy and socialism." The Communist paper *L'Unità* said: " . . . a wave of healthy common sense will no doubt pervade both political and administrative life . . . a greater spirit of solidity and practicality . . . a more rigorous standard of economy and a greater sense of honesty."

10 One of the few exceptions that we know of was a survey conducted by a Bolognese veteran's paper *L'Italiano* which pointed out how much "has changed in the female world," "a change which strongly affects those who during the long lonely days (of the war) dedicated so many thoughts and so many dreams to women." It also posed the question: "Is it simply a momentary infatuation with feminism or is there really a sound basis behind the transformation of traditional customs? Do we in fact feel repulsed to find that the woman at our side, besides being a friend and spouse, is also our companion in political life and in the working environment?" The weekly opens the survey on the reaction to women's franchise with the provocative question: "Should the woman be the boss?" The answers from both men and women were numerous and varied and were summarized as follows: "As impartial observers we are in a position to inform that the great majority of those who completed our questionnaire was not in favor of women entering the political arena. They seemed agreeable to women being politically active in pre-electoral activities and services. For the most part a preference was expressed for the typically Italian woman born to tend the hearth and to be the mother and educator of her children, leaving the male to deal with all other worries and responsibilities . . ." (*L'Italiano* edited by the Veteran's Committee of the province of Bologna – F. Macolino. The first issue printed 7/10/1945).

11 For information on women's status during Fascism, see in Franca Pieroni Bortolotti's *Il movimento politico delle donne, scritti inediti*, edited by A. Buttafuoco, Utopia Rome 1987, her essay "Osservazioni sull'occupazione femminile durante il fascismo;" and Enzo Santarelli's "Il fascismo e le ideologie anti-femministe" in *"Problemi del socialismo,"* 4, 1976. Bortolotti's analyses of the statistics on female employment between 1921 and 1936 focus on the trends in various industrial sectors. It would seem that on the whole, while there was a steady decrease in the number of women working in agriculture, there was a substantial increase in those employed in industry; in spite of the drop in numbers after the expulsion of women from the industrial work force in the postwar period and during the 1931 crisis, the total was 1,377,373, almost what it was in 1911. The number of women in banking and business rose from 226,422, in 1921, to 448,535 in 1936 (from 20.6% of the work force to 28%); in private and public administration (excluding the defense department), the increase was from 13% to 25.3%. In the field of education the slight decrease due to the limits imposed by Fascist legislation (from 70.5% to 69%) was offset by an increase in private teaching between 1931 and 1936 (from 65% to 73%).

12 Victoria De Grazia, *Consenso e cultura di massa nell'Italia Fascista*, Laterza, Bari 1981, a well-documented analysis of Fascist policy regarding leisure time. The author looks at the contradictions between the reactionary effects of official policy and the efforts to establish a broad, popular base and at the superficial and, in the long run, fragile nature of the ideological consensus that was finally achieved. It is worth noting, however, that the number of people who listened to the radio, individually or collectively — while still far lower than in other countries — increased considerably at the encouragement of the regime: radio subscribers leapt from 27,000 in 1926 to one million in 1939.

More recently, at a conference in Milan on "Donna Lombarda," De Grazia, quoting from her new book, talked about the relationship between women and the Fascist regime, underlining the necessary distinction between the regime's authoritarianism, the objective trends of the economic market and the development of a welfare state along the following lines: while the 'Risorgimento' called for the "nationalization of men," the Fascist government demanded the "nationalization of women," but female citizenship was founded on their biological reproductive function and on their spiritual sense of sacrifice and self-denial. See Chiara Saraceno's brilliant "Percorsi di vita femminile nella classe operaia. Tra famiglia e lavoro durante il fascismo" in *"Memoria"* N. 2, 1981, for a description of the effects on the development of the identity of working class women.

13 See *UDI Laboratorio*, quote on page 13.

14 It would be superfluous to describe in detail the well-known evolution of American sociology. Talcott Parson consolidated the functionalist approach with his idea of a stable division of male and female roles overriding the radical, liberal feminine drive described, among others, by Mary McCarthy in *The Group*. The American occupation tried to influence Italian mores in his field as well: Edoardo Anton, who directed radio talks for the PWB controlled radio station, asked Anna Garofalo to host a 15-minute, three times weekly program during prime broadcasting time, dedicated entirely to women. He said: "The Americans give a lot of weight to radio programs for women — they feel that women — especially Italian women — should be addressed in such a way as to help them emerge from centuries of being ignored, of being in a position of servitude. As Allied troops moved from southern Italy towards Rome, they saw women treated with little more than the consideration shown to beasts of burden. They would like us to speak to these women — to tell them about all kinds of things, to make them aware that from now on, they too will be taken into account." Anna Garofalo has recompiled these radio programs for PWB in her book *L'Italiana in Italia*, Bari 1958.

15 Henry Chambre, *Le Marxisme en Union Sovietique*, Paris 1955; a similar interpretation was made by Italian Communists, though much later, in Lacuna Castellina, "L'esperienza sovietica" in *Famiglia e società nell'analisi marxista*, Rome 1964.

16 See S. De Lestapis, "Evolution de la pensée exprimée par l'Église Catholique", in *Renouveau des idées sur la famille*, Paris 1954 (published by the Institut National des Études Demographiques, one of the leading national authorities in the field), for an account of the evolution of the family, family spirituality and within that, a certain vision of women. For a closer look at Catholic spirituality, see Jean Lacroix, *Force et faiblesse de la famille*, Paris 1948, as well as the illuminating pages by E. Mounier in *Il manifesto al servizio del personalismo comunitario*, Bari 1975.

17 John Bowlby's set experiences with wartime child evacuation operations and institutions where eugenic experimentation aimed at creating a master race were carried out, led him to his claim regarding the irreplaceable role of the

mother which he set down in *Soins meternels et santé mentale*, Paris 1950, a
work which greatly influenced the stance the World Health Organization was
to take.

18 The contradiction has been aptly defined by Ernesto Galli della Loggia
    (*Ideologia, classi, costume* in *L'Italia contemporanea*, edited by Castronuovo,
    Torino 1976) as the strange coexistence of "adventure and reassuring nor-
    mality," "in a very painless and effortless conciliation between the old and the
    new;" and by Corrado Barberis: "a veneration of youth which disrupts the
    traditional elements and engenders the transformation of the urban family,"
    side by side with a Fascism which exerted its conservative influence in rural
    areas and reinforced the authority of the head of the family. C. Barberis, *La
    Società italiana*, Milan 1976, pages 56-77.

19 Arrigo Boldrini is particularly concerned with the fundamental role of the
    farming family in the Resistance movement in the Emilia region. He exam-
    ines the patriarchal structure of that society as well as the character of the
    antifascist "azdor." The strategic importance of the family in that particular
    part of the country was linked to the decision to extend the Resistance into
    the plains of Emilia Romagna, a costly move in terms of human life (*L'Emilia
    Romagna nella guerra di liberazione*, Bari 1975); for a closer look at the rela-
    tionship between familial solidarity and the Resistance from a feminine point
    of view, see *La Resistenza taciuta; dodici vite di partigiane piemontesi*, edited
    by A. M. Bruzzone and R. Farina, Milan 1976.

20 In 1945, the daily *L'Unità* published an electoral propaganda pamphlet in
    which Rita Montagnana defended the PCI from the accusation of
    "divorzismo" (supporting divorce), and reminded the reader . . . "the hun-
    dreds of thousands of women whose husbands have been away for so many
    years want nothing more than to rebuild their families, to live with their loved
    ones – divorce is the last thing they want." Rita Montagnana, one of the
    prominent women of the PCI, was at the time the wife of Palmiro Togliatti.

21 In the first of the series of her radio broadcasts (cfr note n. 14) Anna Garo-
    falo began by reading a letter written by the wife of a prisoner of war. "She
    has been waiting for him faithfully because she loves him, but now, as the
    moment of his return draws near, she is wondering what their future relation-
    ship will be like given her state of mind . . . she has learned that she is capable
    of doing most of the things that were once exclusively her husband's domain .
    . . she has realized that the sense of inferiority she had with regard to her hus-
    band, the unconditional admiration, were unfounded, just as were the
    authoritative and condescending attitudes he had towards her." As she her-
    self wrote: "I feel that from now on, after all the things I've seen and done, I
    will no longer be able to stand for such an attitude from my husband and that
    I will want to take my place at his side with a self-assuredness and an inde-
    pendence which I don't know how he will be able to bear." And as Valeria,
    one of the main characters in Alba De Cespedes' *Quaderno proibito* (Roma
    1952), says very succinctly: "During the war, some people understood a
    number of very important things, some did not." And for the effects of
    wartime experiences on women, see Miriam Mafai, *Pane Nero*, Rome 1985.

22 In 1976, (in *Resistenza e storia d'Italia*, Milan 1976), Guido Quazza stated
    that everything that had been said about women's role in the Resistance was
    still limited to a purely rhetorical commemoration: a historiography, mainly
    by women, begins to reveal the enormous degree to which women's participa-
    tion in the Resistance has been ignored. See in particular Franca Pieroni
    Bortolotti, *Le donne nella Resistenza antifascista e la questione femminile in
    Emilia Romagna 1943-1945, in Donne e Resistenza in Emilia Romagna*, Vol.
    II, Milan 1978 and, above all, M. Bruzzone and R. Farina, *La Resistenza taci-
    uta: dodici vite di partigiane piemontesi*, cit. Numerically speaking, it is inter-
    esting to consider the following statistics: there were 35,000 active, fighting
    partisan women, 1,600 were arrested and prosecuted, 623 either died in com-
    bat or were executed, and 2,750 were deported. An official publication (*La
    donna italiana dalla Resistenza ad oggi*, published in 1975 by the Consiglio dei
    Ministri) puts forward the hypothesis that women represented about 20% of
    those fighting. However, if we also take into consideration partisan support
    groups, and that each fighting partisan could count on (depending on the
    area) between three to ten women for help, the numbers increase dramati-
    cally.

23 Much has already been said (see P. Gaiotti, *La donna nella vita sociale e
    politica della Repubblica*) about the importance of the role of women who
    had experiences abroad as exiled Communists and intellectuals such as Maria
    Federici or Josette Lupinacci de Menasce.

24 Bruzzone and Farina recount an episode which has great symbolic value: on
    the occasion of Italy's liberation, a number of partisan commanders avoided
    having women marching in the formations so as to spare them lewd remarks
    and disrespectful comments; some of the women were grateful.

25 Ibid, p. 15ff.

26 Regarding the development of women's Catholic organizations and the rela-
    tive bibliography see under "Movimento Cattolico e questione femminile" by
    P. Gaiotti de Biase in the *Dizionario storico del Movimento Cattolico*, Vol. I,
    Book II, Marietti, Turin 1981; see also *Società, chiesa, e associazionismo fem-
    minile*, AVE, Rome 1988, by Cecilia Dau Novelli. In examining the spread of
    women's movements, it is interesting to note that whereas in 1920 "Gioventù
    Femminile" had 700 clubs with 50,000 members, by 1925 there were 15,800
    clubs with 333,000 members. The 1946 annals of "Azione Cattolica" show
    884,992 members of GF and 369,015 members of Unione Donne; figures
    peaked in 1956 with 1 million 265 thousand members of GF and 630,000
    members of Unione Donne.

27 Cecilia Dau has dealt in detail with the political and, for the most part, eman-
    cipatory commitment within the organization, especially among women from
    Piedmont. See also P. Gaiotti, *Le origini del Movimento femminile cattolico*,
    Brescia 1963.

28 According to Paola Di Cori ("Storia, sentimenti, solidarietà nelle organiz-
    zazioni femminili cattoliche dall'età giolittiana al Fascismo" in *Nuova Donna
    Woman Femme* N. 10/11 1979), and Michela di Giorgio ("Metodi e tempi di

una educazione sentimentale. La gioventù femminile cattolica negli anni venti", *ibid.*), the loss of historical memory can be directly attributed to Catholic women's organizations; more recent and detailed research by Annarita Buttafuoco, which expands on earlier findings by Franca Pieroni Bortolotti, highlights the fact that this cancellation of memory happened earlier and was linked to a general change of direction in the cultural climate, to a nationalistic swing and to the feeling of exhaustion among Italian feminists: "the definitive and radical break with culture and with the experiences of the past occurred, for women's political movements, during the period between the war in Lybia and the outbreak of WWI. I believe this to have been the time during which those profound transformations took place which caused them to become 'omnibus institutions' as Laura Casartelli Cabrini so bitterly describes them." A. Buttafuoco, *Cronache Femminili*, Department of Social, Historical and Philosophical Studies at the University of Siena, Cortona 1988, page 251.

29 Paola Di Cori and Michela De Giorgio, in the essays quoted (which examine the question from a purely feminist point of view) both acknowledge, though with different tones, the decisive role of such an experience. "The GF called on young women to leave home and to embrace the Christian evangelical effort; in a certain sense it proved to be a push in the direction of emancipation. During their training period, they learnt to speak in public; social gathering and pilgrimages had them travelling throughout Italy . . . the various Catholic institutions offered young, single women opportunities for socializing which were undoubtedly instrumental in providing them with a sense of social identity which the Fascist regime afforded only to mothers." Paola Di Cori, cit., p. 120. And according to Michela Di Giorgio: "The rules and the rituals of militancy — the club, the badge, the meetings, the seminars — which were all quite foreign to the usual forms of female co-existence — were so successful because they were innovative and, rather than being a means of instilling obedience, they became the setting for self-expression, a dynamic way of spending one's own time . . .", cit., p. 131.

30 But in his essay "Le organizzazioni di massa e l'Azione Cattolica", in *Cultura, politica, partiti e Costituente* edited by Ruffilli, Bologna 1979, Agostino Giovagnoli reports the comment made by a woman, a representative of the GF: "Professor Gedda has emphasized modern man's excessive emotionalism. Now, instead of working to correct this deformation of feeling, we, in our evangelical efforts, use and extol the very methods and techniques which provoke this emotionalism, running the risk even of augmenting it, and thereby creating an undesirable imbalance." (p. 37)

31 Some of the earliest references to experiences in the GF can be found in Maria Mariotti, "Armida Barelli e la GF in Calabria", AAVV, *L'opera di Armida Barelli*, AVE, Rome 1983.

32 It is this very lack of theoretical assertiveness which explains, for example, how one of the women who was most active in the struggle for women's franchise, Angela Cingolani, might have said in no uncertain terms that "the foundation of women's political right is her mission within the family" (in

Cecilia Dau Novelli, *Il movimento femminile della Democrazia cristiana* in *Storia della DC* edited by Francesco Malgeri, Vol. III, Roma 1988, p. 333).

33 See this text, note 97.

34 There is a sense of women's being 'granted' a right which is evident not only in men's unpleasant paternalistic attitudes, but also in the terms used by women: "recognition" for their merits, the commitment to making "good use" of their rights and "proving themselves" as they did during the war and during the Resistance. (M. Michetti, M. Repetto, L. Viviani, *UDI Laboratorio di politica delle donne*, Rome 1984.)

35 The most recent synthesis of the various stages of relative historiography in P. Scoppola, "*La nascita della repubblica nella storiografia*", in *La nascita della Repubblica. Atti del convegno di studi storici*, Quaderni di Vita Italiana, 3, 1987 which completely ignores any reference to women's entry into the political system. In fact: a) women's franchise strengthened the thesis of the choice of a democracy of consensus over Jacobin democracy. This became the key to a reading of the hegemony in Republican history. (Cf. P. Scoppola, *La proposta politica di De Gasperi*, Bologna, 1977); b) women's franchise supports the hypothesis, that Amendola was the first to consider, that the entry of the masses into history is a typical post-war phenomenon, and represents the biggest innovation in terms of democracy taking hold at the popular level (Amendola was the forerunner in "Dieci anni dopo," in *Rinascita*, 1955, followed by E. Ragionieri and C. Pinzani, *La storia politica e sociale*, in *La storia d'Italia*, vol. IV, Turin, 1976); c) the thesis of the Restoration, above and beyond its political elements, must take into account the new dynamisms introduced into Italian society and the phenomena surrounding women's active participation in political society. (For the thesis of the Restoration, see AAVV, *Dieci anni dopo. 1945-55*, Bari 1955; L. Valiani, *L'avvento di De Gasperi*, Turin 1949; d) women's franchise enriches the outlook on the central role of the parties as mediators of the new civil consensus; e) it proposes the theme that Scoppola (*La nascita della Repubblica*, cit.) suggests as the most recent interpretation, that is a more complex and highly articulated sense of citizenship (cf. P. Gaiotti, "L'accesso alla cittadinanza e il voto alle donne", from the conference *Cittadine: le donne e la Costituzione*, soon to be published).

36 Miriam Mafai, *L'apprendistato della politica*, Roma 1978, p. 66.

37 Already in the 5/14/1944 issue of the *L'Unità* (the official Communist newspaper) there is a brief account of an encounter of Neapolitan women with Togliatti, during which he used the word "emancipation." See also the account of Nadia Spano, Mafai, cit., p. 44.

38 A careful reading of Togliatti's speeches directed at women brings to light a very close connection between women's franchise and the establishment of a new party and the PCI's democratic strategy. "Within the PCI women's franchise was destined to accelerate, by means of internal clarification, the process of opening, renewal and transformation which began in Salerno . . . women's franchise became one with the choice of a democratic path to

Socialism . . . it was a choice which meant a long-term commitment, a patient and difficult achievement . . . destined to do away with any residual sectarian aspirations . . . it destroyed any illuministic, elitist, radical temptations", Mafai, cit., p. 67.

39 Now in Togliatti, *L'emancipazione femminile*, Rome 1973. On the PCI's official position, see A. Tiso, *I comunisti e l'emancipazione femminile*, Rome 1976.

40 We must bear in mind two significant points: the fact that "the Socialist party became popular in the past, when in every farmer's home one could find a picture of Karl Marx next to one of Jesus Christ"; and the proposal, which coincided perfectly with the effort to legitimize the PCI through the epic Resistance, the "millions of copies of photographs of the women who died in the Resistance be made and distributed to all women so that they may keep them with their pictures of the saints." *Ibid*, p. 21.

41 Togliatti appeared to be more reticent and evasive regarding the more problematic aspects of women's condition. He limited his comments to the reaffirmation, along the lines of Engels and Lenin, of the two-way approach: "femminismo dei diritti" (a feminism based on rights) and "forza d'urto della grande associazione unitaria" (the strength of impact of the large unitarian association). *Ibid*.

42 See R. Ruffilli, *Cultura politica, partiti e Costituente*, Bologna 1979, vol. II, p. 283.

43 Cf. P. Gaiotti, *Le origini del movimento cattolico*, Brescia 1963; and A. Valerio, "La questione femminile nei documenti ufficiali della Chiesa", *Nuova DWF*, 16, 1981.

44 The statement of *La Civiltà Cattolica* in 1919 (vol. IV, p. 42) against the PPI proposal in favor of women's franchise is typical: following a significant premise ("without taking seriously the references to a popular sovereignty, which was perhaps an implied platitude of the electoral programs") they asked whether women's franchise "might not threaten to turn women away from their natural mission as educators and comforters of the family, a mission which is much more sublime than that of voter, and catch her up in the whirlwind of political life?". "But on the other hand, we also hear . . . the strength of the opposite argument . . . which portrays women's franchise as a social necessity, by opposing women's supposedly conservative votes to the subversive votes of the socialists, anarchists and similar extremist parties. Contemporary society is in such a bad way that, as when a health crisis reaches its peak, it requires extreme and perhaps dangerous remedies."

45 In Maria Sticco, *Una donna fra due secoli*, Milan 1949, p. 719, Armida Barelli's perplexities and the decision to ask the Pope for enlightenment.

46 For the strategic approach to Italian democracy of Pope Pius XII's Pontificate, see *Pio XII* by A. Riccardi, Bari 1984, and in particular the essay by A.

Acerbi which very clearly defines the relationship between the acceptance of democracy and the confirmation of the Roman Church's supremacy.

47 The speech in *Le encicliche sociali dei Papi*, Roma, 1946.

48 Taken from the testimony of Angela Cingolani (in P. Gaiotti, *La Donna* cit; p. 109). See the correspondence between Sturzo and his friends in Italy in Luigi Sturzo, *Scritti inediti*, edited by F. Malgeri, Rome, 1976. Sturzo expresses to Scelba his concerns about the referendum, "the propaganda aimed especially at women spread by bishops and priests even from the pulpits and perhaps in the confessionals. . . ."

49 Now in *Dieci convegni Nazionali del Movimento femminile della Democrazia Cristiana*, Cinque Lune, Roma, 1966.

50 By contrast with Pope Pius XII's so called "continuismo," it's interesting to note Mons. Montini's awareness of the problems. He recognized the fact that women's franchise represented an "upheaval", a "break" with the feminine tradition, "which is justified with respect to Christian origins" but "a terribly difficult problem nevertheless" (from a speech printed in the November 1946 issue of a CIF newspaper). That people didn't begin to realize what the real problems were with respect to the entry of women into the system of civil liberty can easily be seen by taking a careful look at Catholic newspapers, the most open-minded magazines and the theoretical preparation of the Constituency on the part of the most advanced Catholic group, as the one which drew up the '*Codice di Camaldoli.*' Nothing is said in the "Codice" about the family because "it doesn't constitute a problem" (P. Giuntella, *Il Codice di Camaldoli* in *Appunti*, 1, 1976, p. 26).

51 Cf. G. Ascoli, "L'UDI fra emancipazione e liberazione" in *Problemi del Socialismo* n. 4, 1976. Elena Caporaso attributed the responsibilities to the tendency to "focus the attention on factional struggles" and the isolation of the female members, in her report to the IV National Conference of Socialist Women (now in *Politica del Partito*, Roma, 1954, p. 48.)

52 *L'Avanti* dedicated a special edition to women on 11/6/44; the quote is from the *Manifesto of the PSI Executive Committee*, written especially for the 1st of May 1944, (see *Il socialismo nella storia d'Italia* edited by G. Manacorda, Bari, 1970, p. 765). The different strategies for the Communists and Socialists was so described by Rodolfo Morandi: "The Communists plan to exercise their influence at the right moment through infiltration groups such as "Il Fronte della Gioventù", "La Difesa della donna" and others of the kind. We socialists don't believe that we should risk, in this paper, the interests of an entire class. *The class must take a stand as such*" (the underlining is mine), R. Morandi, *Lotte di popolo, 1937-1945*, Turin, 1958.

53 Spreafico's recent references are still anonymous. "Some objected that such an important decision, which was to virtually double the electoral body, should have been discussed and approved by the Constituent Assembly.

Officially, although various parties greeted with little enthusiasm the reform proposed by the DC, they found it to be in keeping with the trend of things and therefore incontrovertible. But numerous socialists, 'azionisti', republicans, and liberals, all from their own opposing perspectives, warned against the consequences that might have resulted from the relative political immaturity of the feminine electoral body. Some suggested that women's innate conservative tendency might have led them to support the monarchy, or the DC or the Right wing; others feared that women's religious orientation might have strengthened the parties of the masses to the detriment of the minor liberal groups." Alberto Spreafico, "La competizione elettorale e gli esiti del voto", in *La nascita della Repubblica*, from the 'Convegno di Studi Storici,' 4/6 June, 1987. *Quaderni di vita italiana* 3, 1987, p. 184. In *Tempo di guerra* (Roma 1982, p. 226), Pietro Nenni, in making a note in his diary on June 6th of De Gasperi's victory, laments the negative consequences of a decree issued by a government which didn't include the Socialists and the 'Azionisti'. These 'secular' attitudes were historically at the root of the opposition to women's franchise. A. M. Mozzoni, the unrivaled leader of the liberation movement of the 19th century, openly challenged these attitudes. She invited the opposition to ask themselves why the Church had established "such a strong and solid friendship" with women. She encouraged the "wisdom of averting this influence and gaining more prestige for women." Cf. *La liberazione della donna*, edited by Franca Pieroni Bortolotti, Mazzotta, Milan, 1975 p. 180. There appears to have been no support for the significant commitment of qualified women within the liberal movement. Special mention should be made of Josette Lupinacci De Menasce, who gave birth to ANDE (National Association of Women Voters) which was soon overtaken by the stronger women's mass associations. The effort to provide timely and clear information and arouse interest in keeping with the moderate European suffragist tradition, turned out to be out of step with the radical political debate and extraneous to the predominant themes of the liberal campaign. Therefore, middle class women's votes tended to reflect the middle class's own motivations rather than having any specific emphasis.

54 In certain passages of Scalfari's collective biography *La sera andavamo in Via Veneto* (Milan, 1986) we get some indications of how things were. In the author's own words: "We were 'Vitelloni' (lazy good for nothing), a bit snobbish. *Terrible mysoginists*. Very much voyeurs. Rather 'sciroccosi' (air heads)". (The underlining is mine). Better still, further on, we find a description of the debt owed by the group to Longanesi: "Snobbery is really nothing more than a rift with official conformity; it's a challenge in terms of taste which originates within the "establishment" in the name of elegance and spirit: an elitist attitude which asserts the rights of the elite in opposition to the uniformity enforced by the central powers. The words 'snobbery' and 'rebellion' are in a certain sense synonymous." Due to just such a degree of *snobbery* the liberal-democratic culture didn't even consider that it could have counted on several very competent feminist leaders if only they had been given a chance. There were, just to mention a few, women like Josette Lupinacci, Nina Ruffini, Teresita Sandeski Scelba — an historical standard-bearer of Italian feminism — Maria Calogero and many others.

55 Costantino Mortati emphasized, with specific reference to women's franchise, that "the State which endeavors to be rebuilt on a democratic basis must intervene by taking measures which directly or indirectly lead citizens to consider the act of voting as the carrying-out of a duty." Between 1909 and 1921 the percentage of voters had gone down from 65% to 59%. "It isn't inconceivable that these percentages might continue to decline as a consequence of granting the right to vote to women who are less informed about exercising their political rights especially considering the disillusionment and the apathy that the catastrophy of the nation has generated in the hearts of many." See P. Gaiotti, *La donna*, cit., pp. 82 and 247, the outline of the numerous contributions to the debate.

56 Among women of the left-wing, the fact that voting went from being a right to being an obligation was felt as a defeat. M. Michetti "1946 voto amaro: un diritto mutato in obbligo", *Il Manifesto*, 26/6/1986.

57 The structure and the internal evolution of the women's organizations within the PCI and of the 'Movimento femminile' in the DC, are analyzed in detail in the research paper "L'organizzazione partitica del PCI e della DC" produced by the Istituto di Studi e Ricerche Carlo Cattaneo, Bologna 1968, pp. 355 and 417 respectively. It appears there that the PCI "already had in 1946 the highest percentage of women party members in central Italy, a ratio of one out of every three." It was weakly represented in the Tre Venezie and the Mezzogiorno where the percentages went from 9.9% to 15% in 1961. Historically the Left has always been rather weak in southern Italy. The rebuilding process of the Left which appealed to what was left of the traditional unions and farmers' leagues was likely to attract the participation of feminist leadership. The statistics indicate that there were 401,202 women party members in 1946 as compared with 446,659 in 1961. The peak was reached in 1954 with 575,168 members. The organizational data of the DC is vague and imprecise until 1954 at which time there were 462,381 women party members. By 1961 the numbers grew to 487,660, that is from 36.1% to 33.7% of the total members. Membership in the parties meant however something entirely different in the two movements. In the DC, for example, it was mostly a family matter, a formal decision, and only for a small minority did it represent an active, motivated, committed choice. In both parties the separate woman's organizations never prevented women from participating in the general activity, but provided them, rather, with yet another opportunity (and often an extra commitment) for getting involved and exchanging ideas. In fact these women's party organizations, which were originally designed to deal with the presumed backwardness of women, went on to become the breeding ground for discussion and investigation into the woman's question. In both parties the separate organizations sparked endless discussion. The question of working women has often been considered with reservations both by Communist and Christian Democrat women: the fact remains that the prominence of women's organizations was a determining factor in keeping the novelty of women's franchise in the foreground.

58 Lenin, *L'emancipazione della donna*, Roma 1950. Interview with Clara Zetkin. A sense of continuity was also due to "Noi Donne", the official

newspaper of the UDI, which recalled the one founded in 1937 in France by Teresa Noce and Xenia Sereni within the context of the Popular Front movement. See Teresa Noce, *Rivoluzionaria professionale*, Milan, 1973, p. 176.

59 For the origins of CIF, see P. Gaiotti, *La donna* etc. For UDI, see the aforementioned *Laboratorio* etc.

60 Here we see more specifically how important for women was the PCI's choice of "il partito nuovo," open to thousands and thousands of new members. Even if it's virtually unacceptable today to confuse, as was customary in the past, emancipation with an active participation in the party, the existential evidence of many women's personal experiences discourages any facile criticism of the liberating value attributed to the party membership card, e.g. in Emilia. See P. Gaiotti, *La donna*, cit., pp. 34 and 113.

61 Mafai goes on to say, "figuring out their most pressing needs and helping them to resolve them, inevitably required adapting to the current mentality and ways of doing things. It required being or trying to be like others, like other women, a constant effort not to be different, to accept in the final analysis that model of women, the family and interpersonal relationships which prevailed in that society. It was the price to be paid for establishing and consolidating the political connection but also for the trust and respect which were necessary within the PCI, or more precisely between Communist women and feminine masses." Mafai, *L'apprendistato* etc., p. 47. However, both in the DC and in the PCI women have had reservations regarding working among women as a separate branch (for example: Teresa Noce in *Rivoluzionaria professionale*, and Cecilia Dau, quoted).

62 M. Dogan, "Il voto alle donne" in Spreafico, quoted, and La Palombara, *Elezioni e comportamento elettorale in Italia*, Milan, 1963.

63 According to the prefects' predictions ("which were usually based on the pre-fascist situation and on the number of registered members of the various parties") women's franchise, which was considered to be connected to the problem of public order and the freedom to vote, was a "question mark as to whether women were going to faithfully do what men told them to or whether they were going to make personal decisions which were generally expected to be center-right." See F. Fonzi, "Ordine pubblico e libertà di voto", *La Nascita della Repubblica*, quoted.

64 Amalia Signorelli ("Dai taccuini di ricerca sulle contadine meridionali. Sterotipi culturali e volti rimossi" in *Memoria* n. 6, 1982) had some rather remarkable things to say about the way in which in the fifties the Left in particular viewed the condition of women as stereotypically backward: "Common opinion maintained that the greatest resistance to innovation could be expected to come from women; that they were mostly to be held responsible for conservative votes; that southern Italian women tended not to participate in collective activities. Nevertheless, when Banfield defined this characteristic as "familismo amorale" (amoral family feeling) and ascribed it to the entire population of the South, the reaction was one of general

indignation." Amalia Signorelli in her research has traced all kinds of incidents and remarks which strongly contrast with the stereotypes. We quote one woman who in San Cataldo while her husband insistently repeated: "We've been on the side of the cross till now and on the side of the cross we'll stay," serenely added: "The cross has nothing to do with anything. We have the right to vote now, and if they want our vote they have to give us something in return."

65 For a detailed account of the range of these activities in a typical region, see P. Gaiotti, *La Donna*, etc.; also for the meaning that these activities have for women, as expressed by Penelope Veronesi of UDI ("an effort made towards rebuilding our country, in a new, democratic way, like a national endeavor"), and in the words of Maria Federici, President of the CIF ("men consider as secondary certain activities which are destined to become primary. The world needs to pay more attention to the problems of people as such, to problems of the family as such, and not dissipate its energies in that arid and abstract game that has been going on for millennia.")

66 Mafai, *L'apprendistato* etc., p. 35.

67 For the Emilia region among these elements besides the already mentioned "pianurizzazione" (spreading into the plains) which started during the Resistance, the political and union strategies for the rural areas overcame the traditional rivalries between sharecroppers and day-laborers and to some extent small landowners. The result was the political unification of the entire rural environment, which included the female population from the rice-pickers to the sharecroppers (see *Le campagne emiliane nell'epoca moderna*, edited by R. Zangheri, Bologna 1955, particularly G. Ferri's essay; also N. Chiaromonte, "Note sulla politica contadina del PCI," in *Critica Marxista*, 1, 1967); mass mobilization for women was always supported by organized solidarity (a typical example was the hospitality offered to children from Milan, Naples, etc.) and concrete assistance when needed. The atmosphere of a struggle to the bitter end maintained mobilization at a very high level, but in the long run, according to the complaints of some of the leaders of the movements, it accentuated the element of "class" in the mobilization among Communist women. We are reminded of the three women who were elected to the Constituency (Noce, Montagnana, Iotti), the first two of which were confirmed candidates at the head of the electoral list, and the five elected in the 'Blocco del Popolo' in 1948, which included the only socialist elected in the Region, Guiliana Nenni, who got in, despite the low score achieved by the socialist candidates in general. For the Toscana region, see now similar considerations in M. Caciagli e C. Baccetti, "La fondazione dell'egemonia comunista: il voto del 1946 in Toscana" in *Il Triplice voto del 1946*, Napoli 1989.

68 Francesco Traniello: "La Chiesa, etc.," in *La Nascita della Repubblica*, cit.

69 "'Vulimmo o Re' (we want the King) cried the multicolored old double-chinned 'hens' with grandchildren and children hugged close to their breasts or clinging to their skirts; and they marched with a monarchic flag draped across their bodies with the 'Sabaudo' coat of arms covering their enormous

maternal bosoms." Maria A. Maciocchi's description (*Duemila anni di felicità*, Milan 1983, p. 103) is a clear indication of the difficulties in communication between that world and the Left. According to Maciocchi: "The Monarchy was very strong in the South, especially thanks to women. In Naples women were at the head of the march for the Monarchy on the eve of June 2nd, they led the crowd that attacked the PCI federation in via Medina . . . Women marched ahead, dressed in black with the 'Sabaudo' flag draped across their chests like a peplum, holding their little ones by the hand shouting: "Vulimmo o Re! Communisti fetienti! Mort'e famme!" (We want the King! Stinking Communists! Beggars!) They saw them as starving beggars just like them and therefore as rivals that were trying to get their hands on the booty. . . . "

70 "The message that was aimed at the large numbers of women, who experienced the struggle for the Republic as the key to any further changes, was not charged with the kind of spirit that might have triggered in women a more critical attitude to the patriarchal character of Italian society," see *UDI, Laboratorio* etc., p. 15.

71 We get a glimpse of how women felt at the time by analyzing women's reactions to these numbers. For the Christian Democrats, the reaction was disappointment and surprise at the unsatisfactory result which indicated that the presence of women was still considered an exception (Clelia D'Inzillo, "Precisiamo la nostra posizione," in *Azione Femminile* anno II, 14).

72 Serena Piretti, *La repubblica limitata; l'informazione cattolica e la Costituente*, Roma, 1976; also Giovagnoli, *Cultura, politica, partiti, costituente*, cit. p. 342). The first conference of the DC women's movement held in Naples and the first document drawn up by the women's ACLI groups contained a strong appeal in defense of women's role within the family and the institution of the family as such. They made the same demands for equality of employment and career opportunities, equal pay and equal education as were being expressed in the UDI platform (for the ACLI document in which the delegate Maria Federici makes an important contribution, see *Azione Femminile* (the official newspaper for the DC women's movement), Anno I, 27; *Ibidem*, anno I, 7, see also the reportage of the first conference of the DC women's movement held in Naples on April 4, 1945, as well as the collection of UDI documents of the already mentioned *UDI Laboratorio*, etc.).

73 "In the course of the discussion, one had the impression that the men hadn't quite overcome an attitude of mistrust towards women's capabilities, that even the most enlightened and wise of them harbored deep-seated prejudices of the oldest most humiliating kind, and that despite their best efforts a certain awkwardness showed in their words." See Maria Federici, *La donna alla Costituente*, Firenze 1969, Vol. II; who, judging from the Parliamentary annals, is excessively benevolent with those such as Hon. Molé who referred to the Charcot school of thought and to women's anatomical and physiological limitations. See also the tangle of less than noble hypocritical statements, opposed exclusively by Calamandrei and Cappi, which were expressed with regards to the article that sanctioned equality between spouses "with the limi-

tations imposed by the family unity" (Costituente p. 2981 ff). After all, the common Christian thought, as expressed by Guido Gonella (*Azione femminile*, Anno I, 17) attributed to women the identical social status that men have, "in that personal rights are identical," while, "within the context of family life, which requires a hierarchy of position, women's status was one of subordination." Prejudices were expressed openly especially in reference to women gaining access to the judicial system, and they confirmed antifeminist stereotypes held by most members of parliament; a united effort on behalf of female members of parliament due to cooperation between some Christian Democrat constituents and the Left helped to improve the situation.

74 Simonetta Piccone Stella "Per uno studio della vita delle donne negli anni '50" in *Memoria*, 2, 1981. On the basis of Piccone's suggestions, *Memoria* decided to dedicate another issue to the 50's (6, 1982) which supported the same thesis.

75 When in 1956, during a UDI congress, Elena Caporaso first tackled the question of the updating of customs she rightly pointed out: "In this framework of renewal, the essential figure on which evolution hinges is the young woman." In *UDI Laboratorio*, etc., p. 233.

76 Simonetta Piccone Stella cites the interviews edited in Julienne Travers, *Dieci donne anticonformiste*, Bari 1968, as an exemplary document for this attitude.

77 Paola Gaiotti de Biase, *Le donne oggi*, Roma 1957.

78 *UDI laboratorio* etc., p. 225.

79 From 1951 to 1961 the number of women enrolled in schools of higher learning increased from 152,366 to 268,335; in the universities from 38,208 to 53,196. The girls' sections of lyceums gradually disappeared. Of course the trend became virtually explosive, especially after the extension of obligatory schooling in 1963.

80 Simonetta Piccone Stella justifiably refers to a kind of double moral standard for women composed of "lip service to the prevailing order, but in daily practice composed of second thoughts, repenting, backsliding,": "an anxiety-ridden standard."

81 It would be necessary to write another essay on the various images of the female body propagated by the Italian cinema from neo-realism to "big-bosomed" ladies in popular films with strong local color and complex plots, often take-offs of American films. See G. Fink and F. Minganti, "La vita privata italiana sul modello americano," P. Aries, G. Duby, *La vita privata: Il Novecento*, Italian edition, Bari, 1988, and Piera De Tassis, "Corpi immaginati per il proprio sguardo: Cinema e immaginario negli anni '50", *Memoria*, 6, 1982.

82 According to Duccio Tabet ("La famiglia contadina si trasforma," *Rinascita*, p. 195 A. XVIII, 3, March 1961,) "the recourse made by thousands of women doing piece work out of their own homes was a spontaneous expres-

sion of their desire for recognition of their work and a personal income." On piece work done at home seen as a dynamic factor in the condition of women and the Italian economy, see further on. At this point rural areas already registered a change in the general view of the role of women. In the same number of *Rinascita* a father is quoted as saying that he wanted his daughter to study to become a textile expert because "there are very few women who do this."

83 Amalia Signorelli, quoted: "The all-inclusive interpretative schemes of the 50's — the contradiction awkwardness/development, the iron-clad connection between cultural progress and the condition of the salaried worker, so that all other professions were thought to be necessarily linked to conservative attitudes, the very eruption into history of the populace and the subservient (as interpreted by De Martino) which to many seemed postulatory and contrary to the non-historical condition of that world — all oriented the studies of that time as a whole, thus doubtlessly illuminating some fundamental aspects of rural reality, but excluding the understanding of others."

84 See in reference to Catholic women organizations *Donna famiglia lavoro*, edited by T. Tentori (a CIF initiative) Roma 1960 and the later *La donna nella società italiana in trasformazione*, Roma 1966, published by ACLI.

85 In a leftist ideological analysis, Giuliana Dal Pozzo recognizes the merits of some journalists — and in particular of the Turin newspaper *La Stampa* — in protesting the backward condition of women "which they were not up to expressing with regard to other social injustices". "Stampa borghese e realtà filtrata", *Rinascita*, 3, 1961.

86 Paola Di Cori, "Storia sentimenti solidarietà nelle organizzazioni cattoliche", but see also, though in a highly critical context, on the transgressive aspects implicit in Catholic groups: "as long as it keeps within the ambit of ecclesiastical tutelage, any transgression of roles is allowed," *ibidem*, p. 83.

87 Maria C. Giuntella, "Virtú e immagine della donna nei settori femminili", in AAVV, *Chiesa e progetto educativo nel secondo dopoguerra 1945-1958*, Brescia 1988, p. 274 ff. And *ibidem*, p. 287, on route spirituality: "encourage the education of girls not to protect themselves from external risks but to contend with the risks and the difficulties, to venture outside of their own environment and their security, to acquire a sense of independence, of essentiality and simplicity, virtues very different from the modesty generally inculcated in Catholic girls: it is enough to remember the GF's campaigns against fashion, make-up, entertainment and dancing that, despite the efforts to represent an alternative to growing consumerism, in fact came across too strongly portraying an image of defensive, moralistic Christianity." Although its dissemination, however important, was predominant among the urban middle and upper classes, and there has not yet been systematic evaluation of the long-term impact of the Girl Scout movement, one can suppose that it exerted significant influence on Italian female culture, thanks also to its particularly solid theoretical structure. We should remember here that Italy was one of the first countries where to all effects the operation of the Boy and

Girl Scouts was unified. In general, however, these experiences have been given little attention in the historical analyses of the Catholic movement, primarily because of the apolitical nature of the movement.

88 The "Spiritual Family Groups" which represented a radical turning point in *de facto* Catholic family pastoral, arose in 1950 on the model of the French "Equipes Nôtre Dame" from the "intellectual" branches of the AC (F. Franceschetti, "I Gruppi di spiritualità familiare in Italia," *La Famiglia*, May 1957); they never became as popular as they were in France, but the grounding in the parish of the couples involved favored the dissemination of the concepts of family and of the role of women in the context of the family which was essentially egalitarian.

89 Maria Cacioppo, "Condizione di vita familiare negli anni cinquanta," *Memoria*, 6, 1982. What emerges from this analysis is that the following were still rare commodities: electrical appliances, refrigerators, washing machines, etc., the diffusion of consumer goods and the essential stability of shoppers' habits in the course of the decade. There is an interesting discrepancy regarding reproductive behavior between ideal data based on the preferences as to the number of children expressed in interviews (2.7) and real data (2.4).

90 According to Luzzatto Fegiz, *Il volto sconosciuto dell'Italia*, Milan 1956, in 1950, 68 out of 115 housewives still used coal and wood for cooking (92 out of 106 among the lower classes), 7 used gas cylinders (but no one did among the lower classes) and 37 used city gas or electricity (but only 14 among the lower classes). Among 135 asked what they used to clean kitchen utensils, the answers were: ashes-14; lye-35; pumice-29; sand-12; soap-25; soda-25. The situation was destined to change rapidly within a few years.

91 This phenomenon had already begun in preceding decades with the widespread diffusion of bicycles in the plains of North Central Italy among school teachers and office workers, as well as farm hands milk delivery.

92 It is not possible to give figures for the CIF because of its federational character that subsumes various other groups. UDI records a growth in the number of members from 401,391 in 1946 to a million in 1950 stabilizing at an average of about half a million in the 1950's. (Source: *La presenza sociale della DC e del PCI*, cit. p. 220).

93 Those critics were expressed in later years within the UDI itself. See *UDI laboratorio* etc. See also Marisa Rodano "In quanto donna: l'UDI dal 1952 al 1964" in *Esperienza storica femminile nell'età moderna e contemporanea*, edited by Circolo La Goccia UDI, Roma 1988.

94 This led to the end of the Federici presidency that had in great part guided the constitutional acceptance of women's rights by Catholics, but which had also interpreted the function of the organization in terms of strong civil autonomy. See my *Questione femminile e femminismo nella storia della Repubblica*, Brescia 1978.

95 *La presenza sociale della DC e del PCI*, cit. p. 434. And yet the CIF, never reduced its social work to win over the electorate. With regards to this, a reading would be significant of the long battle of rivalry with the Pontificia Opera di Assistenza (POA) in the distribution of national and international funds with the accusations of paternalism and clericalism that circulated among Catholic women's organizations in those years. (The author's personal recollection).

96 The Law of August 26, 1950, protects the working mother physically and economically. The debate among the political parties and within the women's movement, overstating the ideological differences between the government proposal and that of the Left, was deeply felt in the country and gave rise to great Leftist demonstrations, but the final text was eventually approved by the opposition as well.

97 'Operation Sturzo' was an attempt to present at the elections for the municipal council of the city of Rome a unified right-center list that exerted the utmost pressure from the most conservative circles of the Curia to influence DC policies. Opposition to this move and solidarity with De Gasperi were officially expressed, first to Interior Minister Scelba and then directly to De Gasperi, by a delegation of leaders of the GIAC, of the FUCI, of the Movimento Laureati di AC, as well as by the president of the Gioventù Femminile Alda Miceli, the president of the Unione Donne Carmela Rossi, by the president of the Maestri Cattolici Maria Badaloni, thus sanctioning the isolation of the blocking tendency of the Catholic movement's right wing. In a later dramatic audience with these three women, Pius XII defined their gesture "a betrayal" (from the direct testimony of the women involved). In fact records of the Central Committees of Azione Cattolica show that a critical stance regarding the use of civic committees against the DC had already been taken in the past.

98 See *UDI laboratorio* etc., p. 64. One of the elements concerning the characteristic of the Valmarana presidency and the Carazzolo vice-presidency in the CIF was the question of how to define the system of social assistance and its connection with adult education and the promotion of female solidarity.

99 It is however necessary to note how the breach among the unions in 1948 at first indirectly diminished both women's negotiating power in general and that of women's committees within the unions. Particularly in the CISL (Confederazione Italiana Sindacati Lavoratori), once it was no longer necessary, within women's committees, to compete with Communist and Socialist groups, there was a drop in motivation for the mobilization of women unionists.

100 *UDI laboratorio* etc., p. 70.

101 The moderate Consiglio Nazionale delle Donne Italiane (CNDI), established in 1904 in connection with the International Council of Women, drifted towards Fascism in the 1920's, a trend that culminated in the presidency of De Robilant. This accounts for its absence on the scene immediately after the war. In the mid-fifties's, under Nina Ruffini's presidency, it took its right

place again in the Italian women's debate and undertook far-reaching initiatives. The CNDI was an umbrella organization federating women's groups of varying importance.

102 On the ideological level there was a clash between two theories: the Engels-based idea of emancipation by the "inclusion of all women in work outside of the home" and the opposing Catholic proposal of "free choice." This latter thesis, however, was not worked out in detail in terms of the transitions and tools necessary to make women's choice truly free, in particular to guarantee housewives equal and economic and legal conditions. It did however consolidate in the Catholic world the principle of women's full right to work. Official consacration took place at Pisa during Social Week in 1954 under the title *"Today's Families and the Social World in Transformation"* (Maria Federici presented the report). The forerunners of this were: the conferences of the DC Women's Movement (document of the 1st conferences in 1945 and Stefania Rossi's report at the 4th conference in 1950); the ACLI conferences (from the 1st in 1945 to *Il lavoro della donna* in 1957 e *Parità di retribuzione* in 1957). The theoretical analysis development of the conditions for free choice, however, linked with the Vanoni Plan (a personal commitment of the writer who is still proud of it) was essentially abandoned. But the demise of the Vanoni Plan also marked the end of the project designed to give solidarity and rational guidance to the process of economic growth which was soon to emerge with the advent of the economic boom. If the radical thesis for emancipation seems abstract, and impractical, the Catholic thesis was seen at the time more as an effective anti-Communist ploy or as a useful cover for the disagreements about female labor rather than as a concretely planned political objective. Regarding the manifestations of this thesis, see P. Gaiotti, *Le donne oggi*, Rome 1957, and also "Una tesi sulla questione femminile," *Civitas*, December 1958. For an early historical reconstruction besides the cited *Questione femminile e femminismo*, see also Paola Gaiotti, "Una ipotesi e la sua storia: l'emancipazione anche attraverso la condizione di casalinga," *Reti*, 1987, N. 1. On the positions within the DC, *Dieci Convegni Nazionali del Movimento Femminile della DC.*, cit. On the positions of the Left one may refer to the documentation cited in *UDI laboratorio* and Aida Tiso, *I communisti e la questione femminile*.

103 At a CIF conference in 1955 AC's President Carmela Rossi's summary of the as yet unattained objectives (access to all careers, the abolition of the brothels, equal pay and the reform of family laws) confirmed the essential agreement among women of different ideologies; in Cecilia Dau, *Il movimento femminile* cit., p. 359.

104 The first bill was proposed by Angela Merlin in 1953; the debate throughout the country was long and difficult, but women were on the whole in agreement; the principle wasn't approved until 1962.

105 Despite the succession of proposed bills to admit women to all public offices, according to the terms of the Constitution, in 1956 only a single bill was approved admitting women to jury duty. This was the occasion for a great mobilization of women and it triggered a wide-spread debate.

106   Proposed by Maria Pia Dal Canton of the DC and approved in 1959.

107   Italian brothels were modelled along French legislative lines. And, in fact, it was Napoleon III, on the eve of leaving for the second war of independence, who asked for such a "service" as a means of protecting his soldiers. The issue thus became entangled with the same "epic" attempt during the Risorgimento. Strong abolitionist campaigns were waged unsuccessfully by Catholic and lay intellectuals with the participation of women's groups at the turn of the century.

108   The thesis is supported by Michetti, Repetto and Viviani in *UDI Laboratorio* etc., p. 174. They note that the law was rarely cited either in the course of the conference or in accounts of the work of UDI. For a recent feminist interpretation of the debate on the Merlin bill, see T. Pitch: "La sessualità, le norme, lo stato," *Memoria*, 17, 1986.

109   In the Catholic world, despite difficulties, Angela Gotelli took a favorable position in no uncertain terms at the 3rd National Conference of the DC's MF. The difficulties are evident if one considers that a prominent journal such as *Cronache sociali* (23-24, Dec. 1984) published a series of interviews of which the only distinctly abolitionist one was that of Maria Jervolino. Meanwhile an open-minded and authoritative theologian such as Don Guzzetti waxed eloquent about principles and lesser evils without actually taking a stand. Nevertheless one must remember that one of the most distinctly abolitionist texts of the period, L. Scremin, *La questione delle case chiuse*, Roma 1953, was published as part of a widely circulated series by a Catholic publisher as "Studium."

110   "From 1954, the employment of women workers continually increased, going from 4,566,000 in May of 1954 to 5,889,000 in May of 1961 . . . The percentage of women in the total work force increased from 24.1% to 27.9%. The increase involved all economic sectors: in agriculture women workers increased by 33%; by 50% in industry; by 22% in all other activities with an evolutionary rather than transitory character." Thus states Nora Federici, one of Italy's most prominent demographic experts, at a conference on emancipation of Italian women organized in Turin on the occasion of the celebration of the 100th anniversary of the Unification of Italy. See Società Umanitaria, *L'emancipazione femminile in Italia, un secolo di discussioni 1861 - 1961*, Firenze, 1963, p. 119.

111   The agreement between employers' associations and unions which was signed July 16, 1960 still omitted agriculture, however. Putting it into practice was slow and difficult because it involved the entire contractual system and salary structure in all sectors; but it still remains one of the big steps in the long and complicated process of equality for women. Collective agreements followed in 1962 and 1963.   On paper they did away with wage discriminations between men and women and reduced salary categories to five.

112   The acts in AAVV, *Retribuzione uguale per un lavoro uguale*, Torino, 1957.

113 See documents in *UDI Laboratorio* etc.; and also, in Marisa Rodano's contribution at the 8th Conference of PCI; for a comment, see P. Gaiotti "La donna e la famiglia nella via italiana al socialismo", *Donna e società*. Anno I, n. 4.

114 The same phenomenon was to re-emerge in the 70's. Whereas the women of the female revolution refuse it, the small groups of the far Left still feed on the universal concept of class oppression, the supremacy of the economy, Leninism as a model; women anticipated the critique of the classic Left wing ideology destined to become established in the 80's, even if they often limit themselves to transposing in a feminist key a simplistic, dichotomous vision of history. Cf. AAVV, "Il movimento femminista degli anni settanta," *Memoria*, 19-20, 1987.

115 *UDI laboratorio* etc., p. 254.

116 See *UDI laboratorio* where an analysis is made of the disavowal this gave to the strategy of the "right to work" as the basis of the emancipation process. "The harmonization of family and work, which according to the emancipation strategy of UDI could be realized only at the price of great transformations within society as women gradually took on the role of producers, had occurred in the case of work done at home without a blow having been exchanged — without, that is, society having been forced to change its ways" and "without creating economic or social rights for women workers", p. 255.

117 The law on piece work done at home passed on May 13, 1958 established registers of workers and recognized their rights to social security. It made an exception, in rather vague terms, of those types of work that had previously been done in the home.

118 Prandi Cappello, *L'Industria del truciolo a Carpi*, Bologna 1973; but also Adele Pesce, *L'altra metà dell'Emilia Romagna; rapporto sulla condizione femminile*, Milan 1989.

119 G. De Rita, "L'impresa famiglia", *La italiana dall'Ottocento a oggi*, edited by P. Melograni, Bari, 1988.

120 For an extended bibliography on Italy's underground economy, see Maria Agata Cappiello, "Proposta di bibliografia ragionata sull'economia sommersa nell'industria (Italia 1970-1982)", in *L'altra metà dell'economia*, edited by A. Bagnasco, Napoli 1986.

121 The datum was only just balanced by the presence of women in city administrations (but mostly in small communities) and by their first appearances in the government: as under secretaries, Cingolani in '51; Jervolino '54 to '58; Gotelli from '58 to '60; Badaloni for a long time beginning in '59. The minimal presence of women in Parliament was to last, even if with ups and downs, until the legislature of 1983-1987 where women were still 7% of all parliamentarians, just as in 1946; a significant change took place only in 1987 with a score of 10% mostly due, however, to the great battle to balance representation fought by the Communist women who still constitute 30% of the parliamentarians of their group.

XIX

Commentary on Paola Gaiotti's "The Impact of Women's Political and Social Activity in Postwar Italy"

Margherita Repetto-Alaia

Paola Gaiotti's paper reflects the excellent work by the author on women in contemporary Italy, especially since WWII: an area of research which, as the paper points out, is still largely ignored by historians of Republican Italy.   Similarly women's history has tended so far to deny the existence before the 1970s of a women's movement, that is to say, of a self-conscious collective presence endowed with concepts, goals and strategies. Paola's paper represents a contribution to the vast work of historical reconstruction which is needed.

The paper deals effectively with three main groups of issues. First, the stance taken by major parties and political groups between 1944 and 1945 on women's enfranchisement reflected each party's assessment of the political situation, its view of the future balance of power, and the party's goals and strategy.   In reverse, the paper also analyzes the impact of women on the political balance of the Republic and on the political fortunes of the various parties. These issues relate to the conceptualization of the "woman's question" in the different cultural traditions, which is most deserving of investigation. We still lack studies which follow the different traditions of thought concerning feminism, linking the history of such ideas to political history from the eve of WWI until well after WWII. Such studies should include the developments which took place in Italian society during the years of the regime (as different from Fascist propaganda) and in the cosmopolitan enclaves of antifascist exiles.

Secondly it examines the impact on society of women acting both collectively and individually after 1945. The paper draws a first picture of the process of feminization of Italian society, connecting it to trends which go far back into the 1930s (as indicated by the research which has recently been undertaken and which Paola refers to in her work). Thanks to her background, Paola is especially sensitive to the need for research on women in Catholic organizations, which are an essential feature of the pre-WWII picture. Regarding feminization, the paper notes a few directions for further investigation. The history of education, the evolution of the labor market and the welfare system are all still untouched or insufficiently explored.

Finally, the paper explores the historiographical question. The "woman's question" — the author points out — to this very moment has never been used as a measure of the political and social process taking place in the postwar years. As one significant example it is conspicuously absent from the debate in assessing *continuity* vs. *change* between pre- and postwar Italy.

Taking Paola's argument as a whole, I intend to focus on the points which are critical to her historical reading of this period and then indicate my agreement or differences of interpretation of the process and its results.

The lack of a political debate surrounding the enfranchisement in fact masked misgivings which all political groups held regarding the vote for women and their political involvement. The paper implies that those misgivings were basically the same as those which defeated the suffrage campaigns in 1904, 1913 and 1919. From these misgivings came a general consensus held by men in power — political and intellectual leaders alike — to downplay the "novelty" in favor of "continuity." The message was more often that women would prove their maturity by their capacity for reconciling old with new duties. As a result, political enfranchisement was then presented as a *duty* rather than a *right* albeit belated, which would open the road to further recognition of personal and collective liberties.

The lack of a political debate did not however imply lack of attention on the part of some of the most influential personalities in Italian politics and society. Paola Gaiotti quotes Pius XII, thus indicating an area of her own ground-breaking research which however awaits further investigation. Among political leaders, she points to De Gasperi and Togliatti. Although for different reasons each foresaw difficulties for their party arising from women's political enfranchisement, they were explicitly supportive of the decision which brought it about. Both of them made the issue a significant part of their choice of a mass democracy based on popular consensus, in contrast to more radical and elitist views held in other sectors of the political spectrum at the time.

Notwithstanding this "conspiracy of silence", women took advantage of their full political status. Thus the process of feminization unraveled itself. Paola Gaiotti stresses the positive impact it had on many aspects of postwar society, suggesting that among them was the social solidarity logic imbued in many articles for the Constitution. While I agree with the general picture and many of its specific points, I see other elements which call for an overall less positive reading of the breathing space allowed to women as new citizens.

It must be recorded that among political leaders, only Togliatti in 1945 posed explicitly the existence of a problem of women's emancipation in postwar Italy. The founding of the Union Donne Italiane as the mind and motor of this process was indeed the best result of that strategy and it comprised the innovative and far reaching part of the message.

Indeed the founding of UDI would not have been made possible without the physical existence of legions of Italian women who had gone through their own personal experience of emancipation during the war years. Concerning women among organized Catholics, Paola Gaiotti also points to the surviving legacy of currents which we may call "Catholic" feminism, strongly supportive of woman's personal dignity and interested in seeing this idea incorporated in law. That legacy, going back to the early century, in the 1930s had been filtered through the theories and activities of groups among Italian Catholic laity which paralleled those founded in France by Emanuel Mounier and gathered around the journal *Esprit*. Incidentally such views were also present in the original founders of UDI, some of whom came from the experience of the Catholic Communist movement.

Why the energy of this group of leaders belonging to different sectors of the ideological-political spectrum could not be fully unleashed to provide courageous leadership for collective, but also personal, emancipation of Italian women then, and for the generation which soon would be coming of age (roughly mine), is in need of explanation. So is the question of why the issues for woman's personal rights and individual liberties — what Paola Gaiotti calls the "femminismo dei diritti" — soon disappeared from the UDI agenda, leaving the focus entirely on economic and political questions of general interest. The studies on young women in the 1950s — cited by Paola — prove the lack of role models to guide young women in a changing society. Only from the early 1960s were some of us in a position to conceptualize about change and therefore to contribute to the growth of woman's awareness.

Looking from this perspective, some of the paper's other relevant points need reassessment. Paola Gaiotti rightly observes that the "congiuntura familista" — the family oriented ideology — far from being solely an Italian phenomenon, was sweeping through all of Western society after WWII. I agree with Paola that the message, so far as it is to be credited, among others, to American influence, contained a new conceptualization of relationships between spouses and therefore of women's status in the family, which reflected a new status in society. But the message adapted to pre-existing conditions. In the Italian case the new morality indeed found reception in a few of the high speeches addressed to women by the political and moral leaders of the Antifascist Resistance. But reality both cultural and practical was very different, and the new morality would have required support in new codes of law and in economic and social policies as well. The affirmation of equality in the family which had circulated among women in 1944-45, was not clearly reflected in the Constitution. The language of the latter reflected a compromise: I am thinking in particular of Art. 29, of the conflict surmised there between equality and family interest, and the implicit reference to the unequal existing legislation. For the three ensuing decades that article represented a stumbling block on the road to reform of family laws.

All of the above is not to say that the picture drawn by the paper on women's political and social participation does not reflect reality. Indeed, women took advantage of their political enfranchisement and worked to make the new democracy their own province. But we should not miss seeing the forest for the trees. The lack of conceptualization, on the part of women themselves and on the part of society, of the significance of women's personal liberties as women, crippled the process of emancipation at its very outset. In fact the lack of a sustained ideal effort in that direction subsequently made it hard to implement the logic of solidarity contained in the Constitution while upholding at the same time full recognition of the equality for women as individuals.

What are the historical causes behind *all this*? Many of the answers given so far have been more in the form of an ideological rather than an historical explanation.

The freeze due to the Cold War is in my opinion an explanation *a posteriori*, in so far as it does not explain why women didn't build a common ground on other issues beyond the vote in the immediate postwar and during the Constituent period.

Either women were intimidated by conservatism — Catholic or otherwise — or they took part in it, particularly on matters concerning the family and sexuality. Speaking of conservatism on the left, there is no deluding ourselves about the scarce welcome extended to any idea of "feminism" on the part of most militants and a great many leaders. Within the context one must mention Togliatti's firm decision to avoid ideological confrontation with Catholics on crucial issues such as the family and its relationship to the State.

The key to an historical explanation indeed lies with women, with the society of women: intellectual women, women leaders, women at large. Here again I agree with Paola Gaiotti's critique of the negative evaluation of the impact of women on postwar politics. The interpretation of how women cast their vote in the 1946 and 1948 elections based on the clerical vote argument, patronizes and discriminates. Ultimately it implies that the "city" really belonged to men and that it could only lose from admitting women. Paola corrects that conception, however there are questions that need to be addressed, especially in regards to the crucial 1946 elections. Did women respond to a specific message contained in the parties' platforms and/or in the organizational effort spent by the parties in the direction of the female electorate? If so, how was the message construed? If the answer is in the negative — no specific message — what were the events which led to the disappearance of that note of vitality and courageous consciousness of their own rights which one could detect, for instance, in the printed material circulated by women among women in 1944 and 1945, or, for that matter, in the proceedings (never published in full) of the founding convention of UDI in April 1945?

We need a lot more studies of women in the years from 1944 to the end of 1947, of their complex dealings with the parties which presided over the reconstruction. In this regard I would also like to focus attention on the "lay forces." Little has been written about the attitude concerning *gender* among men and women belonging to that sector of the postwar political spectrum. One may recall the controversy in 1945 between Luigi Russo and Joyce Lussu in *Belfagor*. What role did women from that area play? Women such as Joyce Lussu, Maria Calogero, Lucia Corti, Anna Garofalo (to mention only a few) could somehow speak for the surviving tradition of liberal-feminism at its best. That tradition had crossbred with the Socialist tradition in the pre-Fascist times. Women who had inherited that tradition should have been on the cutting edge of society in postwar years. Without going into it in depth, the conclusion seems to be that women were intimidated by the "cultura alta" of the Resistance, which to a great extent remained in post 1945 Italy identified with the lay culture, with the culture of Crocean Liberalism (which filtered even into the populist culture of the left). Again *gender* could be the touch-stone for a deeper understanding of forces shaping Italian postwar society.

In conclusion in examining "continuity" and "change," the paper stresses the latter. By looking retrospectively at a global assessment from 1945 to the present, there is no doubt that "change" is most appropriate. Yet if we look at the period under consideration, there is no denying that much of the potential contained in women's self-awareness and drive for change which had emerged from the war was lost. Women's self-esteem vis-a-vis a male oriented society only surfaced slowly and painfully.

Only a consistent body of intellectual work in the field of women's studies from many different disciplines will deepen an historical understanding of the process of women making room for themselves in modern Italian society. On the other hand, such an understanding is crucial to an in depth investigation of the society of that period and of the 1920s and 1930s as well. A full view of the period from the gender perspective would also allow us to compare the Italian case to that of other European societies. It has long been my opinion that from this point of view there are Italian peculiarities, but not an Italian specificity. On the whole, the *"specificità del caso italiano"* does not apply. For instance, regarding women, over approximately 100 years, the Italian case largely parallels the French. The similarities are striking.

Notwithstanding my quibbles, I wish to thank Paola Gaiotti for her contribution not only through her pioneering scholarship and writing, but also through her struggles for the advancement of our common cause.

XX

The Difficult Path Towards Independence: The Italian Judicial System From the Fall of Fascism to the Early 1960's

Guido Neppi Modona

The thorny point for the judiciary in Italy has always been its relationship to the political power structure. This must be borne in mind when studying the period immediately following the fall of Fascism, but in order to gain a better understanding of this problem we must first examine certain premises on the role played by the courts in earlier periods, beginning with the era of national unification. Any discussion of judicial power and the administration of justice during the fifty year history of the liberal state (1870 to 1922) and later during the Fascist era, must come to terms with the relationship between the judiciary and the executive, and specifically the former's historic relationship of dependence/independence vis à vis the latter. In effect, the major historical research on the judiciary up until the late 1970's has focused either on norms that permitted the executive to exercise some degree of control over the judges,[1] or on concrete interventions by the executive to bend the courts to the political will of the government then in power.[2]

With regards to norms, the position of the Public Prosecutor diverged from that of the judges. Article 129 of the judicial law of 1865 (which remained in force without major revisions until 1941), provided that the "Public Prosecutor (Pubblico Ministero) is the executive branch's representative at the judiciary authority and answers directly to the Ministry of Justice." Hence, the Office of the Public Prosecutor depended hierarchically on the Ministry of Justice, and had to follow its directives.

Such control was exercised through the forwarding of memoranda from the Ministry of Justice to the heads of the Public Prosecutor's Office, notably the General Prosecutor of the Appeal Courts, who, in turn, would send them on to the King's Prosecutor at the Law Courts. This made it possible for the executive to guide and direct the conduct of penal actions in general, by requesting the General Prosecutor to use extra diligence in prosecuting certain categories of crimes (for example, those concerning "public order" or social conflicts), refrain from prosecuting altogether certain others.

If, subsequently, the need arose to intervene in specific trial cases of political and social significance, the Ministry of Justice, often at the request of the Prime Minister and/or the Minister of Internal Affairs, would send specific instructions for the conduct of the trial to the General Prosecutor. Such interference was most frequent in the cases in which social, economic and political conflicts required coordination between the executive and the judiciary. In this manner, the role of the judiciary, and that of the Public Prosecutor's office in particular, became subservient to the government's immediate political needs, especially in case of social conflict and public order.[3]

If the Public Prosecutor depended formally on the Ministry of Justice and thus did not enjoy external independence, the institutional relationship between the judges and the political power was different. The 1865 judicial law formally sanctioned the independence of individual judges from the executive, but the specific practice regarding the juridical status of the magistrate allowed for numerous forms of government stipulations and interference.

The judges were substantially subjected to the control of the Ministry of Justice, particularly in all matters concerning their career and position within the judiciary system. All nominations, assignments, promotions, transfers, designations to administrative offices, and disciplinary actions were controlled by commissions instituted within the Ministry of Justice and hence under the firm control of the executive. The choices made by the judges in the context of their juridical activity were necessarily conditioned by the Ministry of Justice's interference in matters concerning their career and juridical status. The judges had strong reasons to remember that an attitude that was not in conformity with the political needs of the government in power would play a negative role when a promotion, a transfer or an assignment to administrative office was to be decided.

Thus, the Ministry of Justice was empowered to transfer any judge for "purposes of utility" (art. 199, paragraph 2, of the judicial law), a veritable sword of Damocles hanging over the heads of judges who might be considered "inconvenient" because they were overly independent from party politics. Finally, the power to initiate disciplinary actions was given to the Public Prosecutor, who, as we have seen, was hierarchically dependent on the Ministry of Justice.

The advent of Fascism did nothing to change the court's role of subservience to the political regime. The new totalitarian state sought to control every branch of the activity of the public administration. In fact, as regards the judiciary, such need was to a great extent fulfilled through the controls the executive had exercised over the judges under the previous liberal government. It was not until 1941 (royal decree of January 30, 1941, #12), that the Fascist regime undertook to revise the judicial code, and even then, it did nothing more than fine tune and consolidate the system that had been widely accepted practice for already more than fifty years. We can only point out that, beginning with the first years of the regime, the memoranda from the Ministry of Justice, formerly sent only to the General Prosecutor at the Appeal Courts, and to the King's prosecutor at the Law Courts, were now also directly transmitted to the heads of the courts (the chief Appellate Judges and the head judges of the Law Courts). In this fashion, the judges, too, are directly involved in the political injunctions of the government and are called upon to comply with them.[4]

Thus, within the binary perspective of dependence/independence vis à vis the government, we may conclude that the judiciary in Italy never enjoyed true independence from political power, not during the life span of the Liberal State, and certainly not during the twenty years of Fascist control. The Enlightenment concept of the separation of powers that became the foundation for the liberal and legal state in the nineteenth century was implemented for the first time in Italy's history of the administration of justice after the collapse of Fascism.

Recent research conducted in the last ten years on the personal records of judges serving during the 1800's suggest that, when comparing the relationship of the political power to the judiciary, we must take into consideration yet another variable: the integration or separation between the judiciary and the political establishment with particular reference to the judges situated at the top of the judiciary hierarchy.

To speak, as we have done until now, about pressure, interference and controls of the judiciary by the government presupposes a context of separation between executive and judiciary power. Should we conclude, however, that no such separation existed and find in reality a relationship of osmosis and integration between the high judiciary and the governmental political class, the binomial dependence/independence would have to be differently interpreted.

In fact, the examination of the personal records of highly placed judges in the first forty years of united Italy brought to light precisely such a relationship.[5] Until the end of the 1800's, the magistrates called to serve in the highest positions of the judiciary were for the most part of political extraction, that is to say they were designated to tasks of greater responsibility on account of the political merit acquired in the course of their patriotic activities during the period of the *Risorgimento* that preceded the unification of Italy.

We find, moreover, a continual osmosis between the high appointments in the courts and the political offices, in that there was a rotation of the same men for the positions of Minister of Justice, General Secretary or Vice-Secretary of the Ministry, Deputy, Senator, and the judiciary appointments. Thus, the link and coordination between institutional politics and the judiciary appear to be completely natural, given the unity of political, cultural and ideological background of the people appointed in turn to political or judiciary posts. On the one hand, the judges of political extraction constituted the privileged channel through which were transmitted, within the judiciary, the legal politics congenial to the will of the government. On the other hand, the magistrates that acceded to political appointments transmitted directly to the political establishment the needs and the aspirations of the judges, or, at least, of the high courts, whose spokesmen they became on the basis of the law drafts concerning the organization and regulation of the legal system.

This state of affairs changed in the first 10 years of the new century, when the generation of judges whose political origin had participated in the *Risorgimento* began to die out, and when new judges advance their legal careers no longer on political merit, but through competitive examination. Not surprisingly the decline of the role of political appointees brought about institutional and organizational changes which were destined to replace the preceding state of integration between the high courts and the political establishment. In 1907 the High Counsel of the judiciary was instituted, and in 1909 the National Association of the Italian Judges was founded.

Both institutions expressed, although from different points of view, the gradual establishment of the judiciary as a separate body from the political power. At the same moment in which the technical training cut the umbilical cord that tied the judiciary to the political power, the Superior counsel tended to become a self-governing organ of the judiciary, which cooperated with the powers exercised by the Ministry of Justice. In turn, the National Association of Italian Judges, originally emerged as an internal pressure group of the lower versus the higher magistrates, tended to become the spokesman of the judiciary as a whole in regards to the political power.

The potential separation between the judiciary and the political establishment did not, however, necessarily mean an increased independence from the government. On the contrary, in the first 10 years from the 1900's the pressures and the stipulations of the government were intensified, not only with the purpose of controlling the general choices in legal politics, but also of interfering in the practice of individual trials. The judiciary's progressive establishment as a separate body did not translate into the conquest of external independence in relation to the executive. Rather, the latter attempted to find new channels for maintaining control over the judges, to the extent that, during the Fascist regime, the judiciary became an increasingly technical-juridical body whose nonpartisan and neutral character, and hence its separation from the political sphere, was exalted in theory. At the same time the chains of dependence from the executive became increasingly stronger, to the extent that they openly bound the judges, as well.

We may, therefore, take for granted that the binomials dependence/independence from the executive, and integration/separation from the political establishment are not conflictual terms where the relationship to political power is concerned. The separation does not correspond to an effective independence from the executive, but a position of subordination to the political power, as, in fact, it was shown in the last years of the Liberal State, and then during the Fascist period.

The fall of Fascism signaled the beginning of profound changes in the relationship between the judiciary and the political power, changes that would lay the foundation for eventually breaking the traditional bonds of subservience to executive power that had prevailed until then. The first legislative reform of great import was constituted by the royal decree of May 31, 1946, #511, through which the Public Prosecutor's subordination to the Ministry of Justice was rescinded. The minister's administrative power was replaced by a mere surveillance power. For the first time, the Public Prosecutor's institutional separation from the executive was asserted, and the first step taken towards the affirmation of independence — not only formal of the judiciary from the political power.

The complete independence of the entire court system from the executive power was achieved in the 1948 Republican Constitution. In it the judiciary is acknowledged as an "autonomous authority independent from any other power" (Art. 104, paragraph 1); the independence of individual judges is affirmed, establishing that "judges are subject only to the law" (Art. 101, paragraph 2); judges are provided with the fundamental guarantees of irremovability (Art. 107, paragraph 1) and equality, in the declaration that "distinctions among judges are based solely on diversity of functions" (Art. 107, paragraph 3), and that judges are to be designated only through competitive examination (Art. 106, paragraph 1); these same guarantees are also extended to the Public Prosecutor (Art. 107, paragraph 4).

Such solemn declaration of principles is backed by the establishment of institutions that guarantee the effective independence of the judicial from the executive power. The Consiglio Superiore della Magistratura (Superior Council, CSM) was created, and alone vested with the power of self-governing, relieving the government of the powers it had formerly exercised over the juridic status of the judges and which had greatly conditioned any real independence of the courts from the government. In fact, the CSM was empowered in the following matters: hiring, assignment of benches and functions, transfers, promotions, and disciplinary measures (Art. 105), while the Ministry of Justice was given control over the organization and operation of justice-related services (Art. 110).[6]

Two-thirds of the members of the CSM are judges elected by the judiciary from its own ranks and one third are university professors of law or attorneys elected by a joint session of Parliament (Art. 104); this makeup is intended to prevent any excessive detachment of the judiciary from the social body, and especially from the political power structure. The officials elected by the Parliament should, in fact, secure the necessary links with the political establishment and avert the risk of an excessive corporate isolation on the part of the judges.

Thus, with the advent of the democratic-republican regulation, the premises are set for the definitive superseding of the patterns "integration/dependence" and "separation/dependence" which had characterized the relationship of the judiciary to political power in the preceding periods of the history of united Italy.

Among other things, the National Association of Judges, which had been dissolved by the Fascist regime in 1924 was reconstituted as early as 1945. It would energetically claim the value of the independence of the judiciary power, accompanied however by a tendency towards excessive corporate separatism from the social body and from political power. Notwithstanding these premises favorable to an immediate surmounting of the consolidated patterns of the relationship to the political power, those very patterns continued to operate for almost twenty years. The reasons for this are to be found in the nature of the institution, in the failed "defascistization" among the ranks of the judiciary personnel, and in the reigning political climate of the first twenty years of Republican Italy.

The CSM, the judiciary's organ of self-management, a vital element to achieving the needed independence of the courts from the executive, did not become operative until 1958, a good ten years after the promulgation of the Constitution. This was not accidental. The Christian Democratic and centrist governments, which had firm control over post-Fascist Italy for almost twenty years, did not look favorably upon a veritable affirmation of the independence of the courts.

As a matter of fact, the executive's fear of losing a governmental tool, which had served so effectively in the past, was great: through the judiciary, the executive was able to operate political choices which then it would not be called to justify politically, sheltered as it was behind the screen of the judiciary's supposed independence. Thus, for more than ten years after the fall of Fascism, the interference of the Ministry of Justice in the juridical status of the judges continued to exist. In turn, the judges continued to submit to the kind of conditioning to which they had been accustomed since long before the advent of Fascism.

To this institutional orientation one must add the continuity of judicial personnel from the preceding regime. Despite legislative measures taken even before the definitive fall of the Fascist regime by the first governments of post-Fascist Italy, there was no purge of the judiciary, or of the rest of the state administration, for that matter.[7] The judges sitting on the bench after the war of liberation had entered the judiciary during the liberal state and moved ahead in their careers during the twenty years of Fascism, attaining the highest posts in the judicial administration based on meritorious service during the dictatorship. That is to say that they were not, on account of their juridical, cultural and ideological background, the most suited to put into practice the values of independence that the republican Constitution had recognized as the fundamental principles of the judiciary activity of the new democratic system.

The continuity in personnel went hand in hand with the preservation of the structures and judicial organization of the Fascist regime. Notwithstanding the Constitutional principle of uncompromised external independence of the judiciary from the executive, internally the system was still basically the same one defined by the 1941 law, a rigid hierarchy in which the section chief exercised considerable direction and control over the activities of individual judges. From the work assigned to single judges or single sections all the way to the establishment of benches, the power of the head judges of the Law Court and of the Court of Appeal, as well as that of the Prosecutor of the Republic over the lower Court and of the General Prosecutor over the Court of Appeal, remained almost absolute, allowing cautious control of the juridical activity of the single judges or of the benches.

Because the reform of the judiciary, that had been prescribed by the 7th transitional provision of the Constitution, failed, the constitutional principle (Art. 107, paragraph 3), according to which the judges are distinguished only by diversity of function, remained in practice unenforced. The effects of the failed purge and of the continued service of the same judges after the fall of Fascism merged with the preservation of the hierarchical structure of the judiciary sections. Since the section chiefs were judges who had been rewarded for their conformity and loyalty to the Fascist regime, one can easily understand the fundamentally conservative attitude of the judiciary following the Liberation.

The three factors that prevented judicial power from becoming truly independent from the executive after the fall of Fascism can be summarized as follows: the delay before the CSM became operational; and the continuing interference by the Ministry of Justice on the career appointments and the office status of the magistrates; the continuity in the personnel structure and organization of the judiciary especially where they allow for extended power by the section chiefs; and the cultural heritage of judges reared during the Fascist period, who continued to defend the myths of juridic formalism and of a law and courts that were uncommitted and value-free.

The myth of a neutral and value-free law was used after the Liberation to justify the attitude of total disregard, if not open hostility, of the judiciary to the new democratic order. In effect, the very foundations of the judiciary (penal and penal procedure codes, civil code, uniform text on public security laws, prison administration) were still those enacted by the Fascist regime in support of its political and ideological needs. Using juridic formalism as a cover, the courts easily laid claim to a role that essentially resulted in preserving the legislation enacted during the twenty years of Fascism, as well as its underlying values.

The first test of judicial power immediately after the Liberation was the enforcement of special penal legislation to punish crimes of Italians serving in the army of the puppet Fascist Social Republic (1943-45) collaborating with the German invaders during the eighteen-month civil war against the Anti-Fascist Resistance. The forces of the Resistance were well aware that punishment of Nazi-Fascist crimes could not be entrusted to the same judges who had been reared and were practicing during the twenty years of Fascism. So even before the civil war ended, the Comitato di Liberazione Alta Italia [Liberation Committee of Northern Italy (CLNAI)] proposed that the punishment of crimes of collaboration be entrusted to specially designated popular justice agencies, panelled by judges who had not been involved in the past regime. The agency supported by the CLN was called the People's Court of Assizes, wherein judges of political and popular extraction prevailed.[8]

Yet three days before the Liberation, the CLNAI proposal was superseded by a decree from the Rome government (Royal Decree of April 22, 1945, #142) instituting the Extraordinary Courts of Assizes, to be presided by a magistrate of the appeal courts, that is to say by a judge who, because of his age — if nothing else — had to have been trained and promoted during the twenty years of Fascism. Furthermore, the CLNAI proposal provided that the sentences of the People's Court of Assizes could not be appealed, while the governmental decree provided for appeals to the Court of Cassation, and, given its place at the apex of the hierarchy, its judges must necessarily have been connected with the ideology of the past regime.

Again departing from the CLNAI proposal, wherein the exercise of penal action was entrusted to special popular justice agencies, in the governmental decree even the charges were entrusted to public prosecutors, who had been accustomed, on the basis of their mentality and the long tradition of hierarchical subordination to the Ministry of Justice, to obeying the instructions of the executive. Punishing the crimes of collaboration was thus resolved in terms of continuity, both as regards the composition of new judiciary agencies and the mentality of the judges called to act upon the special criminal legislation against the collaborators. This explains the basic failure of judicial interventions against the Fascists responsible for having brought Italy to the depths of a civil war that lasted almost two years. Not enough research has been conducted on the work of the Extraordinary Courts of Assizes at national level, but a special study on the activities of these organs in the Piedmont region[9] provides a rather representative view of the attitudes of the courts, particularly when we compare the local decisions to those handed down by the Court of Cassation.

The basic trend in the courts of Piedmont, i.e. an area where the Liberation War had been particularly bitter and had involved large segments of the population, was to severely punish the "excesses" carried out by Fascist thugs in their fight against the partisans, but to refrain from extending responsibility to the political, administrative and military representatives of the past regime. The "common" crimes, that is to say murders, torture, acts of violence against defenseless populace committed by the militia men belonging to the "black brigades" were severely prosecuted, while the executive officers of the political and administrative apparatuses of the Repubblica Sociale Italiana (Fascist Social Republic) and of the Fascist party seemed to enjoy some sort of immunity.

One has the impression, despite the special legislation against collaborators, that there was prosecution of only those actions that would have been subject to the rigors of the law regardless, such as common crimes governed by the penal code, while the actions of those who had served in positions of authority in the civilian and military agencies of the Fascist Social Republic were presumably lawful, as they were functions performed in the service of formally legitimized apparatuses of the bureaucracy. In other words, the judges that had continued to serve during the eighteen months of the "Republic of Salò" (i.e., the Fascist Social Republic) refused to apply the sanctions issued against former Fascists to the executive officers of other branches of the administration who had also served under the same regime.

The virtual immunity enjoyed by the executive officers of the bureaucratic apparatuses which had constituted the administrative, political and military backbone of the Fascist Social Republic stands in contrast with the prosecution of the heads and the thugs of the various military factions of the Salò Republic, who were guilty of violent crimes. This contrast is explained by the refusal of the courts to enforce the concept of justice implicit in the legislation that contained sanctions against Fascism. Thus, even the courts of a region like Piedmont, deeply involved in the struggle for liberation from Nazi-Fascist rule, closed ranks in a fierce defense of the continuity of the state, its men, and apparatuses, as if it were irrelevant that the juridical values they upheld had been legitimized by the Fascist Social Republic.

We may conclude that a conservative orientation was adopted in the Piedmontese courts, as it presumably did in other regions of northern and central Italy, where the bitterness of the liberation struggle against the Nazi-Fascists had been strongly felt. These courts remained prisoners of the juridic formalism and judicial neutrality in which they had been trained for twenty years, even though they did not disregard the fiercest and bloodiest episodes of the civil war against the partisans. They did, however, respond to the most immediate claims for justice raised by the population oppressed by eighteen months of civil war.

Vastly different are the conclusions one logically makes regarding the judges of the Court of Cassation, who were not only conservative in their defense of the men and apparatuses of the past regime, as explained earlier, but who were themselves parafascist.[10] In fact, the Court of Cassation has been ascribed responsibility for systematically undermining the attempts to punish the most ferocious and atrocious crimes committed by the Nazi-Fascist "black brigades" through a series of scandalous annulments of the sentences handed down by the Extraordinary Courts of Assizes. It must be added that the same court relaxed beyond any reasonable limit the application of the amnesty conceded by the Minister of Justice Togliatti in 1946 concerning some categories of crimes of collaboration, an amnesty whose manifest purpose was to hasten the process of national pacification.

Here, the effects of the failed "defascistization" of the top level of the courts were particularly obvious: the judges of the Court of Cassation, who had not experienced personally the Nazi-Fascist barbarity, and had made major compromises with the regime, not only chose to defend the continuity of the formally legitimized administrative apparatuses of the past regime, but carried on a cover-up of the worst crimes committed by the "black brigades."

Closely linked to the attitude of the courts towards crimes of collaboration were the trials instituted against the partisans. Here, the problem of continuity with the penal legislation and judicial structures of the Fascist regime becomes even more evident. The main characteristic of the so-called trial of the Resistance is to have been conducted exclusively by the regular bodies of the judiciary instituted in 1941, and by the judges that had been in service during the regime, who had to apply the rules of the Fascist penal code of 1930, and who had not been purged.

In this regard, the great jurist and Resistance fighter Piero Calamandrei spoke of the "magisterial professional naiveté" and "juridic ingenuity . . . of legislators emerging from the clandestine struggle," who missed the opportunity of giving "firm recognition to the new legality resulting from the order established by the revolution" and who left "almost the totality of the legislation from the old regime unaltered, in the face of which all the revolutionary actions of the combatants in the clandestine war and in the war of liberation were made to appear not as heroic acts in defense of the homeland against invaders but as the criminal acts of 'rebels'." Thus, he added, "three years after the liberation, there is not yet in Italy a legislation that would give full recognition to the partisan war!"[11]

These words were written in 1947, when only the first hints had appeared, of the anti-partisan repression which was then to have greater development in the new political climate following the defeat of the "Popular Front" during the election of April 18, 1948. They synthesize the juridical and political premises of the trial of the Resistance. In this context, the contradiction between the new democratic institutions and the continuity with the laws and the juridical structures of the old regime is, if possible, even more marked than the one that produced the essential failure to enforce the sanctions against the Fascist crimes.

While special legislation provided for the punishment of the crimes of collaboration, the trial of the Resistance was made possible, in fact favored, by the preservation of that "legality" that the partisans had defied in the eighteen months of armed combat against the Nazi-Fascist order.

The logical consequence of the failure to give judicial recognition to the legitimacy of the armed struggle for the partisans during the War of Liberation flowed from the 1930 penal code, which had not been revised after the collapse of Fascism, so that their actions continued to be considered "common" crimes: from robbery to extortion, from crimes against persons to those against property, and from kidnapping all the way to homicide. Moreover, the failure to give judicial recognition to the legitimacy of partisan actions rendered possible the pressing of charges in civil courts, with the purpose of obtaining from the partisans compensations for damages regarding requisitions, soliciting contributions, etc., which during the times of the Liberation War had been absolutely necessary to the exigencies of the struggle against the Nazi-Fascists, but that failed to be upheld by specific legislation after the Liberation.

In the absence of an appropriate law that would generally declare that all the actions of the partisans in the course of the Liberation War were not criminal — with the exception of such actions of which the goals were extraneous to the objectives of the Resistance — the legislators of free Italy, even before April 25, 1945, resorted to amnesty. This meant that those actions were considered crimes, but that the State, in recognition of the exceptional political and military contingencies in which they had been committed, was waiving their prosecution through an act of clemency.

Between April 5, 1944, and June 22, 1946 (the date of the already mentioned amnesty of Togliatti, which also encompassed the crimes of collaboration), numerous decrees of amnesty for the "crimes" of the partisans were emitted. These decrees were subject to so many conditions that their application was rendered difficult and controversial.

In particular, the various legislative formulae adopted in the amnesty provisions did not minimally take into consideration the "natural" propensity of the courts to deal with the "crimes" committed by the partisans by adhering to the continuity of the legal system inherited from the Fascist regime while ignoring the revolutionary significance of the Liberation War. The ambiguity and discretionary character of the conditions to which the application of the various amnesty decrees was subordinated seemed to serve the purpose of inviting the judges to exercise their traditional role of punishing any crime committed, including those of partisans. In the first decree, amnesty is given on condition that the crime be ascertained to have been committed to the end "of liberating the mother country from German occupation," and that it had been concretized in "armed action for the driving away of the German troops from the sacred soil of the mother country," or "in actions directed towards frustrating the war activity of the German troops." Its terms allowed not only discretionary, but value laden judgments often alien to the mentality and the technical-juridical background of the judges.

These are the legislative premises on which the ordinary courts operated in conducting the so-called prosecution of the Resistance,[12] especially after 1948, when the change to moderate centrist government was accompanied by an actual intent to punish and squelch the partisan movement. Using the sentences handed down by the Piedmontese courts until 1960 as a reference point,[13] we see many points in common between prosecution of the collaborators and that of the partisans.

On the one hand, the courts refused to apply standards of judicial review to the political, administrative and military organizations of the past regime; on the other hand, by relentlessly adhering to a formalistic methodology in categorizing the actions of the partisans, they demonstrated a significant lack of understanding of the unique context in which the partisans had acted. They failed to understand that, though clumsily written, the amnesty decrees were intended to avoid incrimination of partisan fighters. In both cases the post-Fascist era judges refused to exercise the role of judicial review the republican legislature had entrusted to them.

It appears paradoxical that beginning in 1948 and continuing until the end of the fifties the courts initiated trials against the partisans for the crimes of illegal possession and transport of weapons, in other words, for actions constituting an indispensable premise in the War of Resistance. From today's perspective, it seems incredible that the judges did not understand the anachronistic and outrageous character of the charges against those who, carrying or hiding weapons, were daily risking their lives.

But if we analyze the cultural context in which the judges were exercising their profession, and the role, assigned to them by the Fascist regime, of mere technical interpreters of criminal law, our incredulity will diminish. In fact, within the framework of a rigorous technical juridical interpretation of the Fascist penal code, the judges resorted to criteria of reasonable benevolence in the case of the "crimes" committed by the partisans, just as they did for any other common crime, with the purpose of rendering less oppressive the consequent sanctions. Generic attenuating circumstances are frequently conceded also in the case of homicide, let alone the downgrading of armed robbery to the less grave felonies of theft or receiving of stolen goods.

Within these limits, it does not seem appropriate to place upon the courts the responsibility of the trial of the Resistance, nor that of the failure of the sanctions against Fascism. Nonetheless, in interpreting the highly ambiguous legislative messages of the political authorities, the courts used only the formalistic canons at hand, refusing to engage in any political mediation when dealing with anti-Fascist issues.

The attitude of the judges in these two basic issues of criminal justice that prevailed for fifteen years after the fall of the Fascist regime explains why it was not until the sixties that the Italian courts learned to use the new values of independence and autonomy from political power guaranteed in the republican Constitution. Notwithstanding constitutional principles, the historical tradition of a judiciary that was subservient to the executive power — but was culturally accustomed to hide this state of dependency behind the myth of the neutrality and the technical nature of law — continued.

In other words, the continuity of men, structure and judiciary organization was stronger than the new constitutional order of the relationships between the judges and the other powers of the state. For the judges emerging from twenty years of Fascist rule it was easier to continue interpreting their role as that of loyal enforcers of the political will of the current government. Since these governments, from the ousting of the left in 1947 through the next fifteen years of Christian Democratic and centrist hegemony, were firmly committed to ensuring the continuity of the judicial order inherited from the Fascist regime and postponing implementation of the new constitutional values, it was only logical that the Italian courts would support conservatism and defend continuity.

Moreover, it must be remembered that the Constitutional Court, one of whose tasks was to assess the possible conflict between common law and constitutional principles, began to function only in 1956. Until that date, the task of evaluating the constitutional legitimacy of common law was entrusted to the Court of Cassation, i.e. precisely to those judges who had been among the main authors of the Fascist code and legislation. Once again, as it had happened in other periods of Italian history, the subordinate role of the judiciary in regards to the political governmental order was carried out through the emphatic corporate separation of the judiciary body from the rest of society. It was, above all, the top level of the courts who imposed this separation, in order to avoid risking the independence recognized by the Constitution to the judges of the Italian Republic putting an end to their traditional subordination to governmental political power.

Once again, the myths of the technical nature and of the neutrality of law were used to hide the political role played by the courts in support of the political aims of the government in charge. If the duty of a judge is limited exclusively to applying laws that are already in effect according to the interpretative canons of judicial formalism, then there can be no alternative to the opinions rendered by the judges on the Court of Cassation, at the apex of the judicial hierarchy, nor can we point to the politically conservative role played by judicial power.

Only in the mid-sixties was the monopolistic cadre presiding over the Court of Cassation broken and an effective ideological and political pluralism emerged. During the famous meeting of the National Association of Judges held in Gardone in 1964, judges for the first time claimed their role of interpreting the existing legislation in light of the Constitution. It was also at this meeting that currents surfaced within the association, the first expression of the charged ideological, political and cultural position now reflected in the courts.[14]

It was precisely in the mid-sixties that progressive and left wing currents within the courts lay claim to the judicial power of controlling the legality of the operation of the executive, of the public agencies and of the governmental parties. For the first time in the judicial history of Italy, the values of effective independence from executive power were affirmed, and the courts claimed full rights of operating on the basis of an ideology different from that of the political forces of the government.

This new perspective entailed a profound change in the relationship of political and social forces. It replaced the one-way integration with the political establishment that had characterized the first thirty years of Italy's judicial history after national unification; no longer was there merely a formal separation from politics and the hiding behind judicial formalism as a cover-up, whether intentional or not, of subservience to the government in charge. There are now true forms of pluralistic relations with the various political powers as provided in the Constitution, regardless of their position in relation to the government. On the one hand, this means the overcoming of those forms of separatism from society that had until then fostered a climate of corporate isolation of the judiciary; on the other, it assured the attainment of an effective independence from the executive, by means of a pluralism of relationships with the political forces, even those of the opposition.

The Constitution's intention of guaranteeing the effective independence of judicial power did not become reality until fifteen years after its promulgation, when the continuity of men and judicial structures inherited from the Fascist regime was finally broken.

Starting with the mid-sixties, there was reversed the traditional dependence of the courts on the executive, and the dependence of the individual judges on the section chiefs and officers at the top of the judicial hierarchy. These include: the beginning of the CSM's and the Constitutional Court's functioning; a new set of standards governing promotions and advancement in the profession, free from the oppressive influence of the high court judges in the judicial merit and promotions commissions; the retirement from top judiciary offices of the generation of judges who had been trained during the Fascist regime; and a new political climate that recognizes greater legitimacy to opposition from the left.

This complex of factors finally allowed the overcoming of the negative connotations which had until then characterized the binomials integration/separation and dependency/independence. Actual independence from the executive power is now accompanied by a pluralistic integration with all political forces: the judges can finally play the role, assigned by the Constitution to the judiciary, of controlling the legality of the operations of all state apparatuses, and of enforcing the rules of legality also in the case of governmental parties and the political establishment.

The independence from the executive, which, accompanied by the corporate separation from society and nurtured by the myth of judicial formalism and of an apolitical nature of the law, had been a merely formal value until the mid-sixties, is now conjoined with the recognition of the legitimacy of interpretations that do not necessarily endorse the political interests of the government.

Judicial inquiries into the political and administrative misconduct of national and local government agencies, occurring with increasing frequency from the early seventies onward, are not tuned to the political interests of the current governments; the reason for this may be that the guarantees for actual independence from the executive are accompanied by a process wherein the courts enclose the ideologies, the requests for justice and the political undercurrents of the entire civilian society.

The absolute institutional novelty of this relationship between the courts and the political power structure was not immediately understood by the government's political forces, and was left to expand undisturbed until the early eighties. Only at the beginning of this decade have the political parties begun to show signs of growing intolerance for the new role of the courts, submitting proposals for an institutional reform of the relationship between the judiciary and the executive that would revive some of the patterns for earlier periods of Italian judicial history.

It is not by chance that there is some movement in the direction of limiting the effective independence of the judiciary from the executive. The objective is to sever the new pluralistic binate relationship of independence/pluralistic integration with all political forces, and return to a pattern where the courts would again play a subservient role in the government's body politic.

Notes

1 Piero Maravelli, *L'indipendenza e l'autonomia della Magistratura in Italia*. Milan: Giuffrè, 1966.

2 M. D'Addio, *Politica e magistratura (1848-1876)*, Milan: Giuffrè, 1966. G. Maranini, *Storia del potere in Italia, 1848-1967*, Florence, 1967. G. Neppi Modona, *Sciopero, potere politico e magistratura, 1870/1922*, Bari: Laterza, 1979. N. Tranfaglia, *Dallo stato liberale al regime fascista*, Milan: Feltrinelli, 1973 (155-184; 281-290).

3 Regarding government intervention in strikes and in trials of political significance, see G. Neppi Modona, op. cit.

4 G. Neppi Modona, "La magistratura e il fascismo," in *Fascismo e società italiana*, Turin: Einaudi, 1973 (125-181). G. C. Jocteau, *La magistratura e i conflitti di lavoro durante il fascismo (1926-1934)*, Milan: Feltrinelli, 1978.

5 For this approach to the judiciary's relationship to political power, cfr. P. Saraceno, *Alta magistratura e classe politica dalla integrazione alla separazione*, Rome: Edizioni dell'Ateneo, 1979; P. Saraceno (ed.), *I magistrati italiani dall'Unità al fascismo. Studi biografici e prosopografici*, Rome: Carucci Editore, 1988; P. Venturini, *Un "Sindacato" di giudici da Giolitti a Mussolini. L'Associazione Generale tra i Magistrati Italiani, 1909-1926*, Bologna: Il Mulino, 1987.

6 On constitutional principles, on the structure of judiciary power and on the relations between the judiciary and other powers of the state in the Italian Republic, see A. Pizzorusso (ed.), *L'ordinamento giuidiziario*, Bologna: Il Mulino, 1974. A. Pizzorusso, *L'organizzazione della giustizia in Italia. La magistratura nel sistema politico e istituzionale*, Turin: Einaudi, 1982. F. Bonifacio, G. Giacobbe, La magistratura, Commentary (articles 104-107 of the Constitution), vol. II, in G. Branca (ed.), *Commentario della Costituzione*, Bologna: Zanichelli, 1986. V. Denti, G. Neppi Modona, G. Berti, P. Corso, La magistratura (Commentary to Articles 111-113 of the Constitution), vol. IV, in G. Branca (ed.), *Commentario della Costituzione*, Bologna: Zanichelli, 1987.

7 On the failure to purge administrative and judicial agencies, see C. Pavone, "La continuità dello stato. Istituzioni e uomini," *Italia, 1945-48. Le origini della Repubblica*, Turin, 1974.

8 G. Neppi Modona, "La legislazione CLN del Piemonte," *Aspetti della Resistenza in Piemonte*, Turin: Book Store, 1977 (307-374).

9   G. Neppi Modona (ed.) *Giustizia penale e guerre di liberazione*, Milan: Angeli, 1984.

10 Basic reading on the role of the Court of Cassation is A. Battaglia, *I giudici e la politica*, Bari: Laterza, 1962 (69-101).

11 P. Calamandrei, "Restaurazione clandestina," *Il Ponte*, 1947, pp. 965-966.

12 A. Battaglia, op. cit., p. 102 f., in the chapter devoted to the judges and the trial of the Resistance.

13 S. Testori, "La 'repressione' antipartigiana e la magistratura piemontese (1946-1959)," in G. Neppi Modona (ed.), *Giustizia penale e guerra di liberazione*, cit. (173-206).

14 For a historical reconstruction of the role of the courts in Republican Italy, see A. Pizzorusso (ed.), *L'ordinamento giudiziario*, cit. (13-63); D. Pulitano, *Giudice negli anni '70*, Bari: De Donato.

XXI

Parallel Administrations:
The State and the Parastate

Sabino Cassese

The political developments that occurred in the twenty years following the Second World War can be divided into clear-cut periods: 1945: the end of the war; 1948: the enactment of the Republican Constitution; 1948-1958: centralism; 1958-1963: acceptance
of the left-wing forces; 1963 on: central-left government.

The same cannot be said for administrative developments. Seen
in this light, the years from 1945 to 1963 do not appear as a unified
period. On the one hand, the dominant theme of the epoch would
seem to have been continuity; on the other, however, the time
period in question gives the appearance of a phase of preparation.
To be more precise, these years lack one of the characteristics generally possessed by periods defined as historic: a *"dies a quo"*,
meaning a starting point (in the conclusion of this paper we will
see, however, that 1963 does represent an authentic turning point
in the country's administrative history).

Much has been written about the continuity between the Fascist
and the post-war administrative bodies. At the time the fact was
widely bemoaned and criticized, and historians have analyzed it in
the years since (one need merely mention the work of Federico
Chabod and Claudio Pavone). Indeed, the continuity in question
was not only formal, affecting the State and its institutions, but also
substantial, meaning that it regarded both the men and the administrative apparatuses involved.

In the event, as early as the government of Salerno (1944), the
efforts of the government involving the state administration were
geared towards restoring institutions, purging them of Fascists and
returning to the system of the pre-Fascist period. Though some

new institutions were introduced (the High Commissioners' Offices, for example) these were merely designed as temporary measures. Indeed, the idea of establishing a "State of National Liberation Committees" (CLN) soon met with failure.

The effort described above, however, was only partially successful. While the removal of Fascist elements resulted in the abolition of the superstructure of the corporate state and the restoration of municipal liberties, the effort had only a slight effect in terms of personnel, given the failure of the purge and the minimal influence exercised on the overall management of the administration by the injection of crippled and handicapped individuals, patriots, veterans, orphans, widows, etc. into its ranks.

A large portion of the state operations underwent no significant modification. The Fascist "Welfare" system, for example, "remained basically unaltered throughout the 1950's. . . . The underlying trend was therefore substantial continuity in the basic institutional principles and regulations, as well as in the organizational and administrative patterns."[1]

Nor did the total number of state employees undergo significant modifications. Between 1945 and 1963, the figure for the percentage of government employees for every 100 thousand citizens grew by only half a point (from 2.3 to 2.8). While government employees did obtain a new set of rules and regulations, these were based on principles that had been consolidated by the Fascist Council of State in the area of public employment. In the previous eighteen-year period the ranks of state employees had grown by one point (from 1.3 to 2.3), and the same rate of growth was experienced in the fifteen years that followed.

The ministerial structures themselves remained essentially untouched. The most important changes were: the merger – though a far less than perfect one – of the War, Navy and Air Force ministries into the new Ministry of Defense, a transformation performed in 1947; the establishment, during the same year, of the Ministry of the Budget, which was considered merely a "temporary expedient" by De Gasperi; the establishment in 1951 of the Ministry of Bureaucratic Reform; the 1957 establishment of the Ministry of State Holdings; the 1958 establishment of the Ministry of Health and the 1959 establishment of the Ministry of Tourism and Entertainment.

Even the Constitution failed to modify the situation. On the one hand, the work of the Constituent Assembly confirmed what was defined by Nenni as the "division of labor" between the Assembly — which was assigned to prepare the future, meaning the Constitution — and the government, designated to exercise both legislative and administrative power. On the other hand, the Constitution remained in a state of torpor up through the "Constitutional Thaw," which did not take place until the 1960's.

To sum up, the years from the end of the war to the advent of central-left government appear as something of a continuation of the preceding period. Though the First World War had signalled an important turning point in the country's administrative history, the Second World War, despite its highly visible effect on the national territory and on Italian society, does not seem to have produced significant changes in the State's administrative structures.

If we shift our focus from the state administration to the state-controlled agencies and corporations, the outlook seems to change. Here is a review of the principal modifications. The years 1945-1950 are of little importance, being characterized by what amounts to administrative immobility. The only noteworthy developments to occur during this period were: the reorganization of the National Autonomous Highway Agency — ANAS (1946); the strengthening of the Banca d'Italia, which was assigned powers over currency, together with the establishment of the Italian Exchange Office — UIC (1945), followed by the disbandment of the Inspectorate of Credit and Savings, whose monitoring powers were shifted to the central bank (1947); finally, the Togni Law on financing to industry provided on favorable terms (1948) and the Tupini Law on the public works projects of the municipalities (1949).

The Fanfani Plan of 1949 was a watershed event for working-class housing and the establishment of INA-housing. A distinguishing characteristic of this and other initiatives undertaken during the same period was the fact that the new programs were not assigned to the state administration but to public agencies that had been established "*ad hoc*".

Apart from housing, the areas where the initiatives were concentrated included agriculture, aid to Southern Italy, energy, highways, state holdings and financing to the economy provided on favorable terms. In each of these areas, one or more public agencies were established.

In the case of agriculture, the period of reform began with the agricultural reform and the assignment of land to small farmers (1950), after which it continued with the laws on mountain areas and on small agricultural plots (1952), not to mention the initiatives involving assistance to working farmers (1953). A large number of agencies were established: those founded in the previous years — such as the Flumendosa Agency (1946), the Agency for the Development of Irrigation and Land Transformation in the Apulia, Lucania and Irpinia Regions (1947), the Sila Program (1947), the Fund for the Formation of Small Farming Plots (1948) — were followed in 1951 by the agencies for the Po Delta, the Maremma marshlands, development in the Apulia, Lucania and Molise Regions, and the special Department for Land Reform under the Flumendosa Agency; still later, in 1954, the Fucino Agency was founded, followed by the Autonomous Agency for Reclamation, Irrigation and Land Improvement in the Provinces of Arezzo, Perugia, Siena and Terni (1961).

In terms of aid to Southern Italy, the Southern Italian Development Fund was established in 1950, while three special credit institutes — for continental Southern Italy, Sicily and Sardinia — were founded in 1953 (ISVEIMER, IRFIS and CIS). In the same year, the Institute for Industrial Credit to Southern Italy was reorganized, and in 1955 legislation was passed for industrial financing in Southern Italy and the island regions. Finally, in 1957 the activities of the Southern Italian Development Fund were expanded from agriculture and public works to include industry as well, and in 1957 and 1962 two laws were passed on industrial financing in Southern Italy and the island regions.

As regards energy, 1953 witnessed the founding of the National Hydrocarbons Agency — ENI, together with the Sardinian Electrical Agency. In 1957, legislation governing hydrocarbons was passed, and in 1960 the National Committee for Nuclear Energy — the CNEN — was established.

As far as highways are concerned, the related plans dates from 1954-1955. Its execution was entrusted to the Institute for Industrial Reconstruction — IRI — at a time when state-held corporations were enjoying a significant revival.

After the La Malfa and Giacchi studies of the early 1950's, state-held enterprises were considerably strengthened in the period between 1953 — the year ENI was founded — and 1957 — the year the Ministry of State-held Enterprises was established. The large public holding companies experienced particularly strong growth in the areas of steel, construction, telephone service, radio and television broadcasting and the electro-mechanical industries. The state-held enterprises played an important role in the "Program for Increasing Employment and Income in Italy during the Ten-year Period of 1955-1964", better known as the Vanoni Plan. The establishment of the Ministry of State-held Enterprises was followed by that of the Autonomous Agency for the Film Industry, the Autonomous Agency for Thermal Spas and the Autonomous Agency for the Management of Mining Enterprises (1958).

The policy of supplying the economy with financing at advantageous terms was decided upon following the short-lived managerial drive of 1951 (laws on the monitoring of production potential and the control of production activities, consumption, prices and wages). Noteworthy initiatives were undertaken by the governments of De Gasperi (VI and VII) and Fanfani: legislation on medium-term credit to small industries, to agriculture, to mining concerns, to the chemical industry, to the steel industry and to the hydrocarbons industry (1951); legislation for economic development and increased employment (1952); measures for credit to medium and small-scale industrial enterprises (1954); legislation on the financing of industrial concerns in Southern Italy (1957); legislation for the financing and the establishment of advantageous terms for the re-employment of personnel laid off by steel companies (1956); legislation offering incentives for medium and small-scale firms and handicrafts enterprises (1959); measures for the financing of industry in Southern Italy (1969).

A large number of credit institutes are related to the above measures: the Credit Institute for Medium-term Financing to Medium and Small-scale Enterprises in the Piedmont and Val d'Aosta Regions, the National Institute for Financing Reconstruction, and the Central Institute for Medium-term Credit, all of which were founded in 1952; the Sardinian Industrial Credit Institute was founded in 1953, as were the Credit Institutes for Medium-term Financing of Medium and Small-scale enterprises in the regions of Umbria, Lombardy, the Marches and Latium; finally, the Institute of Sporting Credit was established in 1957.[2]

Only two of the administrative modifications performed during this period failed to produce a plethora of "*ad hoc*" administrations: the liberalization of foreign trade ushered in by La Malfa in 1951, which allowed Italy to return to the international markets, and the country's signing of the Rome accord of 1957 establishing the European Common Market. It should be noted, however, that both these measures were directed at freeing Italy from its policy of self-sufficiency and opening up the related markets. Even La Malfa's liberalization was accomplished without introducing any thorough-going innovations in the relevant legislation, which, in terms of both the exchange of merchandise and the exchange of currencies, was still based on the principal that whatever was not expressly authorized was to be considered prohibited. For the most part, the liberalization involved merchandise, merely broadening – though to a significant extent – the range of merchandise for which import and export authorization was to be granted in a preliminary, general sense (so-called "customs" authorization).

The state (or ministerial) administration therefore remained essentially unchanged during the early postwar period, up through the 1960's. The government-controlled agencies and corporations, on the other hand, grew considerably, and this represents the principal contradiction of postwar Italy.

For that matter, the contradiction appears even more acute when one considers that the immobility of the state administration was accompanied by the economic "boom:" "the years of the 'boom' witnessed the most marked deterioration of the public administration, especially in the financial and technical fields, precisely because the country's economic progress exposed the inability of the bureaucracy to keep pace with overall growth."[3]

Parliament decided to refrain from entrusting new tasks to the state administration, aware of the fact that these tasks would not be performed. There was a lack of confidence and trust in the ministerial bureaucracy. On the one hand, the miasma of procedures that the administration had to follow was no secret. One need merely recall the words used by De Gasperi in Parliament to present the legislative proposal for the establishment of the Southern Italian Aid Fund in 1950: the agency — the Southern Italian Aid Fund — was established so that it might operate "under a unified, consistent set of directives, with the necessary flexibility to adopt the planning and the execution of its efforts, with all due speed, to changing economic and social demands." In 1962, the Minister of the Budget, Pella, attempted to modify the state accounting system, one of the principal causes of inefficiency in the ministerial administration, but without success.

Apart form the lack of confidence, there was most probably a lack of trust as well. The ranking officials of the bureaucracy had been selected, and received their professional experience, during the Fascist period. A parallel bureaucracy, namely that of the government agencies, whose personnel could be recruited from among trusted individuals, without the need to hold public competitions, appeared to be the more reliable option. It is symptomatic of the situation that this period saw Luigi Sturzo and Ernesto Rossi begin their debate — though from different points of view — regarding superfluous government agencies, which were seen as a hindrance to the economy and an abuse of the political system. There is a second factor that should be emphasized: far from representing a novel development, the growth of the non-ministerial administrations simply marked the continuation of a trend that appeared in the 1920's and took root in the 1930's. One need merely perform a comparison: during the period 1945-1963 a total of 170 individual agencies and 12 category agencies were established. During the period 1926 to 1944, a total of 287 individual agencies and 26 category agencies were established, meaning that the government-controlled agencies and corporations did not represent an innovation. Indeed, during the postwar period they grew at a lower rate than they had under the Fascist regime.

This lends further strength to the hypothesis presented at the beginning of this discussion: namely, that the early postwar years did not represent a unified period, but merely marked the continuation of the trends initiated in the 1930's. Despite the political transformation, the social upheaval and the damage wrought by the war, the administrative structures continued for almost twenty years along the path first taken in the 1930's.

True changes did not occur until later, at which point they opened a new chapter in the country's administrative history. The transformations were, in part, the result of the cycle of economic growth: the "boom" had led to a rise in both expectations and available resources. The prevailing passions and ideas had changed. Italy had become a predominantly industrialized country. To a certain extent, however, the changes were also the fruit of the avenues originally opened during the grey days of the early postwar years: mainly, the liberalization of foreign trade and the creation of the European Economic Community.

Can it be said that the administrative modifications followed the social and constitutional changes at a distance? Or do such transformations take place only when economic developments have reached a critical threshold, a point at which enough energy and resources may be set free and then applied to the public sector? Or is it true that we continue to be enchanted by history's grand events (wars, changes in political regimes) and fail to pay due attention to the enduring presence of the public institutions that provide the underpinnings for day-to-day life? As things stand, these questions still await an answer.

Notes and References

1 M. Ferrera, "Italy", in *Growth to Limits: The Western European States Since World War II*, P. Flora, ed., De Gruyer: Berlin-New York, p. 391.

2 See F. Merusi, ed., *La legislazione economica italiana dalla fine della guerra al primo programma economico*, Milan: Franco Angeli Editore, 1974, and A. Orsi Battaglini, ed., *Amministrazione pubblica e istituzioni finanziarie*, Bologna: Il Mulino, 1980.

3 D. Bartoli, *L'Italia burocratica*, Milan: Garzanti, 1965, p. 157.

XXII

Interventions by Joseph La Palombara and Leopoldo D'Elia Following the Presentation of Guido Neppi Modona

In the afternoon session of October 21, 1989 of our Symposium on Postwar Italy presided over by Giovanni Sartori of Columbia University, Guido Neppi Modona presented a paper. Sabino Cassese could not attend the meeting, however his paper is included here. We are unable to publish formal papers in response to Modona's and Cassese's presentations, but both Joseph La Palombara of Yale University and Leopoldo D'Elia of the Italian Senate made interesting observations which follow.

Joseph La Palombara

Just a couple of comments involving two or three points. First, there is a striking difference between the Italian Constitution of 1948 and the American Constitution in that the Italian Constitution invites the judiciary to become involved in the political process in ways that were historically not intended in the United States. Evoking John Marshall in "Marbury v. Madison" is a very good point, namely the separation and balance system that the founders in Philadelphia in 1787 thought they were putting together, did not in any explicit way suggest this. Although there are historians who believe that Hamilton's scheme was clearly and quickly articulated by Marshall, there was nothing in the written Constitution that suggested that judges ought to become as deeply involved in the political process, as the concept of judicial review implies.

Furthermore, I think it is a strength of the Italian Constitution — and I would be interested in knowing whether my friend and colleague Elia agrees with this — that it is explicit on this score anticipating that judges are going to be very definitely and richly (and I think appropriately) part of the political process. There is not any pretense of the kind that Beccaria articulated, that there is something out there in the ether that ordinary human beings cannot discover, that judges can. And the question then is not so much whether judges are in the political process, but there are a couple of other questions. One would be, the way in which they behave politically, and the ability of other institutions to deal with that behavior — it seems to me that's the critical question.

I am concerned about the United States at the moment, not so much because of what the Supreme Court does, and it has recently done, for example in connection with the issue of abortion. I think they have been doing exactly what they have done for a good many decades in the United States. I am concerned that some of the other branches of government in this system no longer have the capacity to produce that centripetal tendency toward equilibrium that has been, I believe, the saving grace of the American Constitutional system. What I find distressing in the Italian debate over the role of the judiciary and of judges, is the tendency to make only the judiciary the object of criticism that somehow or other they have gone beyond the limit of their function. Abstractly and conceptually one can divide these functions of government, I think that the process of government requires that we recognize that judges inevitably not only interpret, but also make law, and I say thank goodness that they do. The point then is — and here I repeat myself, but I think it is something worth considering — not to look at the judicial branch in isolation, the point is to see the judicial branch as it relates to other branches of government. To Vanni [Sartori] I would say that the problem with evoking the common law is that the common law produces, in the cradle of the common law, a parliamentary system that argues a legislative supremacy. Our system, while it derives from that common law tradition, does not accept the idea of legislative supremacy, but quite definitely singles out two other branches, and in the process of singling out two other branches for attention, politicizes them. I think that is healthy for our system of democracy, I am not sure how it would work elsewhere. But the role of judges, it seems to me, in the United States was deliberately obscured at the beginning of our

Constitutional history. John Marshall provided clarification and I think it has been a benefit, but I think the benefit lies in our recognizing that judges make law on occasion.

Leopoldo Elia

My friend Sartori has called me to task, creating undoubtedly a little embarrassment for me, since the Committee I chair at the Senate is examining several law proposals that directly concern the reform of the Supreme Council of the Judiciary. I would like, however, to distinguish between two issues: as far as the past is concerned I will refer to the debate that took place, but I must point out that during the centrist era important laws were passed, such as the so-called Piccioni Law of 1951, which separated, at least as far as compensation and benefits were concerned, the personnel of the Judiciary from other public employees. Thus the Piccioni Law opened the way for the distinctive treatment of the Judiciary, which was then carried out through laws of ever increasing significance for this type of personnel. Leaving aside the past, however, the gravest problems arises not so much from the independence of the single magistrates, which is a constitutional requirement, than from the basic premises, from the context in which the independent judge must operate. I will limit myself to three points. The most difficult context is the legislative one, because even if we tend to adopt a strict interpretation of the judge's role as applying, implementing the laws, we must admit that these laws in the last ten-fifteen years have been very vague, generic in certain cases, and their implementation has been very uncertain as was, for instance, the case of the rent control and stabilization law. Not to mention that in other situations, e.g. in terms of labor-relationships, the fields from which the judge had to make his choices were too wide. It seems to me that I heard some hints in this direction being made in the report we listened to this morning.

The clauses that for Anglo-Saxon judges are more common — the call to reasonableness, to the balance of interests — for Italian judges carry too strong a dose of discretionary power. Thus the decreased responsibility of the legislator has a counterpart in the too great responsibility of the judge. This is, therefore, the first point, a very delicate one, of the relationship between the legislative power and the exercise of the juridical power.

A second aspect concerns the selection of the personnel of the Judiciary. With the so-called Breganze Law, many (except in certain exceptional cases) of the most important assignments, not to mention financial raises, are made solely on the basis of seniority. There is no selection within this group. It is said that "there cannot be a selection of the bureaucratic type." It is true, but we know that in the Anglo-Saxon system selection is made in a completely different way, since the appointments are made either from among renowned lawyers, as in England or by popular vote, or in some other way. When the hierarchy is of bureaucratic, not elective, type, or when it is not a question of the Bar, as it is in the Anglo-Saxon system, the difficulty arises in putting together aspects that compound two evils, that is a criterion of the bureaucratic nature with a non-existent internal selection, by means of which rain falls on the good and the bad both, on the capable and the incapable in the same measure. I agree that these laws have been given in order to guarantee independence from the promotion committees that had used their power in ways that bordered on political or caste bias. But an absolute lack of judgement criteria for the performance of the judges may constitute, as in other domains in Italy, the implementing of the principle that La Palombara has developed in his recent book: in Italy, the demand is for equal treatment and recognition rather than for equal opportunity, ignoring the quality of the performance that would justify or not such recognition. It is a very difficult, very sensitive, ground, I realize, but I have to point out this difficulty in reconciling independence, as seen by the Breganze Law, with the possibility to assign delicate tasks to the more capable judges.

And finally, a last question concerning the role of the Supreme Judicial Council. This role is, today, very controversial. We go from some minimalist correctives, which appear to be proposed even by left-wing parties — such as the reduction of favoritism in the election of the members of the Council — all the way to more radical changes in the election system itself, such as giving less room to factionalist maneuvering, and modifying in depth the election system, which is to an extreme degree proportional, as everything else is in our country.

Then, there are those who propose more radical reforms, such as the participation here, too, of the Chief of State, who would intervene in the composition of the Council — for purposes of balance — as Chief of State, instead of merely as President of the CSM (*Consiglio Supremo della Magistratura*, Supreme Judicial Council). Thus we would come closer to the structure of the Constitutional Court: a quota of members would be designated by the President of the Republic — for the most part from among the judges, in order to maintain a majority of judges; a quota by the Parliament; and one by the Judiciary. This, too, is a most steep ground, but the very fact that these proposals of law have been drafted shows that if we go from history to future perspectives, the matter is still open, and it will be extremely difficult to arrive at a balanced and adequate solution.

XXIII

Roundtable Discussion on the Symposium on Post World War II Italy Chaired by Frank J. Coppa

Transcribed by Joel Blatt

Margherita Repetto Alaia: Let us begin our last piece of work for the day and for the entire symposium. I will briefly introduce the chair of the roundtable discussion, Professor Frank Coppa. Dr. Coppa is Professor of History at St. John's University and a prominent historian of Modern Italy. He is the author of a series of monographs, and biographies of Giovanni Giolitti, Camillo Cavour, Pope Pius IX, and Cardinal Antonelli. He has also contributed chapters to numerous other books, essays, and articles. He is also the Editor-in-Chief of *The Dictionary of Modern Italian History*, published by Greenwood Press in 1985, and *Modern Italian History: An Annotated Bibliography*.
Here is Professor Coppa.

Frank Coppa: During the course of its work, the Organizing Committee recognized that in a two day conference on Postwar Italy, we could not possibly address all of the important issues. The Committee felt that some forum was needed to provide a place where other matters and issues might be considered, while providing an opportunity to utilize the expertise of a number of members of the community of Italian-American and Italian scholars. Hence the origins of this roundtable discussion. Unfortunately, we simply do not have the mechanism to undertake what we had initially envisioned, a true roundtable discussion during which we could discuss outstanding matters, so we have had to adopt a rather different technique. We are therefore asking this distinguished panel to address either issues that they felt were not fully explored, or issues that were not really addressed at all in this postwar period. I would implore the members of the panel in making comments or inquiries not to speak for more than four or five minutes at the very most, thus allowing the other members of the panel to respond.

The members of the panel include: Jared Becker, Assistant Professor of Italian at Columbia University, who is the author of the volume *Eugenio Montale*. Currently he is working on a book on Gabriele D'Annunzio. Joel Blatt, Associate Professor of European History at the University of Connecticut, Stamford Campus, who has published a series of articles on French reaction to Italian Fascism and is currently working on a number of books on this broad theme. Joel served as Chairperson of the Columbia University Seminar on Modern Italy from 1981-1984. Ronald Cunsolo is Professor of History at Nassau Community College, and he also served as Chair of the Columbia University Seminar. He has published a series of articles on Italian nationalism in such journals as the *Rassegna Storica del Risorgimento* and the *Journal of Modern History*. His volume on Italian nationalism to be published by Krieger Press is scheduled to appear shortly. Alexander De Grand is Professor of History and Chair of the Department of History at North Carolina State University. He has published volumes on the Italian Nationalist Association and the rise of Fascism in Italy, on Angelo Tasca, on Giuseppe Bottai, and he is currently working on a biography of Giovanni Giolitti. Mary Gibson is an Associate Professor of History at the John Jay College of the City University of New York and is currently the Chair of the Columbia Seminar on Modern Italy. Her volume, *Prostitution and the State in Italy, 1860-1915*, was published by Rutgers University Press. Ira Glazier is Professor of Economic History at Temple University and Director of the Center for Immigration Research of the Balch Institute. The recipient of numerous grants and awards, he has published on various aspects of Italian economic life. Frank Rosengarten is Professor of Italian at Queens College of the City University. He has published a volume on Vasco Pratolini, another on Silvio Trentin, and one on the Italian Anti-Fascist Press. He is co-Editor of the journal, *Socialism and Democracy*. Salvatore Saladino is Professor Emeritus at Queens College of the City University of New York. He has a series of articles and volumes including *Italy from Unifi-*

cation to 1919 and *A History of Modern Italy*. Professors Peter Lang, Roland Sarti, and Emiliana Noether could not be here. But Professor Joseph La Palombara who teaches Political Science at Yale University, and also is an internationally recognized scholar on comparative politics and an authority on the Italian economic and political system, is here with us. He is the author of more than a dozen books as well as numerous scholarly articles.

Some years ago, on the occasion of the fortieth anniversary of Italy's Republican Constitution, Renzo De Felice, in an article in the *Corriere Della Sera*, claimed that the Italian Republic did not differ all that substantially from the Giolittian Liberal State and aroused even further controversy by claiming that the Republic retained many of the features of the Fascist regime or at least some of its innovations. Let us begin today's discussion by examining what the Republic owes to Liberal Italy and what it has retained, both in the positive and negative sense, from Mussolini's Italy. At this point, I invite any member of the panel to address that particular issue or, if they'd like, to raise any other issue about this period and the Conference. In turn, we might have any member of the panel or audience respond. I ask that each member identify himself or herself. We would encourage this very devoted and patient audience which has been steadfast and has remained until the eleventh hour both to pose questions and indeed to come forward and to comment on any aspect of the conference or any issue that they believe was not sufficiently addressed.

Cunsolo: Thank you Professor Coppa. In my opinion I would say that there is at least this one thing the Italian Republic owes to Liberal Italy, and that is the liberal parliamentary regime. Much had been said against the operations of the Italian Parliament, and yet after Fascism the Italian Republic accepted the liberal parliamentary regime. And if I may point out one important reason why, I think it was the stand that Giacomo Matteotti took in Parliament in exposing the outrageous tactics used and employed by the Fascists in attempting to swing elections. By assuming that position and later by being martyred by the Fascists, Giacomo Matteotti sanctified Parliament. He underscored the importance of Parliament as a place where individual deputies could speak out even at the cost of the penalty of their lives. And so I think that there is at least this one connection between Republican Italy and Liberal Italy.

Another point I would like to make, if allowed to do so, is that at least at the very beginning of the conference the expression "the Catholic world" was used and it was used repeatedly. But it seems to me that once the assumption is made of "the Catholic world," and you begin to penetrate it, you find so many divisions, factions, and exceptions that the term loses its historical validity. Who speaks for "the Catholic world"? It is a multiplicity of elements and components that are involved. "The Catholic world" is no more united, no more monolithic or massive or unilateral or one-dimensional than let us say, the Protestant world.

I have another comment that I would make concerning the emphasis that was placed on the role of political Catholicism, Catholic organizations, and Catholic laity in the reconstruction years. It is amazing, at least to me, the experience that has over-taken the Catholic movement in Italy. It is almost a "rags to riches" story. Within a period of about eighty years, Italian Catholics went from total abstentionism, at least in political elec-tions, to selective participation, let's say by 1904. And then when the Republic comes you find the almost total involvement of Italian Catholics in politics. I think that a lot more needs to be said of this process. After all, Catholics had to sort out their emotions. What about the attitudes of the Popes, particularly Pius IX, who had issued the *"non expedit"*, what led his successors to change their minds? What did that mean? Certainly there were many journals, many resolutions adopted, pastoral letters, and also talks by Bishops. But how did the average Italian Catholic in the street come to rationalize and accept this *voltafaccia*, this 360 degree turn from total abstentionism to complete involvement? And then of course there is the other side, the secular forces — what about the Anti-Clericals? How did they accept the total participation of the Catholics within the political process? Of course you can say, as was said, that there was the fear of Communism, the fear of Stalin-ism, and perhaps there was also much CIA pressure. That provides an explanation of sorts. But insofar as the average Italian is con-cerned, whether he was Roman Catholic or secular, how did he re-spond? How was he able to accept and tolerate this change that had taken place within the Italian Catholic movement? Thank you.

Rosengarten: First of all, I would like to commend the high quality of all of the interventions that we have heard since the beginning of the Conference. As a whole when they are published as proceedings, they will form an extremely important and useful contribution to our understanding of modern Italian history. Having said that, however, I would like to raise a few questions that in my opinion were left either unanswered or only slightly touched and that might have enriched the discussion. My field of expertise is literature and literary and cultural history, principally the period of the 20th Century. I am far from an expert in political or economic history, but I have read as much as some, as many, people. With regard to literature and culture, I felt that with the exception of Professor Verucci (and now I am commenting on the Conference), who did mention the important journals, *Lo Stato Moderno* and *Il Ponte*, after the war, that there was a striking lack of attention paid by the speakers, perhaps unavoidably because one cannot cover all bases, to the very vigorous revival of literature and culture, particularly in the field of the novel, poetry, and cinema after the war. This is indebted to the tremendous contribution of the Resistance and in general of the Antifascist forces that had come into play and come to fruition during the four years. As a matter of fact, one of the questions that was raised by Frank Coppa concerned the "paese legale" and the "paese reale" question. If you want to know about Italy as "paese reale" as opposed to the "paese legale", you really have to read some of the important novels such as *La luna e i falò* and *Cronaca di poveri amanti*. I made a list of some of the works of Carlo Levi, Ignazio Silone (I could go on — Leonardo Sciascia, and so on) to really get an understanding of some of the less obvious social realities of Italy that are not covered quite so well in standard and conventional political history. So that is one point that I wanted to make.

Another point has to do with democracy and reconstruction. I am not one to deny that there was reconstruction nor am I denying that there was a return to certain democratic institutions that were established by the Liberal State and destroyed by Fascism. However, I felt that in general there was a rather uncritical treatment of the concept of democracy as it was reborn in Italy. By uncritical, I mean that the discussion of democracy remained on an institutional and formal level. Had it not been for the intervention of Professor Neppi Modona at the end this afternoon, we might have even left here with the impression that there was a complete restoration, a completely satisfactory recreation of democracy in Italy. Now this was not the case. As a matter of fact, this brings me to another point that I felt was insufficiently dealt with, and that is the historical connections between post-Fascist, Fascist, and pre-Fascist Italy. This was touched upon here and there. But I think that the connections are much deeper, much more complex, much more contradictory than one would have thought by listening to many of the presentations. I think that this is an important point. So in a strange kind of way, as good as the presentations, the papers, were, there was in some way a lack of historical perspective. In other words, we had a kind of parcelling out of various aspects, but there was no sense of coordination; now, again, this may have been inevitable, but I bring it to your attention.

Let me close by saying one last thing on the issue of the interconnections between the national and the international dimensions as affecting Italy after World War II. I reread Norman Kogan's political history of Italy since 1945 to refresh myself on certain points, and particularly the first 150 pages of the book. I can assure you, assuming that Norman Kogan is a reliable historian and political scientist and I believe he is, the degree of United States' interference, blackmail, threats, and other forms of intervention in Italian politics were incredible, massive and determinant in many respects with regard to Italian politics. I feel that the theme was inadequately treated here. On the other hand, I am not denying the authenticity and originality of Italy's own restoration of freedom and so on. But that interplay, the dialectical interplay between the national and the international, it seemed to me was missing. I would have liked to have heard more of that. Let us see how some of my colleagues here at the table and the rest of you in the audience respond. Thank you.

Becker: Some of the things that Professor Rosengarten has just said struck a responsive chord with me, perhaps because we have been talking in the interlude. So maybe this reflects a conspiracy between me and Professor Rosengarten. Listening to Senator Elia's and Professor Vacca's contributions, I was impressed and kind of fascinated at the way the two factions which Eugenio Montale referred to in the late 1940s as the Chierico Rosso and the Chierico Nero now seem to have shifted or been moved so decisively toward the center in retrospect. So De Gasperi and the Christian Democrats are not so much the Destra as is commonly assumed, and indeed the Christian Democrats are anxious to welcome the Communists into the fold of parliamentary democracy as a means of democratizing them. Meanwhile, according to Vacca, we have a PCI which is much more reformist than revolutionary, believing in a mixed economy, and entering the logic of parliamentary democracy. Well, not surprisingly given these attempts to shift things toward the center, there were some skeptical reactions here. I heard a cry of *doppiezza* at one point, and as Professor Rosengarten says, the calculated exploitation on the part of the Americans and the results that they had in Italian politics, the exploitation of the red scare by people like Tarchiani. So I was a little dismayed to see the other day that Professor Vacca seemed to be a little isolated at a certain moment during the session on Friday, and I hope, I trust, that he will take comfort in the fact that his Gramsci, after all, as it turns out forty years down the road, is not so marginalized a figure. The publication of *The Prison Notebooks* in translation and the use of Gramsci which is by now quite widespread in the Anglo-Saxon world is probably not the treatment reserved for an author associated with a narrowly doctrinaire position. And by contrast Crocean historiography, which was mentioned in the discussion of the lay forces, seems to be in retrospect quite limited in importance. While Gramsci talked about the well known elimination of the revolutionary movement in modern European and modern Italian history in Croce's histories, there is also the less than satisfactory treatment of Fascism as parenthesis and a general hostility on Croce's part to any culture more modern than Carducci. Perhaps all of these weaknesses in Croce are connected. In addition to Gramsci, and the publication of *The Prison Notebooks* after all is one of the great publishing events of this period under consideration here, I also think that consideration is due to another kind of work, which has also endured from that moment of the late 1940s in Italy. That is neo-realist film and narrative. We heard talk about the influence of *Il Ponte* and *Il Mondo*, but surely there is also wide influence for neo-realist film and narrative, although I think that the influence is ambiguous. Well it is influential obviously if you have someone like Giulio Andreotti who so stridently took to task a film maker like De Sica. And then the financial pressures existed in neo-realist film makers. That is another interesting chapter here. *Bicycle Thief* by De Sica in 1948 has a rather interesting position, I think, because you see a scornfulness for the Christian charitable organization which ignores the unemployed desperate worker. But also you have the presentation in the background of the local section of the Communist Party which really appears more as background noise, completely unhelpful, babel. And so this is perhaps De Sica's version of the Terza Via, and I think that it is one sign of the ambiguities that are not recognized yet in neo-realist film and narrative. Thank you.

Saladino: But not at all *"feroce."* I was struck today by a number of comments that seemed to emphasize a theme of continuity of Italian history. With regard to the parliamentary system, for example, it was there before 1922. It survived in a transformed corrupt form even as late as 1939, and it was revived after 1945. And the question occurred to me, what choice was there in fact in 1945-1946 if not a return to the parliamentary system in one fashion or another? It didn't have to be a parliamentary democracy; conceivably it could have been a presidential republic. But a parliament of sorts was inevitable, or was it inevitable? Could other structures of government have been formulated in 1945-1946, other and outside of the parliamentary? I'm not going to give any answers; I'm just meandering in my own mind and expressing myself openly. I don't know the answer.

We were told also that despite the obvious changes in the juridical system after 1946, here, too, we have a continuity, of personnel if nothing else. The judges, many of them at least, were there before 1922, continued after 1922, and some survived even beyond 1945 — may even be around still today. Judges have an extraordinary longevity.

And political parties. As I remember, in 1919 there were three major political parties, in addition to the old Liberals who died very quickly. There remained the Popolari, the Socialist Party soon to break up, and the Communist Party. There are today these three parties, somewhat transformed, and a group of others quite smaller in composition. And I wonder how it is that the political geography has changed really so very little. Again the theme of continuity, which then raises in my mind the Crocean question: was the Fascist period really "parentesi storica"? Was it really only a parenthesis, which could almost be disregarded, neglected, historically ignored? Or does it require more profound examination by us today to determine how much of what occurred during these twenty years survives in institutions and in the minds of the Italian people.

Blatt: At the end of the war, Piero Calamandrei, who has been mentioned during the conference, was the representative of the family of Carlo and Nello Rosselli in the trial of some of the men responsible for the assassination of the two brothers. In his concluding plea, Calamandrei, looking at the accused, asserted:

> Disgraziati, you more than us, because you wanted to kill them and they have risen immortal; and in the slime of this trial, they wear a halo. Are the Rosselli brothers dead? No. It is you who are dead, you on that bench and the sad ghosts who are behind you, but Carlo and Nello, sweet friends, youthful and smiling, are here (profound commotion in the courtroom). Beside us, they watch all this immense ruin, this emptiness, but their faces are clear, their eyes serene, and they say: 'Non Mollare!' (Don't give in).

I use that to raise a question. Did the Rosselli brothers die in vain? What was the weight of the Resistance in the reconstruction? Did they provide the stones, indicated in the beautiful passage from Nello Rosselli that Margherita placed on the program, the stones upon which we can walk in freedom? What role did they play? And my general question is this: In the reconstruction what was the weight of the different forces: the past, the Resistance, the major currents of Italian political life at the fall of Fascism, Fascist remnants, fears, emotions, ideals, pressures from outside — the United States and Russia both — the economic demands of everyday life, and others? I'm interested as a historian in how we weigh these different components. Thank you.

De Grand: I have three very brief points that I wanted to make. One relating to Professor Vacca's and Professor Tamburrano's papers. The failure of the Left in the immediate postwar period, it seems to me, had two causes that Togliatti realized very rapidly, and this was one of his strengths. One was the failure of left-wing economic thinking during the interwar period. The Left really didn't seem to have an adequate economic theory coming out of the 1930s, and it was really at the mercy of more liberal, more bourgeois economic theory in the postwar period. The second problem of the Left was that the Left thought during the interwar period mainly in terms of an autonomous Italy. They did not see what kind of postwar, and it was probably impossible to see. I think that Togliatti's great strength was that he recognized the new political configuration more rapidly than anyone, or most people, in the Socialist or Communist parties and was able to react to it.

A second thing that occurred to me was that we talk a lot about the continuity of the State. But it seems to me an interesting idea might be the continuity of Italian society. I believe that the Italy inherited by the Republic in the immediate postwar period was more like the Italy of the 1920s and 1930s than the Italy of today. The economic miracle was that great dividing point, and Italy changed more rapidly in those years than in all the years before. But what we are looking at is an Italy where the same mentalities, the same ferociousness of the class struggle, the same bitter alienation from the State existed. And it seems to me if we talk about that in the pre-Fascist era, and in the struggles against Fascism on the part of workers and peasants, we can't leave it out in the immediate postwar period and sort of factor it out. And that somehow has to be factored in as a pressure on the Left to take positions that it did and to maneuver between this pressure. I think that Professor Vacca brought this out earlier.

And then, a final point that occurred to me was that the Left really did not leave the government of its own volition. It was ousted. And it seems to me, in the context of the similarity between societies, from the continuity of society, and the continuity of the state, the particular bitterness and disappointment and defeat of the period from 1948 to 1955 was never conveyed. It is almost as though Scelba, and Siri and Paolo Bonomi, and extremely conservative politicians who really sought to turn back the clock were pushed aside as inconvenient old-fashioned furniture, but they were there, and they were major figures in this period, and their names hardly ever come up any more.

Just one last thought very rapidly. There seems to emerge from the Conference the thought that because things worked out well and because everybody is very satisfied today about the way they worked out, that in a sense we read back and say this is the only way it could have occurred. I'm not absolutely certain about that. If Togliatti made some mistakes, it was probably in not pushing harder in the 1944-1945 period. But the question comes to mind — would that have made that big a difference or not? It seems there was room for maneuver; there was room to impose other ways of doing things. Thank you.

Gibson: As I understood our mission, it was to focus on one or two papers to comment upon so we wouldn't go on too long. So I'm sorry to slight the papers yesterday, but I chose the two that seemed to be closest to my interest although I am more a specialist in the 19th Century than the 20th. The papers I chose to comment upon were those by Professor Neppi Modona on the judiciary and by Professor Gaiotti on women. I tried to consider what was common between them, and what seems to have emerged is the notion of continuity and change. And I think Professor Neppi Modona showed in a very interesting way how there had been continuity between Fascism through at least the 1950s of personnel, organization, and judicial philosophy in the judiciary, and therefore the Constitution was not really implemented until the early 1960s. One thing that has come up many times today is the Rocco Code, and that interests me a lot, and if it interests anyone else maybe we could discuss in greater detail why it has been so hard to get a new penal law because the law is, of course, in contradiction with parts of the Constitution. Now unfortunately Professor Sabino Cassese could not come today, but I did read his paper and I found a striking similarity with that by Professor Neppi Modona in the sense that he talked about the bureaucracy in general and pointed out the striking continuities in personnel. He also made a point that in the *parastatale* sector there seems to be a great growth in contrast to the ministries, to the seeming rigidity and unchanging structures of the ministries, but that had also begun in the Fascist era so has a kind of continuity about it. And I thought it was quite interesting at the end of his paper when he cautioned we historians not to be too dazzled by dramatic kinds of changes like the end of wars and renaissance of political activity if this means that we ignore various kinds of continuities like administrative continuities, which certainly had great effect on everyday people's lives in Italy.

This, in a way, brings me to Professor Gaiotti's paper, which I thought very successfully combined attention to both continuity and change because she analyzed that period in reference to women on various levels. She showed for instance, on the political level, that the parties tried to characterize the introduction of women's suffrage as simply continuity, which is, of course, quite interesting, and that they all in some way blocked, or tried to control, women's votes so that their political participation did not really increase, if you look, for instance, at the number of Deputies and Senators, in any striking way until the late 1970s and 1980s. And yet she also argued that in social and economic terms there was a great change in women's lives. For one thing they were working in much greater numbers than before, and I think she was probably right to mention that this was probably true of the international context. Certainly in the United States you might say that there was a great propaganda effort after the war to return women to the home and give men back the jobs. And everyone until ten or fifteen years ago thought that happened until they looked at the statistics, and found that, in fact, there had been a fundamental change in women's lives in the United States, that they were working in great numbers, and there wasn't that kind of a going backward that we assumed had happened. So perhaps as we discuss some of the other papers that I have not touched on, we might try to reconsider some of these topics that have come up in the conference in the more expanded perspective; in other words to focus not just on the leaders and what they said, but what always particularly interests me, how these ideas or these issues might have actually affected Italian citizens, both men and women, in their everyday lives. And this would in some way broaden the way we look at these issues. Thank you.

Glazier: I'm not a specialist on contemporary Italy, but I think that I would have to agree with most members of the panel that between Liberal Italy and the Republic there was a great deal of continuity as well as some change. Now I would somewhat restrict or modify the question to consider or compare perhaps also the issue of postwar reconstruction; that is to say post-World War I and post-World War II. There, I think quite clearly that we are dealing with very dissimilar situations. It presents a rather interesting comparison, however. After World War I, we have a situation with a great amount of instability; economic policies, for example, such as autarky and so forth, create conditions which are really very unfavorable to growth. After World War II, we find that perhaps Italy's economic performance was better than her political performance. I'm speaking still of the reconstruction period, but I would also like to extend the reconstruction period up through at least until 1963. During the course of the conference I did not find much interest or much analysis of developments subsequent to 1948 or 1949. Now as we all know very important structural changes did occur in Italy in the reconstruction period of the 1950s, the details of which I won't burden you with, but which concern technology, employment, productivity, and modernization of the service sector, and, of course, the South. But at the same time I think that it is important to recognize that certain appointments with the future were made in the post-reconstruction period, at least in the economic sphere, which were not kept or which remained to be kept. We were speaking at lunch with Professor Treu who reminded us that certainly the problems of the South are no longer what they were in the 1950s and 1960s; that is to say we can now discriminate a South which is developing, and perhaps even a South which is developed. We must make distinctions between what happens in Calabria, what is happening in Calabria and the Basilicata for example, with developments in Abruzzo, in Campania, in Sicily, and so on. But these are very important issues which I would hope would form part of another conference, also deserving attention in the matter of postwar reconstruction. Thank you very much.

La Palombara: I really came to engage my friend Cassese in conversation today and I'm deeply sorry that he had been called away. Still, I want to say just two or three things. One is that I think that the most important thing about Fascism's legacy to the Republic is that Fascism happened. It was an experience that had some consequences that I think are not marginal for postwar Italy. One was the nature of the Special Tribunal and what happened to most of the people who came before it, who were given opportunities to meet together and to talk and to write and to plan. Someone mentioned the translation of *The Prison Notes*. *The Prison Notes* would never have been written in Germany under the Nazis. And there was something about the regime that in a sense not only was very Italian but managed to create a permissiveness that made it possible for something called "the parties of the arco costituzionale" to emerge after World War II. In recent years, and I think perhaps correctly, it has been argued that it is no longer good enough if you are trying to establish democratic credentials to identify yourself as an Antifascist. And I think that probably makes sense. But I think in the immediate postwar years and for some decades after the postwar, it was very important for people to gain a certain Republican legitimacy by simply being able to qualify under the label *antifascista*. So I think that the particular configuration of Fascism in political terms and indeed the particular way in which the judiciary functioned under Fascism helped to create a basis for Republican development that I think would have been quite different.

The other legacy that I'd like to point to and it is suggested by De Grand's comment on the economic side — it seems to me that Fascism did very little to modify, and indeed if anything, solidified, a relationship between economics and politics that makes Italy even today a country of extremely primitive capitalism; that is to say the nature of the relationship between the public and private sector in Italy goes back to liberalism and is reinforced in a curious and even perverse way by Fascism's economic policies in the early 1930s. That is to say, willy nilly, that structure that we associate with the public sector IRI, but not just IRI anymore — I write about this in my book. I say at one point that the place in the world where if you think you are an entrepreneur you would want to be an entrepreneur, is in Italy — it is structured to assure you against bad management, because if you really are a bad manager, you can dump your badly managed industry on the state. And also where if you are skillful enough, you can in fact pick up for a song some public sector industry where public managers have managed so well that the industry has become profitable. I don't know of any other market system where that particular nexus operates; that is to say where entrepreneurs who are failures can save themselves from disaster by having the general public pick up what it is they have